THE KU KLUX KLAN IN THE CITY
1915-1930

T0097100

THE KU KLUX KLAN
IN THE CITY
1915-1930

KENNETH T. JACKSON

With a New Foreword by the Author

Elephant Paperbacks
IVAN R. DEE, PUBLISHER, CHICAGO

THE KU KLUX KLAN IN THE CITY. Copyright © 1967 by Oxford University Press, Inc. This book was originally published in 1967 by Oxford University Press and is here reprinted by arrangement.

First ELEPHANT PAPERBACK edition published 1992 by Ivan R. Dee, Inc., 1332 North Halsted Street, Chicago 60622. Manufactured in the United States of America and printed on acid-free paper.

Library of Congress Cataloging-in-Publication Data:
Jackson, Kenneth T.
    The Ku Klux Klan in the city, 1915–1930 / Kenneth T. Jackson —
1st Elephant pbk. ed.
        p.   cm.
    Originally published: New York : Oxford University Press, 1967.
    "Elephant paperbacks."
    Includes bibliographical references and index.
    ISBN 0-929587-82-0 (alk. paper)
    1. Ku Klux Klan (1915–)—History. I. Title.
HS2330.K63J3   1992
322.4'2'0973—dc20   91-32287

To the memory of my father
KENNETH GORDON JACKSON
(1907-1961)

Foreword to the 1992 Edition

No institution or organization in American history is more associated in the public mind with lawlessness and criminal behavior than the Ku Klux Klan. Although the Klan has typically given lip service to motherhood, virtue, patriotism, temperance, and the legal authority of the state, the reality of Klan doctrine, activities, and membership has long been quite different. Indeed, for more than 125 years the Invisible Empire has been the very symbol of intolerance. Created in Pulaski, Tennessee, immediately after the Civil War, the Ku Klux Klan took as its initial purpose the restoration of white supremacy to the former Confederacy through intimidation and violence. The primary targets of the secret order were former slaves who aspired to the freedom and dignity supposedly guaranteed by the 13th, 14th, and 15th Amendments. Fortunately, the United States government took vigorous action against this first Ku Klux Klan, and it survived only a few years. It was completely dormant by 1873.

The second, and by far the largest and most important, of the three major Klan movements was organized in Atlanta in 1915. It grew to enormous size between 1920 and 1925, when its membership was variously estimated at between two and five million and when its ranks included such prominent citizens as the governors of Texas, Indiana, and

Oregon and the mayors of Atlanta, Indianapolis, and Denver. The primary targets of this crusade were Catholics, eastern and southern European immigrants, African-Americans, and Jews, with the evil forces of the papacy in Rome deemed the most threatening to America. This Klan declined rapidly in the late 1920s, especially after campaigning against Al Smith in 1928, and it finally went out of existence in 1944.

The third Ku Klux Klan was born in Atlanta in 1946, and it continues to survive, if not thrive, in the 1990s. It is different from the first two Klan movements because it has always been extraordinarily fragmented and because it has never exercised the influence of its predecessors. There are at least a half-dozen separate Klan groups currently operating, and none of them has an active membership of more than 1 percent of the Klan total in the 1920s. Indeed, when a former Klan leader, David Duke, made a much-publicized run for governor of Louisiana in 1991, his failure to win was ascribed less to the stridency of his program than to his earlier association with such a discredited group as the Ku Klux Klan.

Perhaps Duke's marginality in Louisiana and the nation suggests the truth of Abraham Lincoln's dictum that you can fool all of the people some of the time and some of the people all of the time, but you can't fool all of the people all of the time. The wonder, however, is that so many people have been fooled for so long by the various organizers of the Ku Klux Klan. In the 1920s they were fooled into thinking they could turn back the clock and return America to a time when it was presumably white, Protestant, rural, and prosperous. After World War II they were fooled into believing that the Reverend Martin Luther King, Jr., was an agent of the Kremlin, that African-Americans who wanted to spend the night in an ordinary motel or sit at a lunch counter were dangerous revolutionaries, or that an occasional bomb or murder could slow the forces that were changing the United States forever.

Since this book was first published a quarter of a century ago, many new inquiries have appeared on one or another aspect of Klan history. Particularly notable have been Robert A. Goldberg, *Hooded Empire: The Ku Klux Klan in Colorado;* William D. Jenkins, *Steel Valley Klan: The Ku Klux Klan in Ohio's Mahoning Valley;* Kathleen M. Blee,

Women of the Klan: Racism and Gender in the 1920's; Elizabeth Wheaton, *Codename Greenkil: The 1979 Greensboro Killings;* and Kevin Flynn and Gary Gerhardt, *The Silent Brotherhood: Inside America's Racist Underground.* All describe a white supremacist organization committed to upholding Christian identity and racial pride, and all take us well beyond the understanding of the secret order that was common in the 1960s. But they have not substantially modified the thesis of *The Ku Klux Klan in the City.* Quite simply, the urban klaverns of the Invisible Empire dominated the organization and provided the bulk of the leadership and the financing. They also provided a large portion of the total membership.

Readers will note that this book has retained the word "Negro" rather than "black" or "African-American." If I were writing in the 1990s I would of course use different terminology. In this case, however, the text is that which originally appeared in 1967.

KENNETH T. JACKSON

January 1992

Preface

The traditional image of the Ku Klux Klan is that of hooded night-riders preserving white supremacy in the rural South. If applied to the first and the third of the three Klan movements in American history, this image is basically correct. The original "Invisible Empire" was organized by Confederate veterans in 1866 and shrank neither from intimidation nor from violence in a successful effort to prevent former slaves from exercising their recently acquired political and economic rights. Similarly, the most recent Ku Klux Klan, which has proliferated into several distinct movements since its rebirth in 1946, is heavily oriented toward the maintenance of white supremacy and has consistently been most active in opposition to the Supreme Court's school integration decision of 1954.

But the usual stereotype has little validity as it relates to the largest and most significant of the three Klan movements. The Invisible Empire of the 1920's was neither predominantly southern, nor rural, nor white supremacist, nor violent. It was fathered by an Atlanta fraternal organizer and first gained prominence on the national scene in the turbulent years after the close of World War I. Following closely in the nativist tradition of the Know-Nothing party of the 1850's and the American Protective Association of the 1890's, albeit increasing their intolerance, the Ku Klux Klan presented itself as the defender of Americanism and the conservator of Christian ideals.[1] It received a charter in 1916 as a "patriotic, secret, social, benevolent order," but found ample occasion to denounce Catholicism, integration, Judaism, immigration, and internationalism as threats to traditional American values. Enrolling over two million members between 1920 and 1926, the Klan commanded almost as much support as organized labor and was described with considerable accuracy by journalist Stanley Frost as "the most vigorous, active, and effective force in American life, outside business."

Four decades have passed since the Invisible Empire began its long decline, but few scholars have ventured to penetrate its secrecy. As a result of our fragmentary knowledge, students of the subject have agreed only that the secret order was politically oriented and at least as strong outside as within the South. Important questions regarding the total size and distribution of membership, the nature of the Klan's appeal, the extent to which it shifted prejudices from one section of the country to another, and the socioeconomic status of the typical Klansmen remain unresolved. There has, however, been no lack of conjecture.

Among the theories of the Klan movement none has been so persistent or so widely accepted as the notion that the Klan was a rural and small-town organization that can best be understood in terms of a general rural reaction against the rise to dominance of great cities in American life. Dartmouth sociologist John Moffatt Mecklin clearly formulated this theory in 1924:

> The Klan draws its members chiefly from the descendants of the old American stock living in the villages and small towns of those sections of the country where this old stock has been least disturbed by immigration, on the one hand, and the disruptive effect of industrialism, on the other.[2]

[1] With regard to the American Protective Association, Professor Donald Kinzer has recently shown that it was not anti-Semitic, that it admitted foreign-born citizens to membership, and that it "flourished on, rather than engendered, sentiment for immigration restriction." Kinzer, *An Episode in Anti-Catholicism: The American Protective Association* (Seattle, 1964), p. 247.
[2] J. M. Mecklin, *The Ku Klux Klan: A Study of the American Mind* (New York, 1924), p. 99.

Professor Mecklin saw the explanation of Klan growth in a combination of rural ignorance and small-town monotony; why else would poor folk be sufficiently impressed by burning crosses and mysterious paraders to exchange sixteen dollars for a sheet? Cities were supposedly almost free of Klan influence because their heterogeneous populations, impersonal relationships, and complex patterns of life created a more tolerant and less superstitious society. Mecklin was a shrewd observer of the American mind, and his interpretation has been accepted with only slight alteration to this day. For example, William E. Leuchtenberg, in his popular *Perils of Prosperity*, argues that Klan strength was greatest among small-townspeople who felt themselves eclipsed by the rise of the city, a position taken also by Arnold Rice in *The Ku Klux Klan in American Politics* and by George Mowry in *The Urban Nation, 1920-1960*. Richard Hofstadter, Walter Johnson, Frank Tannenbaum, Andrew Sinclair, John P. Roche, and David Shannon are among other distinguished scholars who have followed this traditional interpretation.[8] The small-town thesis seems to be supported not only by logic and common sense, but also by founder William Joseph Simmons himself, who declared in 1920 that "the great city as at present constructed corrodes the very soul of our American life." He concluded that "overgrown cities are in themselves a menace." His successor as imperial wizard, Hiram Wesley Evans, took a similar position, arguing in 1925 that white Protestants were in a death struggle with the city, center of cosmopolitanism and foreign influences.

Since 1962, however, two studies have questioned the Mecklin thesis. In a trenchant dissertation on the Klan in Arkansas, Texas, Oklahoma, and Louisiana, Charles C. Alexander hypothesized that a general "quest for moral and social conformity" enabled the

[8] Richard Hofstadter, *The Age of Reform: From Bryan to FDR* (New York, 1955), pp. 291-2; Walter Johnson, *William Allen White's America* (New York, 1947), p. 375; Frank Tannenbaum, "The Ku Klux Klan," *The Century*, CV (April 1923), 878-9; Andrew Sinclair, *Era of Excess: A Social History of the Prohibition Movement* (New York, 1964), p. 18; John P. Roche, *The Quest for the Dream: The Development of Civil Rights and Human Relations in America* (New York, 1963), p. 86; and David Shannon, *Between the Wars: America 1919-1941* (Boston, 1956), p. 80.

secret order to register its "greatest strength and most notable successes in the booming cities of the Southwest." But he argued that
the Klan was an outlet for rural-minded America and that to a large
extent it was a reaction against such homegrown evils as the rise
of the city.[4] Alexander was followed in 1965 by David M. Chalmers,
whose *Hooded Americanism: The First Century of the Ku Klux
Klan* represents the first successful attempt to survey the movement
on a nationwide basis. Although suggesting that the Klan was "no
stranger to urban life" and was "a factor in the life of cities from
Philadelphia to Phoenix," Chalmers basically adhered to the small-
town interpretation and probed the implications of his urban re-
marks little further than the observation that rural migrants tend
to carry country values and prejudices with them to the city.[5]
Neither Alexander nor Chalmers proposed to focus attention upon
the city. Therefore, they did not seek to evaluate the distinguishing
characteristics or relative strength of rural and urban Klan chapters, to investigate systematically the socio-economic status of
city Klansmen, to describe problems and tensions unique to urban
life, or to delimit the differences, if any, between "city" and "small
town" or between their interpretation and the traditional Mecklin
thesis.

The purpose of this book is to examine the unnecessarily obscured urban aspect of the Invisible Empire and to test the hypothesis that kleagles (recruiters) were as active and successful
in establishing Klans in large cities as in "towns" of fewer than
75,000 persons. A further objective is to evaluate the influence of
urban Knights (Klan members) over the movement as a whole
and to determine the particular residential areas within large
cities from which the Klan drew recruits. Whenever possible, the
size and meeting places of urban Klans, the nature and extent of

---

[4] Charles C. Alexander, *Crusade for Conformity: The Ku Klux Klan in Texas*
(Houston, 1962), p. 9; *The Ku Klux Klan in the Southwest* (Lexington, 1965),
pp. 20-32; and "Invisible Empire in the Southwest: The Ku Klux Klan in
Texas, Louisiana, Oklahoma, and Arkansas, 1920-1930" (unpub. Ph.D. diss.,
University of Texas, 1962).
[5] For instance, in his discussion of the Mississippi Klan, Chalmers maintained,
"Here, as elsewhere, the Klan was a town phenomenon. . . ." Chalmers,
Hooded Americanism: The First Century of the Ku Klux Klan (Garden City,
N. Y., 1965), p. 66.

their fraternal, social, coercive, and charitable activities, the type and character of publications they sponsored, and the extent of their participation in municipal and state politics will be indicated. Because interviews, chapter records, or even precise precinct returns could not always be secured, this work is confessedly incomplete, and in places very painfully so.

My method of study is to consider in detail the Klan experience in Atlanta, Chicago, Dallas, Denver, Detroit, Indianapolis, Knoxville, Memphis, and Portland and to discuss more generally the movement in other cities. As a matter of definition, a community is herein considered as urban only if (1) it had a 1920 population exceeding 75,000, or (2) it was part of a principal standard metropolitan area of more than 100,000 persons in 1920.[6] Suburban areas such as Harvey, Illinois, are therefore regarded as urban, while small cities such as El Paso, Texas, are considered to be "towns." Footnotes and bibliographical suggestions are minimal; scholars seeking more extensive documentation are referred to the author's doctoral dissertation, which is available on loan from the University of Chicago.

Because it is more important here to understand than to condemn, the text does not ring with denunciations of intolerance. The task is to examine the fears, prejudices, and activities of rank and file members. In the final analysis, the Klan was not alien to society or un-American. If it were, the problem would have been much simpler. Rather the Klan was typically American. It prospered and grew to national power by capitalizing on forces already existent in American society: our readiness to ascribe all good or all evil to those religions, races, or economic philosophies with which we agree or disagree, and our tendency to profess the highest ideals while actually exhibiting the basest of prejudices. To examine the Ku Klux Klan is to examine ourselves.

---

[6] The official definition of a standard metropolitan area is a central city of at least 50,000 inhabitants plus surrounding area. A "principal standard metropolitan area" in 1920 would have a central city of 50,000 inhabitants and a total population of more than 100,000. Donald J. Bogue, *Population Growth in Standard Metropolitan Areas 1900-1950* (Washington, 1953), pp. 4-10.

Contents

Figures

Tables

THE KU KLUX KLAN IN THE CITY
1915-1930

I

THE INVISIBLE EMPIRE

The liberties of a people are never more certainly in the path of destruction than when they trust themselves to the guidance of secret societies. Birds of the night are never birds of wisdom. . . . The fate of a republic is sealed when bats take the place of eagles.

Josiah Quincy

On March 3, 1915, the first full-length motion picture in American history was released for exhibition. Directed by David Ward Griffith and based upon a novel of the Civil War and Reconstruction by Thomas Dixon, *The Birth of a Nation* depicted the Lost Cause as a hallowed one. It related the story of a vanquished South, rescued at the last moment from the tentacles of scalawags, carpetbaggers, drunken Union soldiers, and unprincipled freedmen by the hard-riding horsemen of the Ku Klux Klan. A technical masterpiece that was often factually inaccurate, *The Birth of a Nation* was ultimately viewed by more than fifty million people and had a vast influence in the shaping of popular misconceptions about the critical Reconstruction period of American history. In 1922, Walter Lippmann ventured the opinion that "no one who has seen the film, and does not know more about the Ku Klux Klan than Griffith does, will ever hear the name again without seeing those white horsemen." [1]

Although *The Birth of a Nation* electrified audiences throughout the United States, nowhere was the reception more enthusiastic than in the Old South, where for decades the film was brought back for additional showings. Men yelled, whooped, cheered, and on one

3

occasion even shot up the screen in a desperate effort to save Flora Cameron from her black pursuer. Climactically, white-hooded riders galloped across the screen to the accompaniment from the theater orchestra pit of the "Poet and Peasant" overture or "The Ride of the Valkyries."

The Birth of a Nation had already played in Knoxville, Chattanooga, Spartanburg, Asheville, and a dozen other southern cities when it opened in Atlanta on December 6, 1915. On that memorable evening, cheer after cheer broke forth from "one of the largest audiences that ever crowded through the door of an Atlanta theater." In an unprecedented three-week engagement the film broke all existing attendance records in the Georgia capital. Alongside the newspaper advertisements of the movie was an occasional announcement of a "high class order for men of intelligence and character."

Less than a fortnight before the opening of *The Birth of a Nation* in Atlanta, a strange spectacle took place a short distance from the city on the imposing granite crest of Stone Mountain. Led by William Joseph Simmons, a tall, clean-shaven, two-hundred-pound fraternal organizer who was to persuade theater manager Bill Sharpe to grant him free admission to see *The Birth of a Nation* time and again,[2] sixteen men ascended a rocky trail to found a memorial organization to the Klansmen who had performed so gallantly in defense of white supremacy two generations earlier. A cool Thanksgiving breeze whipped an American flag, while a crude burning cross illuminated the Bible, carefully opened to the twelfth chapter of Romans.[3] Against this backdrop the small group swore allegiance to the Invisible Empire, Knights of the Ku Klux Klan. One week later they received a preliminary charter from the state of Georgia.[4]

1

The Founding Father

Although the thirty-four charter members included many "solid" citizens of Atlanta, the first four years of the Klan's existence were marked by only sporadic success and frequent financial difficulty. A co-founder of the organization, Jonathan B. Frost, whose offer to finance recruiting and publicity was rejected, embezzled several thousand dollars of the accumulated funds and almost brought the secret order to financial ruin.[1] Nevertheless, an Imperial Proclamation was issued in 1917, directing the attention of the world to the Klan's "tender sympathies and fraternal assistance in the effulgence of the light of life and amid the sable shadows of death."[2]

"Colonel" Simmons (the title was honorary in the Woodmen of the World), the guiding spirit behind the founding of the Klan and its first imperial wizard, was richly endowed with neither character nor ability. In addition, there was nothing in his background to suggest that he would be heard from in later life. The son of a country physician, he was born on a farm near Harpersfield, Alabama, in 1880. He served in the Spanish-American War, and although one admiring author contended that "he advanced more rapidly in military knowledge than the other men of his company," his genius went unrecognized since he did not rise above the rank of private.[3] Returning to civilian life, he experienced a religious conversion at a rural revival meeting and embarked upon a career in the ministry of the Methodist Episcopal Church, South. After several years as a circuit rider in Florida and Alabama, Simmons left the cloth because the Methodist Conference of Alabama refused to award him a large church of his own. The ex-preacher then became a field representative and salesman of fraternal insurance for the Woodmen of the World.[4] His varied career also included a brief term as Instructor of Southern History at Atlanta's faltering Lanier University.

Certainly in the earliest years of the Invisible Empire, Simmons intended that the secret order be no more than a genuine fraternal lodge, with largely ritualistic activities and a selective membership policy. He therefore busied himself with formulating a secret jargon and administrative structure commensurate with this plan, often copying verbatim from the ritual of the Reconstruction Klan. When finished, the Imperial Wizard gathered his handiwork together in a highly classified, 54-page pamphlet known as the *Kloran*. Simmons told his followers that the *Kloran* was "THE book" of the Invisible Empire, and he admonished them never to take the document "where any person in the foreign world may chance to become acquainted with its sacred contents."

But Simmons set a poor example for his men. More concerned with protecting his own financial interests than the mysteries of the Klan, the Colonel copyrighted the *Kloran* on January 16, 1917 (copyright number 2 Cl A 448991), and duly deposited two copies with the Library of Congress. In the coming years therefore, when candidates for initiation swore themselves to eternal secrecy, the object of their oath was available in the nation's capital for any who might wish to examine it.

Whether the membership before 1920 was selective or not is purely problematical, but it most certainly remained small, and according to one observer, "had less strength in Atlanta then the B'nai B'rith." [5] Not enough money was pooled by the founders to publicize the Klan widely, and then, too, the Imperial Wizard insisted upon his superficial secrecy. Expenses often exceeded income, and the Colonel met the deficit with his own money. Of these difficult days he later recalled: "There were times during those five early years, before the public knew of the Klan, when I walked the streets with my shoes worn through because I had no money." [6] An unbelievably egotistical individual, Simmons did not wait for posterity to recognize his achievement, constantly reiterating that, "I was its sole parent, author and founder; it was MY creation—MY CHILD, if you please, MY first born." [7]

Perhaps as a reward for his loyal efforts, Simmons endowed his position with very considerable power. As Imperial Wizard he could appoint and remove all national officers, issue and revoke chapter charters, and formulate the ritual and dogma. He divided the Invisible Empire into eight domains, each consisting of a group of states and each presided over by a grand goblin, whose powers were considerably less impressive than his title. The Klan hierarchy proceeded downward to the state organizations or realms, thence to the provinces, and finally to the local chapter or klavern, the smallest administrative unit. Here only was Americanism interpreted to mean the democratic election of officers.

Public attention prior to 1920 was only rarely directed at Simmons's brainchild, which was active only in Mobile, Birmingham, Atlanta, and Montgomery. When a strike threatened the shipyards of Mobile in the summer of 1918, white-sheeted figures prevented a work stoppage by abducting a labor leader and threatening "idlers and draft dodgers." In Birmingham, virtually the same pattern was repeated when a strike leader disappeared just as a walkout seemed imminent at the great mills in the suburbs of the city. In addition, Klansmen demanded more police action against the criminal elements of Birmingham and so terrified local hoodlums that the police chief advised Nashville authorities to organize a klavern. In Montgomery the secret order warned loose women to keep away from the soldiers at Camp Sheridan, and in Atlanta it participated in a Confederate reunion.

Despite such sporadic and generally favorable publicity, the Invisible Empire remained confined to Alabama and Georgia and as late as 1920 could best be described as just another indolent southern fraternal group. With a total membership of less than two thousand, there was no indication that the Knights of the Ku Klux Klan, from among hundreds of secret societies and patriotic fraternities, would vault to national prominence.[8]

2

National Expansion

Fate intervened in the spring of 1920, however. Two enterprising promoters had cast a long, interested glance at the hooded fraternity, recognizing its financial, as well as patriotic, potentialities. Edward Young Clarke, an unimposing dark-haired man in his early thirties, and Mrs. Elizabeth Tyler, a crafty, rotund divorcée, had won some success with promotional drives for the Red Cross, Salvation Army, and Anti-Saloon League. They noticed the Klan's floundering condition and reasoned correctly that it could greatly broaden its appeal by exploiting the fears and prejudices of uncritical minds against the Catholic, the Jew, the Negro, the Oriental, and the recent immigrant. They formed the Southern Publicity Association and entered into negotiations with the Imperial Wizard, reaching agreement on June 7, 1920.[1] According to the terms of the contract, Clarke was to be appointed imperial kleagle as head of the Klan's Department of Propagation. As such, he would receive two dollars and fifty cents for each new recruit, an arrangement that would occasionally yield him thirty thousand dollars per week.[2]

Once free to put his booster techniques into practice, Clarke quickly transformed the dormant order into the militant, uncompromising instrument that soon scourged the nation. His new appeal to fear and prejudice proved remarkably successful; within eighteen months there were over one hundred thousand new members, and the Invisible Empire had established strong chapters in the Southwest, Midwest, and the West Coast. In a report to Colonel Simmons in 1921, Clarke declared that in three months his organization had added 48,000 persons to Klan rosters, prompting the observation that, "In all my years of experience in organization work I have never seen anything equal to the clamor throughout the nation for the Klan." [3]

The chief elements in the propagation effort were kleagles, or recruiters, more than two hundred of whom were in the field by the summer of 1921. First contacting their personal friends, the kleagles then aimed at Protestant clergymen, who were offered free membership and complimentary subscriptions to Klan periodicals. Invitations to membership, often typed on expensive stationery to feign exclusiveness, were then mailed to Masonic groups, patriotic societies, and fraternal orders. [4] Ambitious kleagles also utilized Klan propaganda films such as *The Face at Your Window* or arranged for Klan lecturers to speak on the principles of "one hundred per cent Americanism." Masters in the use of such glittering phrases as "the tenets of the Christian religion," "pure womanhood," or "just laws," the professional recruiters preyed upon the fear that the country was in danger from organized elements within. Painting the KKK as the organized good of the community, the kleagles promised to combat these pernicious influences and to return the nation to older values. The only avenue open to true patriots was the Ku Klux Klan, and the individual kleagles, who were allowed to retain four dollars of each recruit's ten-dollar klectoken, seldom rejected the application of a patriot. [5]

The impressive initial success of Klan recruiters was closely related to the peculiar mood of the American people early in the 1920's. The exaggerated idealism that accompanied World War I had conveyed the belief that the campaign in France represented nothing less than a struggle to make the world safe for democracy. But the Armistice did not bring the millennium. With the reduction once again of Europe to a group of squabbling nations and with the repudiation of the League of Nations by the U. S. Senate, disillusionment inevitably resulted. To a large extent the old wartime hatred for the Germans was now translated into a peacetime suspicion of everything foreign. Attorney General A. Mitchell Palmer had alerted the nation to the threat of the Bolshevist, the radical, the terrorist, and the anarchist in the Red Scare of 1919. But the arrest and deportation of a few of the undesirables did not ease the general feeling of uncertainty. Neither did a sharp recession in the summer and fall of 1920. Caused by resistance to high wartime prices and by marked reductions of purchases from abroad, the crisis resulted in numerous bankruptcies and large scale unemployment. Americans yearned for a respite, for a return to "normalcy." Support for Warren G. Harding seemed one route to the past; membership in the Invisible Empire was another.

The first nationwide notice of the Ku Klux Klan came in the fall of 1921. On September 6, after months of research by Rowland Thomas, the New York *World* began a three-week exposé of the secret order, with particular emphasis on its more violent aspects. Carried by eighteen leading newspapers, including the *St. Louis Post-Dispatch, Boston Globe, Pittsburgh Sun, Cleveland Plain-Dealer, New Orleans Times-Picayune, Seattle Times, Daily Oklahoman, Houston Chronicle, Dallas Morning News,* and *Columbus* (Georgia) *Enquirer-Sun,* the articles documented Klan purposes, ideals, and practices. The *World* estimated its combined strength in forty-five states as five hundred thousand,[6] and, on September 19, 1921, it chronologically listed 152 separate outrages attributed to the Invisible Empire, including four murders, forty-one floggings, and twenty-seven tar and feather parties.

Partly as a result of the *World's* coverage, the United States House of Representatives was induced to investigate the alleged misdeeds of the Klan. Testifying before the Committee on Rules, Post Office Inspector O. B. Williamson related that available Klan records indicated collections of $860,363 between June 1, 1920, and September 24, 1921, and Imperial Cashier N. N. Furney admitted that the secret order's financial accounting was confused.[7] But the most important witness was the Imperial Wizard himself. Impressively dressed in a dark business suit, the six-foot two-inch Klan potentate testified that the Invisible Empire neither endorsed nor participated in violence of any sort, and he reminded the committee that the Klan's oath and ritual were a matter of public record. Re-emphasizing its patriotic and benevolent purposes, he asserted that the outrages attributed to the Klan were in reality committed by criminals and trouble-makers hiding behind the robes of Klansmen. After this point by point refutation of charges made against the Klan, Simmons dramatically swore "in the presence of God," that if the Ku Klux Klan were guilty of a hundredth part of the charges made against it, "I would from this room send a telegram calling together the grand kloncilium [executive council] for the purpose of forever disbanding the Klan in every section of the United States." The Colonel's testimony was successful and no punitive congressional action was recommended, perhaps because Atlanta Representative W. D. Upshaw introduced a bill calling for a similar investigation of the Knights of Columbus and other "secret" societies.

Paradoxically, the net effect of the investigations of the *World* and Congress was that the Invisible Empire received a great deal of gratuitous and much needed advertising. The publicity was a boon to recruiting. Many persons outside the East were inclined to look with favor upon the secret order merely because a great New York daily had seen fit to condemn it.[8] The previously unnoticed Klan became a familiar conversational topic in areas far removed from the nearest kleagle, and the national headquarters in Atlanta was deluged with applications, many of them on facsimile blanks printed in the New York *World*. Within four months more than two hundred local chapters were chartered, and within one year membership burgeoned from one hundred thousand to almost one million.

But success brought with it an attendant struggle for power that exposed the incompetence and corruption at the Imperial Palace. Unrest dated from the exposé of the New York *World*, which revealed the details of Imperial Kleagle Clarke's arrest in 1919 (intoxicated and partially clad) with Mrs. Tyler on a disorderly conduct charge.[9] Although Clarke could only offer the fumbling excuse that his over-zealous wife was responsible for the incident, Atlanta Klansmen purchased all three thousand available copies of the New York *World* in the Georgia capital in a futile attempt to protect his reputation. Charging that "Southern womanhood has been slaughtered," the Atlanta Klan's weekly newspaper told its readers that the attack upon Mrs. Tyler's good name meant that, "Your mothers, sisters, and daughters are unsafe from the millionaire newspaper owners."

Imperial Wizard Simmons was undoubtedly troubled by the indiscretion of his subordinates, but he was unable or unwilling to refuse them support. When four prominent northern Klansmen called for the resignations of both Clarke and Tyler, the petitioners were themselves banished, and when Chattanooga Klan No. 4 passed a "treasonable resolution" against the two promoters, the charter of the Tennessee chapter was revoked. Dissension subsided with the resignation of Mrs. Tyler due to failing health, but the controversy resumed in September 1922, when Clarke, who by his own admission had been arrested many times, was jailed in Indiana for the possession of liquor immediately after having made a speech in Muncie on "law enforcement."

By repeatedly affirming his loyalty to Clarke and refusing to eliminate graft and corruption, Simmons ultimately exposed his own incompetence. A dreamer rather than an administrator, the Imperial Wizard had achieved some notoriety within inner circles as a drunkard. Ill-suited to superintend the affairs of a large organization, he failed to give proper aid to state officials and was accused of misappropriating large sums of money. A six-month vacation from May 10 to November 10, 1922, proved to be his undoing, and by the fall of 1922, a strong anti-Simmons faction had developed.

On the evening of November 26, immediately prior to the opening of the first national klonvokation (national convention) in Atlanta, Imperial Night Hawk (national investigator) Fred Savage, Indiana Grand Dragon (state commander) David C. Stephenson, Texas Grand Dragon H. C. McCall, and Arkansas Grand Dragon

James Comer met at the Piedmont Hotel to map strategy for a light-ning coup. They decided to dupe Simmons into accepting an ex-alted but meaningless position, while the real power was taken from his grasp.

At three o'clock in the morning on November 27, 1922, Stephen-son and Savage were dispatched to "Klankrest," the expensive home of the Imperial Wizard at 1840 Peachtree Road. Awakening Simmons, the visitors solemnly related that his character was going to be attacked on the convention floor, that gunfire would inevita-bly result, and that the convention would be wrecked. The aston-ished Simmons was told that the one way to avoid tragedy was for him to refuse to offer his name for renomination, accepting instead the post of emperor, with tenure for life. In the meantime, as Ste-phenson and Savage suggested, it would be advisable to select a temporary Imperial Wizard until a permanent solution could be found.

The gullible Simmons accepted this recommendation, and on the following day he unwittingly abdicated his throne. His "temporary" successor, who was to serve as imperial wizard for seventeen years, was former exalted cyclops (chapter president) of powerful Dallas Klan No. 66 and great titan (district commander) of Texas Province No. 2. Hiram Wesley Evans, who reportedly possessed "the deter-mined convictions of Martin Luther, the kindness of Lincoln, and the strategy and generalship of Napoleon," [10] served as imperial wizard for almost three months before his former boss realized the extent of the trickery. It was difficult for Colonel Simmons to adjust to his new position of impotence, because "not long after Evans got in I noticed a coldness among all the office help. I didn't have any office to go to. I just had to sort of hang around the place even though my title was Emperor." [11]

No longer in control of the men's group, Simmons decided to organize a women's branch of the Ku Klux Klan. On April 7, 1923, he proclaimed the creation of "Kamelia" and named himself as its "El Magus," or highest official. According to the Colonel, who imme-diately began accepting applications for membership, Kamelia was the answer to a long felt need for a unifying body for the nation's white Protestant women.

Table 1

DISTRIBUTION OF KLAN MEMBERSHIP BY MAJOR
GEOGRAPHICAL REGIONS*

Region	1922 Percentage	1924 Percentage
North Central (Indiana, Ohio, Illinois)	6.4	40.2
Southwest (Texas, Oklahoma, Arkansas, Louisiana, New Mexico, and Arizona)	61.0	25.6
South (Entire South east of Mississippi River, including Kentucky and West Virginia)	22.2	16.1
Midwest (Minnesota, Iowa, Nebraska, Kansas, Missouri, Michigan, and North Dakota)	5.0	8.3
Far West (Oregon, California, Idaho, Utah, Washington, Colorado, and Wyoming)	5.1	6.1
North Atlantic (New York, Delaware, New Jersey, Pennsylvania, Maryland, and New England)	0.3	3.7

* Report of the Imperial Kligrapp (secretary) at the 1924 Klonvokation, reprinted in Edgar I. Fuller, *The Maelstrom: The Visible of the Invisible Empire* (Denver: The Maelstrom Publishing Co., 1925), p. 125.

Unfortunately for Simmons, Kamelia did not please the Evans administration, which itself was planning to absorb a half-dozen female patriotic societies then functioning in various parts of the country. After all, the women represented a new source of revenue and votes. Imperial Wizard Evans was thus angered by Simmons's unauthorized act. He forbade all Klansmen from associating with Kamelia and announced that it had no connection whatever with the Ku Klux Klan.

The split between the founder of the Invisible Empire and its highest national officer was now complete. In well-publicized verbal assaults, each faction charged the other with treason and disloyalty. Simmons took advantage of Evans's temporary absence from Atlanta in April 1923 to take possession forcibly of the Imperial Palace. Evans rushed back to the city, a complex legal battle ensued, and the courts temporarily administered the affairs of the Klan.[12] An out-of-court settlement was finally reached on May 1, 1923. Evans was to retain the post of imperial wizard, but the rights of Simmons to the ritual, regalia, and signs of the Klan were recognized. In return for his copyrights the founder of the secret order was to receive one thousand dollars per month for life, a figure that was later altered to a flat $146,000.[13] The Colonel continued to snipe at the Klan until the issue was finally resolved with his banishment from the Invisible Empire on January 5, 1924. After repeated failures to organize other secret fraternal orders, William Joseph Simmons died quietly in Luverne, Alabama, in May 1945.

The well-publicized and bitterly fought struggle among high national officers brought irreparable harm to the Invisible Empire, particularly in the cities. Each faction sought the support of local chapters, and many urban Klans split down the middle on the Evans-Simmons issue. Thousands of previously loyal members resigned or simply stopped paying dues when they realized that the Klan might simply be a money-making institution.

There were, however, certain advantages in the transfer of Klan leadership because Imperial Wizard Evans initiated a number of much needed reforms. Removing his opponents from positions of influence, he canceled the lucrative propagation contract of Edward Young Clarke, placed individual kleagles on a salary rather than a commission basis, and restricted the wearing of white robes to regular chapter meetings. Announcement was made that henceforth the secret order would advance its program by organized po-

Table 2
STATEMENT OF KLAN ASSETS AND LIABILITIES BY SIX-MONTH PERIODS*

	July 1922	Dec. 1922	July 1923	Dec. 1923
Cash	$ 79,765.06	$194,185.72	$ 637,854.14	$ 840,337.39
Notes Receivable	6,807.78	8,161.60	10,196.19	42,232.84
Accounts Receivable	76,138.93	59,608.48	124,777.73	166,953.95
Permanent Assets	222,518.73	252,718.15	309,229.56	409,643.11
Supply Inventory	11,383.87	9,543.58	6,415.80	82,093.78
Other	6,556.81			12,500.00
Total Assets	$403,171.18	$524,217.53	$1,088,473.42	$1,553,761.07
Accounts Payable	$ 73,513.94	$ 72,126.03	$ 830.00	$ 29,505.96
Notes Payable	137,091.03	112,866.03		
Other	36,622.62	11,465.00	1,300.00	1,655.00
Total Liabilities	$247,227.59	$196,457.06	$ 2,130.00	$ 31,160.96
Surplus	$155,943.59	$327,760.47	$1,086,343.42	$1,522,600.11

* The Imperial Night-Hawk, August 29, 1923, p. 1; and The Imperial Night-Hawk, January 23, 1924, p. 1.

litical action and that Klansmen participating in lawless activities would be immediately banished. Moreover, Evans informed the nation that, far from being an un-American hate-mongering institution, the Klan was in reality a benevolent and patriotic society. Emphasis was therefore placed on the positive elements of klankraft (concepts and relationships): education, temperance, the flag, Protestantism, morality, and charity.

Although there was no formal connection between the Invisible Empire and any religious denomination, Fundamentalism was the central thread of the Klan program. Declaring that "America is Protestant and so it must remain," the KKK glorified the "old time religion," rejected evolution and higher criticism, and admonished its members to attend church regularly. Protestant clergymen were reminded that Klansmen accepted the Bible as the literal and unalterable word of God. As proof of their devotion, masked Knights frequently appeared unannounced before quiescent congregations for the purpose of making a well-publicized donation.

An almost natural corollary to the Klan's religious orientation was its effort to become a bulwark against "modernism." The wearing of short skirts by women and the "petting" in parked automobiles and dancing in smoke-filled rooms by both sexes were indications of an erosion of traditional customs and values. At the root of the problem was "Demon Rum." The Eighteenth Amendment had supposedly banished liquor from the United States forever; in actual practice the Volstead law lacked adequate enforcement provisions, and many Americans proved quite unwilling to accept abstinence. The illicit manufacture and sale of intoxicants assumed immense proportions, and, according to temperance organizations, brought along such attendant vices as gambling and prostitution. The Invisible Empire unhesitatingly affirmed that it stood foursquare for law enforcement and against bootleggers, moonshiners, and "wild women."

The Klan's campaign against moral laxity earned for it the allegiance and support of many women. The ladies auxiliaries in such cities as Denver, Portland, Indianapolis, and Dallas were indispensable elements in hooded political success, while thousands of additional women offered "one hundred per cent Americanism" their silent endorsement. Klan lecturers often dwelt upon the virtues of motherhood, chastity, and temperance and emphasized the importance of "clean motion pictures and decent literature." Offering to protect the "purity of womanhood," the Invisible Empire promised to see to it that "the young man who induces a young girl to get drunk is held accountable." The appeal was summed up by the following popular broadside:

> Every criminal, every gambler, every thug, every libertine, every girl ruiner, every home wrecker, every wife beater, every dope peddler, every moonshiner, every crooked politician, every pagan Papist priest, every shyster lawyer, every K. of C., every white slaver, every brothel madam, every Rome controlled newspaper, every black spider—is fighting the Klan. Think it over. Which side are you on?

The third basic element of the Klan's positive program was "practical patriotism" or Americanism. Obsessed with the external displays of national pride, the secret order was always alert for evidence of disloyalty. Among its most frequent activities were presentations of American flags to schools, churches, and private institutions. Moreover, the Klan reflected traditional isolationist sentiment against one-worldism. It fought the League of Nations and the World Court and argued that "American questions should be settled in America by Americans."

Strongly committed to the theory that a sovereign nation should train its own future citizens, the Invisible Empire fought for the extension of the public school system. Terming the little red schoolhouse "the cornerstone of good government and the secret of our prosperity as a nation," it charged state legislators with niggardly appropriations and even supported the controversial Sterling-Towner federal aid to education bill. Although devoted to the "eternal separation of church and state," the Klan decreed that the Bible should be read daily in every classroom and produced statistics showing a relationship between the burglary insurance rate of selected cities and the number of years the scriptures had been part of the public school daily routine.

But Protestantism, motherhood, morality, patriotism, education, and other positive attitudes did not represent the sum total of the Klan program. There was another, and more seamy, side to "one hundred per cent Americanism." Officially, the Invisible Empire denied all hates, but by its definition of membership it appealed to citizens who cherished them. Nativism and racial consciousness have had a long tradition in the United States; the Ku Klux Klan merely awakened smoldering prejudices by capitalizing upon white Protestant fear of Catholicism, Judaism, and racial amalgamation.

Among Klansmen in almost every state and section, the most basic and pervasive concern was the Pope. Catholics were regarded not simply as communicants of an idolatrous church, but as citizens who placed their love and devotion to the Vatican above their allegiance to the United States. It was widely held that the Pope was a political autocrat with a ravenous desire to extend his temporal as well as spiritual influence across the Atlantic. Klan orators spoke of a not far distant Romanist uprising, and the "confessions" of Helen Jackson, an "escaped nun," were often distributed at Klan rallies. Wild rumors told of Protestant girls being held captive in convents, of Catholics gaining control of the strategic heights surrounding Washington, and of Knights of Columbus drilling at night and storing arms in the churches. Nor were those the only reasons that Catholic patriotism was suspect; were they not responsible for all three presidential assassinations and for 90 per cent of the desertions in World War I? Skeptics were warned that Catholics could be manipulated by priests and reminded of traditional Papal interference in the political affairs of Europe. According to the Klan, Catholics were fanatics, who, if given the chance, "would again forge a tyrant's chain, revive the Inquisition, and fire the faggots around the martyr's stake as they were in the habit of doing in times gone by."

Thus was the Catholic Church painted as the deadly enemy of free institutions, to be opposed not so much for her religious beliefs as for her dark and deadly political machinations. According to Imperial Wizard Evans, "The real objection to Romanism in America is not that it is a religion—which is no objection at all—but that it is a church in politics; an organized, disciplined, powerful rival to every political government." Invariably, the Invisible Empire opposed all Catholic candidates for political office. While Klansmen would not assert that an individual's membership in the Roman Church would make him less efficient as a councilman or congressman, there was always the argument that the election of every additional Catholic hastened the day of the Papal takeover. Men who accepted ecclesiastical authority were held to be poor guardians of democratic government and individual liberties. Insisting upon the impossibility of being both a good Catholic and a good citizen, the Klan labeled the Roman Church "fundamentally and irredeemably, in its leadership, in politics, in thought, and largely in membership, actually and actively alien, un-American, and usually anti-American." The most vicious invective was reserved for the Society of Jesus (Jesuits), which the *Kourier* labeled as "the deepest, darkest, and most damnable association of political and religious pirates which the world has ever seen."

Jews were less numerous, and therefore less threatening, than Catholics, but they also failed to pass the test of "one hundred per cent Americanism." The Jewish people were criticized for their racial and religious cohesiveness, and their business leaders were blamed for unfair competition. The Semite was characterized as a parasitic shop keeper rather than "a pioneer, an empire builder, a maker of nations." Most importantly, he was an internationalist, who, according to the Klan, would not in a thousand years form basic attachments comparable to those the older type of immigrant would form within a year.

Closely related to anti-Catholicism and anti-Semitism was the Klan's crusade for the restriction of immigration. After 1890, hundreds of thousands of Italians, Poles, Russians, Czechs, Slavs, and Serbs answered the Statue of Liberty's invitation to "huddled masses, yearning to breathe free." But these newcomers were quite unlike the northern and western Europeans who had earlier populated the continent. Overwhelmingly Catholic and Jewish, they were often penniless when they reached Ellis Island. Moreover, they congregated in big-city ghettoes, supported urban bosses, clung to Old World traditions, established scores of foreign language newspapers, and sympathized with "radical labor agitators." The Klan cited World War I Army intelligence tests to "prove" that Italians, Slavs, and Greeks were mentally inferior to Anglo-Saxons and Scandinavians and, because of their autocratic heritage, incapable of self-government and unworthy of American citizenship. Referring to aliens as "the most dangerous of all invaders," the Klan predictably labeled the melting pot a "mess of sentimental pottage" and a "silly and deadly philosophy."

The Negro was less threatening but no more acceptable to "one hundred per cent Americanism" than the undisciplined and unchastened immigrant. "Every instinct, every interest, every dictate of conscience and public spirit, insist that white supremacy shall be forever maintained." Thus did Hiram Wesley Evans state the unequivocal position of the Ku Klux Klan with respect to the place of the colored man in American life. Justifying this attitude in terms of the survival of the fittest, the secret order boasted that "each race must fight for its life, must conquer, accept slavery or die." Such evolutionary doctrine would seemingly have run counter to the Fundamentalist beliefs of many Klansmen, but Darwin was apparently orthodox when presented in terms of racial superiority. The KKK regarded the Negro as a mental pygmy, unable and unwilling to perform any but the most menial tasks, and ever anxious to prey upon the purity of white women. As expressed by Klan lecturer R. H. Sawyer, "The Negro, in whose blood flows the mad desire for race amalgamation, is more dangerous than a maddened wild beast and he must and will be controlled." Immediately after World War I, the impression was common among white people, both North and South, that a "new Negro," anxious for social and economic equality, was coming home from France. The widespread uneasiness was reflected in savage race riots in Chicago and Tulsa and in a rapid rise in the number of lynchings in 1919. In most cases, the fears were unfounded and the Negro accepted his former station. But in cities with rapidly growing non-white populations racial feeling was intensified during the 1920's.

It was upon this aggregate of positive and negative issues that the American people were invited to membership in the Ku Klux Klan. Anti-Catholicism was almost everywhere the basic issue, but the kleagles were adept at adjusting prejudices to suit local requirements. Their tactics were successful, and at torchlit ceremonies throughout the country, hundreds and sometimes thousands of over-eager patriots took the solemn oaths of allegiance to the Invisible Empire. The initiation consisted of forming a single file, walking from one ceremonial station to another, listening to verbose passages, and swearing an oath. With the right arm raised, and kneeling on one knee, new members swore never to betray a fellow Klansman, save in instances of treason, rape, malicious murder, and violation of the Klan oath, and promised to uphold free speech, free press, separation of church and state, just laws, and the Constitution. The entire ritual was carefully worded to exclude all aliens:

> Only native-born, white American citizens, who believe in the tenets of the Christian religion, and who owe no allegiance of any degree or nature to any foreign government or institution, religious or political, or to any sect, people, or persons, are eligible for membership.

On the surface, the Ku Klux Klan posed a challenge only to Catholics, Jews, Negroes, and recent immigrants. In a broader sense, however, "one hundred per cent Americanism" challenged all citizens because it questioned the ideals of the entire nation. The United States had achieved much by 1920: highly industrialized, prosperous, and stable, it was a symbol everywhere of religious and political freedom and of the Lockean ideal of equality before the state. The Ku Klux Klan challenged these principles and announced a membership goal of ten million white Protestants, who would accept the notion that certain religions and races and ethnic groups were "more equal" than others. The question was basic, and the answer of the American people was long in coming.

II

THE SOUTH

The mind of the bigot is like the pupil of the eye; the more
light you pour upon it, the more it will contract.

Oliver Wendell Holmes, Jr.

According to Southern folklore, the chaotic decade following the
surrender at Appomattox demonstrated forever the absolute necessity of preserving Negro subservience. Scalawags and carpetbaggers supposedly betrayed their race, and it was the Ku Klux Klan,
as the instrument of the righteous, which restored the South to its
former condition and protected its women in their hour of need. As
one daughter of the Confederacy noted: "No brighter chapter in all
her [the South's] history, no fairer page, will ever be read than that
which tells of that illustrious and glorious organization called the
Ku Klux Klan." [1]

When the Invisible Empire was reborn in 1915, William Joseph
Simmons took full advantage of the luster and "immortal fame" of
its Reconstruction predecessor. As if it were not sufficient to copy
the name, ritual, and garb of the earlier order, Simmons often reit-
erated that his Klan was a living memorial to the white-sheeted
veterans of the "tragic era." Such tactics insured the initial respectability of the KKK, and the region that stretched from the Potomac
to the Rio Grande (including West Virginia, Kentucky, and Oklahoma) eventually contributed almost 700,000 Klansmen to the Invisible Empire, or 34 per cent of the national total. [2]

The former Confederacy was, of course, as varied as it was vast, and in reality there were many Souths, each molded by a peculiar milieu. There was the South of the eastern seaboard, of the Mississippi Delta, of the Gulf Coast, and of the Texas Plains; there was the South of the planter, the field hand, the textile worker, the businessman, and, of course, Jim Crow. But for all its internal dissimilarities, the South was a land apart and easily the most homogeneous of American sections. It was overwhelmingly Protestant and native born; the Bible Belt and the Cotton Belt were scarcely distinguishable, and only Louisiana and Florida contained large numbers of immigrants and Catholics. Secondly, the South, more than any other section, was rural. The region accounted for two of every five American farmers, and Mississippi, Alabama, and South Carolina were the least urban of all states. Thirdly, perhaps because of its agricultural dependence, the South was poor, and often miserably so. In public education, public health, and standard of living it ranked at the bottom, and it could claim few universities or cultural institutions of distinction. Finally, and as many writers have suggested, most importantly, the South was the home of fully 80 per cent of the nation's ten million Negroes in 1920. Of all the ingredients of the "southern way of life," white supremacy was the most essential.

Despite the pervasiveness of the race issue, however, it was neither the exclusive nor the predominant *raison d'être* of the Klan in the South. The Negro had reached a nadir in the South in 1920; he either accepted his old place in the social spectrum or moved to northern cities. Anti-lynching bills were repeatedly and successfully filibustered, and the NAACP was as yet weak and ineffectual. In rural areas of high non-white concentration, such as the Mississippi and Alabama black belts, the Invisible Empire was close to impotence. Rather it was the Catholics that seemed to offer the most immediate threat. They were organized; Negroes were not. As Gunnar Myrdal explained in 1944:

> In the plantation areas where the social and political subordination of Negroes is solidified, there is not much need for special organizations of vigilantes to effectuate the extra-legal sanctions.

The Ku Klux Klan and similar secret societies thrive, rather, in the border regions and in industrial communities.[3]

What were the border regions and industrial communities where the Klan prospered? Because the South was the most rural of American sections, the Mecklin interpretation would seem to indicate that most area Klansmen could be found loitering around a village store. To be sure, the secret order did find some success in southern towns, and William Alexander Percy has left a memorable account of its impact:

> But in the Klan fight the very spirit of hatred materialized before our eyes. It was the ugliest thing I have ever beheld. You didn't linger on the post office steps or drink cokes with random companions: too many faces were hard and set, too many eyes were baleful and venomous. You couldn't go a block without learning by a glance that someone hated you. . . .[4]

But Percy's native Greenville, Mississippi, like most other southern towns, was not a bastion of Klan strength. There were no atrocities, no whippings, no threatening letters, and no masked parades in Greenville, and the local klavern failed in its great effort to elect one of its own as sheriff. Rather it was in the sizable communities that the Invisible Empire won its greatest pecuniary and political success. By northern standards, southern cities were not large in 1920. Only New Orleans had 300,000 people, and only eight others had more than 100,000. But southern cities were thriving. The New South of Henry Grady had finally taken hold. Textile mills, railroad shops, warehouses, and factories were creating a new way of life in the urban South. As a result, in Atlanta, Memphis, Knoxville, Dallas, and a dozen other cities, the kleagles of the Klan were not to be disappointed.

3

Atlanta: The Imperial City

A recurrent theme in the history of the Ku Klux Klan has been its continuing relationship with the city of Atlanta. In 1915 and again in 1946, the secret order was reborn in the Georgia capital, and throughout the entire period Atlantans have exercised a disproportionate influence in Klan affairs.

With a population of more than two hundred thousand, about 2 per cent of whom were foreign-born whites, the imperial city of the Invisible Empire was a very lively entrepôt and mercantile center in 1920 and ranked as one of the largest and most urbane cities in the South. Although a recipient of both white and Negro immigration between 1910 and 1920, Atlanta's population remained approximately one-third Negro. The "capital of the Protestant world" [1] was a stronghold of the Methodist and Baptist churches and was the seat of publication prior to World War I of Tom Watson's anti-Catholic and anti-Semitic journal, *The Jeffersonian*. Long known as a city of "joiners," the Georgia metropolis was dotted with lodges, mystic societies, and fraternal halls. The Imperial Wizard was himself a member of some fifteen secret organizations, including the Masons, Royal Arch Masons, and Knights Templars, at the time he founded the Invisible Empire.

The original charter of the modern Ku Klux Klan, granted July 1, 1916, was signed by twelve persons, all from Fulton County: William Joseph Simmons, H. D. Shackleford, E. R. Clarkson, Jonathan B. Frost, R. C. W. Ramspeck, W. L. Smith, G. D. Couch, L. M. Johnson, W. C. Bennett, A. G. Dallas, J. F. V. Saul, and W. E. Floding.[2] Prominent in local fraternal affairs, these men were soon joined by some of the city's "better" citizens, with the result that the Invisible Empire had a strong urban flavor from the beginning. In addition to Imperial Wizard Simmons, who had lived in Atlanta for a dozen years before founding the secret order, most high national officials were long-time residents of the Georgia capital. Imperial Kleagle Edward Young Clarke, whose brother Francis was managing editor of the *Atlanta Constitution,* married into a prominent local family and had resided in the city for many years. Imperial Kligrapp (national secretary) Louis David Wade of suburban Decatur, was a native of Oswego, New York, but had moved to Atlanta at age fifteen and later launched a successful career with the Southern Bell Telephone and Telegraph Company.[3] Imperial Klabee (national treasurer) H. C. Montgomery, a graduate of the Northern School of Optometry in Chicago, was well known in business circles and owned a large Atlanta optical store. Elected chairman of the Fulton County Board of Commissioners of Roads and Revenues, Imperial Klonsel (attorney) Paul S. Etheridge was a prominent member of the Atlanta bar, an alumnus of Mercer University, a deacon in the Baptist Church, and a future Superior Court judge.[4]

Among other Atlantans associated with the Invisible Empire were Mrs. Elizabeth Tyler, vice chairman of the Georgia Committee of the Republican Party; John A. Boykin, solicitor general of the Atlanta Judicial Court; E. D. Rivers, later governor of Georgia; and scores of minor politicians.[5] Although not a southerner by birth, Grand Goblin F. L. Savage, director of the Klan's Department of Investigation, was no small-towner. A native of Boston, he operated the Savage Detective Agency in New York City for thirteen years before joining Colonel Simmons's staff.

The first "imperial aulic" (office) of the Invisible Empire was in a loft of the Georgia Savings Bank Building in downtown Atlanta. Large black letters proclaimed to any passerby the location of Klan headquarters, a disorderly, unpretentious room where Simmons usually worked alone. In four years the office was twice relocated, first to the Silvey and then to the Haynes Building.[6]

Rapid membership growth made possible a marked improvement in the Klan's physical facilities after 1920. E. Y. Clarke opened a separately administered recruiting office in the Flatiron Building, and Imperial Wizard Simmons took up residence in a thirty thousand dollar home at 1840 Peachtree Road, a gift from Klansmen in recognition of his early service.[7] The most auspicious Klan acquisition, however, was a $75,000 white mansion known as the Imperial Palace. Purchased in 1921 and located at 2621 Peachtree Road, in a fashionable and shaded residential area six miles north of downtown Atlanta, the impressive headquarters soon became a mecca for visiting dragons, titans, and cyclopes. Kleagles continued to report to the Flatiron Building, where Clarke chose to remain in order to avoid interference from Simmons.

Although overshadowed by national headquarters, Atlanta's powerful Nathan Bedford Forrest Klan No. 1 was an important factor in the life of the city. During the lean years before 1920, local leader Benjamin H. Sullivan often invited the Imperial Wizard to preside over meetings of "the mother Klan of the Invisible Empire." There it was Simmons's custom to draw two revolvers, place them on the table before him, and shout to his subjects, "Bring on your niggers!"

Atlanta members rarely engaged in public demonstrations prior to 1920. Their first appearance came during a Confederate Reunion on October 10, 1919, when they paraded down Peachtree and Whitehall behind Civil War veterans. Three months later Klan No. 1 gathered in force at a giant temperance bonfire celebrating the birth of Prohibition and the death of "King Barleycorn." Marching with the Anti-Saloon League, the silent Klansmen bore torches and "chilled the marrow in the bones" of onlookers. Klan orators emphasized that the secret order stood for "fair and impartial enforcement of all laws, not only of the prohibition law, but of all statutes."

Law enforcement was apparently subject to various interpretations by Klansmen. Less than two months after the temperance demonstration, J. C. Thomas, a lunch-counter operator, received anonymous threatening letters warning him to "leave alone" a woman with whom he was associated in business. Disregarding the threat, Thomas was subsequently assaulted by four men and taken to a lonely suburban wood near the Lakewood Amusement Park. Unfortunately for the assailants, however, Thomas possessed a knife and was skilled in its use. He killed Klansman Fred Thompson and scattered his other attackers. A grand jury refused to indict Thomas for the death of Thompson, but did indict two of his abductors for assault with intent to murder. They were acquitted and no reference was made to the Klan. But the driver of the car, Homer Pitts, later became a California kleagle, and his attorney was appointed grand goblin of the Pacific Domain.

Violence was certainly not the only activity of local Klansmen. As the home of the first Klan chapter in the nation it was only natural that Atlanta should spawn the first "one hundred per cent American" newspaper. The *Searchlight* appeared on June 22, 1919, under the joint sponsorship of the Klan and the Junior Order, United American Mechanics.[8] Owned by Mrs. Tyler and edited by attorney James O. Wood from the eighth floor of the Georgia Savings Bank Building, the Protestant weekly was progressive by Klan standards. It scored movie censorship as a "curtailment of our liberties," supported wage increases (but not the right to strike) for coal miners, favored public aid to dependent children, and, through staff correspondent Grover C. Edmundson, ridiculed the hallowed doctrine of states rights. Discussing Senator Hiram Johnson's bill for federal regulation of child labor, Edmundson chided representatives of southern states who "seem to forget that the Civil War is over, and that the old hallucinations about the rights of States belong properly to history and not to this generation."

The *Searchlight* was orthodox on most other matters, raging at caustic Baltimore editor H. L. Mencken, encouraging the "deportation of undesirables" to their "European habitats," and denouncing the international Jew. White supremacy was so widely accepted as to require no special preachment, but the *Searchlight* did encourage the development of a race consciousness that would teach the white man "to hold his blood too sacred to mix it with that of another and inferior race." Obsessed with the notion of Nordic superiority, the weekly newspaper anticipated the Yale discovery of 1965 by seeking "the elimination of the Columbus legend" and the recognition of Leif Ericson as the discoverer of America.

Selling for five cents on newsstands throughout Atlanta, the *Searchlight* was an indispensable source of local and national Klan news. Popular even among non-Klansmen, the newspaper attracted a considerable amount of advertising, and local Knights were admonished to "see if you can find what you want advertised in the Ku Klux Press." This was a distinct possibility in Atlanta, because the *Searchlight*'s advertisers included Studebaker, Coca-Cola, the Elgin Watch Company, used car lots, taxi companies, chiropractors, physicians, drug stores, grocers, attorneys, lunch rooms, dry goods merchants, and even Marcell, "the Mineral Man," who for five dollars could cure anything from itch and bad blood to "women's trouble in general."

White supremacy was a basic tenet of the Klan in the South, but urban klaverns took up the cudgel even more vigorously against Roman Catholics. In Atlanta, the *Searchlight* warned often of the papal menace and frequently printed such one-line embellishments as, "What are nearly a million Knights of Columbus arming for?" and, "Do the K.C.'s intend to shoot religion into the heretics?" In 1922, the Klan attempted to intimidate the Atlanta Board of Education into dismissing Catholics from teaching assignments and threatened the lives of demurring board members (Klan-leaning Carl F. Hutcheson and Julia O'Keefe Nelson needed no such encouragement).[9] Local employers were urged to fire Catholic workers, while merchants with "Roman" sympathies were boycotted. Even the city council was infected with the fever, passing in September 1921 a resolution denouncing the Knights of Columbus as an un-American order. Mayor James Key vetoed the motion.

Unquestionably, the most colorful and controversial anti-Catholic in Atlanta was Imperial Kludd Caleb A. Ridley, the national chaplain. From his inner city pastorate at Central Baptist Church just southwest of the central business district, Ridley frequently boasted to his congregation of laborers and factory workers, "I am a Klansman and proud of it." When out of Atlanta on Klan speaking engagements, he often yielded his pulpit to Imperial Wizard Simmons or Imperial Klokard (lecturer) William J. Mahoney. A vigorous campaigner for Klan political aspirants and a confirmed white supremacist, Ridley recommended "the white robe and the fiery cross" as the best method of keeping the Negro in check. But the Pope was his real enemy:

> I can't help being what I am racially. I am not a Jew, nor a negro, nor a foreigner. I am an Anglo-Saxon white man, so ordained by the hand and will of God, and so constituted and trained that I cannot conscientiously take either my politics or my religion from some secluded ass on the other side of the world.[10]

The Reverend Mr. Ridley's well-publicized Klan activities eventually brought him into conflict with fellow clergymen. In June 1923 the Atlanta Baptist Ministers Conference withdrew fellowship from him for "conduct unbecoming a minister of the gospel" and threatened to expel the Central Baptist Church from the Atlanta Baptist Association unless action were taken by the congregation. Supported by the *Searchlight*, Ridley promptly charged the ministers conference with hatred for the Ku Klux Klan, and he resigned his pastorate, despite a vote of confidence from his church. He became a full-time lecturer for the Invisible Empire, but in October was arrested for driving while intoxicated when police officers found two flasks of corn liquor in his car. The charge finished Ridley as a Klan speaker. Three months later he "cut loose financially and otherwise from every secular organization and fraternal order" and humbly petitioned the Atlanta Baptist Ministers Conference for reinstatement. Not expecting the sort of position "I hitherto have held," Ridley asked "that in some small way I be permitted to come back as a plain preacher of His plain words."

Few Atlanta ministers were as outspoken as Ridley either in praise or denunciation of the Ku Klux Klan. In general, those who tolerated the Invisible Empire were financially aided by Klan members, as when Klansmen appeared with an offering at the close of a revival service at the Atlanta Christian Church, while vigorous opposition awaited those who took exception to the Klan program. The Reverend C. B. Wilmer of St. Luke's Episcopal Church, a persistent antagonist of the secret order, was attacked in the *Searchlight* and investigated in two states by police officers in an effort to blacken his name. Dr. Plato Durham, a Methodist minister and a professor of theology at Emory University, was branded a Negrophile by the Klan, and the Reverend M. Ashby Jones was denounced for permitting a Negro to attend an interracial committee gathering in his home and for calling that Negro "mister" in the presence of a "body of fair womanhood of Atlanta." [11]

With few exceptions, public opposition to the Klan was rare in the Georgia capital. Federal Judge Samuel H. Sibley, however, told the Atlanta Kiwanis Club that Klansmen were no better than violators of prohibition laws and the "radical wing of organized labor," a remark which led the *Searchlight* to label Sibley "a small man in a big job." Noticeably silent were the metropolitan newspapers—the *Constitution, Journal,* and *Georgian*—none of which followed the vigorous anti-Klan lead of Julian Harris's *Columbus Enquirer-Sun.* The heavy influence of militant Americanism and Kluxism in Atlanta did stir the city's Greek community into forming the American Hellenic Educational Progressive Association in 1922. A secret and middle-class organization which espoused assimilation, adoption, and conformity, the AHEPA gained impressive strength in the South and Southwest during the decade.[12]

The probable explanation for Atlanta's relative acquiescence in Klan growth was the realization that the Invisible Empire contributed substantially to the city's economy. As the home of both the Georgia and national organizations, the Atlanta operation offered employment to at least fifty kleagles and several hundred office and factory workers. In addition, the usual stream of minor officials to Peachtree Road became a flood at convention time. In May 1922, several thousand Klansmen descended on Atlanta for the seventh klonvention, which featured a downtown parade, a pilgrimage and barbecue at Stone Mountain, and a reception at the home of the Imperial Wizard. A more significant national gathering was the Imperial Klonvokation, which met for the first time November 27-29, 1922. One thousand delegates and an even larger number of unofficial visitors crowded the city to hear Simmons, Clarke, and Evans, expound on the phenomenal progress of the Invisible Empire.[13]

Among the more important and profitable functions of the Atlanta establishment was the production of official robes. White paraphernalia was required equipment for the well-dressed Klansman, and the individual member was forbidden, on pain of expulsion, to produce his own uniform. Simmons arranged for official production in the factory of Atlanta Klansman W. E. Floding until April 1923, when the contract was given to C. B. Davis's Gate City Manufacturing Company.[14] Considerable internal criticism centered on this private monopoly, so the Invisible Empire in 1923 constructed its own three-story, twenty-thousand-dollar robe factory in Buckhead, less than a mile from the Imperial Palace. With efficient operation and a production rate that eventually reached several thousand robes per day, the basic price of a uniform was reduced from $6.50 to $5.00, a sum that still allowed for substantial profit. An adjacent factory housed the Klan printing office, which after 1923 published *The Imperial Night-Hawk*, the *Kourier*, and all imperial decrees, proclamations, and pamphlets.[15]

Atlanta also stood to gain from the most grandiose scheme ever hatched by the dreaming Simmons. In 1921 plans were announced for the conversion of Lanier University, a Baptist institution that had ceased operation during World War I, into a national college for the "sons and daughers of Loyal Americans." With a scheduled endowment of one million dollars, "The University of America" would require of all students Bible study and a course in United States constitutional principles. Well located in northeastern Atlanta on forty acres near fashionable Druid Hills and Emory University, the institution expected each state to erect one building from "the imperishable rock of Stone Mountain" so that the American mind could be mobilized for its patriotic task. A special feature would be a building known as the "Hall of the Invisibles." Unfortunately for the Klan, the requisite funds were never raised and the elaborate plans never emerged into reality.[16]

Locally, the Klan was prospering under Exalted Cyclops Henry J. Norton. With substantial strength in the southeast quadrant of the city, and west of the Georgia Institute of Technology in the northeast, the Atlanta klavern enrolled at least fifteen thousand members by 1923 and boasted of the largest fraternal hall in the city. That the basis of its newer membership was lower middle class may perhaps be inferred from the *Searchlight's* occasional denunciations of "well organized commercial clubs" and "the autocratic chamber of commerce." [17]

Hopeful of creating a favorable public image through charity, Klan No. 1 contributed one hundred twenty-five dollars to a fund for former slaves on Christmas Day 1921, and shortly thereafter gave one thousand dollars to Agnes Scott College in suburban Decatur and twenty dollars to Decatur Junior High School. Picnics, barbecues, and outdoor sports were popular with local Knights, who met regularly on Thursday evenings and usually held initiations in Piedmont Park on Stone Mountain. On solemn occasions, such as the death of a fellow member, Atlanta Kluxers would approach the bier, offer the Klansman's prayer, and leave a wreath in the shape of a cross. Female patriots were also energetic, parading through the streets fully robed like their male counterparts.

The pride of Nathan Bedford Forrest Klan No. 1 was its mounted unit and magnificently uniformed drum and bugle corps. First appearing in the 1922 Labor Day Parade, the Klan marchers wore tight breeches and white shirts. Their blue capes were emblazoned with a fiery cross and the Klan's coat of arms, and their bright nickel helmets were topped by gilded spears. Masks dropped from the visors, effectively concealing identity while allowing for the insertion of an instrumental mouthpiece. The proud drum and bugle corps traveled as far as Indiana to participate in special parades and served as an effective publicity device for the Atlanta klavern.

Klan political involvement in southern cities differed greatly from the situation in the North. Negroes rarely voted, and Catholics were few in number, so the principles of "one hundred per cent Americanism" often reflected the views of a majority of the electorate. As a result, opposition to the Invisible Empire generally revolved around personalities. In Atlanta, as elsewhere in the South, the distinction between Klan and anti-Klan was sometimes blurred.

As early as 1921, the New York *World* reported that the entire official community of Atlanta was "honey-combed with Kluxters, reaching from the lowest to the very highest public servants." [18] The congressional investigation revealed that three members of the city government (including Walter Sims and James O. Wood on the city council) were acknowledged Klansmen, that many others were openly sympathetic to the order, and that the police department was heavily infiltrated. Because Mayor James L. Key was not among these confreres and in fact prohibited masked parades, the Klan made its first important Atlanta political foray in 1922.[19]

Of the six candidates for mayor, attorney Walter A. Sims was the only acknowledged citizen of the Invisible Empire. A city councilman, Sims demonstrated an intense concern with the "Catholic question" and on several occasions called for an investigation of the Knights of Columbus. He advertised regularly in the *Searchlight* and campaigned for white supremacy, the Christian religion, and "the inviolate protection of our southern womanhood." [20]

Police Chief James L. Beavers, labeled by the Klan as "the most incompetent chief of police Atlanta ever had," was the most vociferous of Sims's opponents for mayor. Out to see that the Klan issue was not dodged, Beavers declared that he was "absolutely and unalterably against any and every attempt by the Klan to control, influence, or enter into politics." Despite such pronouncements, Beavers finished fourth in the September 6 primary. With 5792 votes Klansman Sims gained a large plurality and faced a runoff election with three-time former mayor James G. Woodward. Attracting the support of Atlanta's moderate elements and the endorsement of the Civic Forum, Woodward asserted that "any man that makes a political plea on a platform of religious prejudices is unfit to be a mayor." Sims only became more vigorous in his anti-Catholic diatribes. He dubbed Woodward the Knights of Columbus candidate and charged the Roman Catholic Church with seeking the destruction of public schools and spending fifty thousand dollars in the campaign.

The vote on September 20, 1922, was the heaviest yet cast in an Atlanta runoff election and was closer than the Klan had expected. But the result was a victory for the Invisible Empire over "un-American" forces. Sims outdistanced his seventy-year-old opponent by a vote of 7244 to 6273, completing a Klan sweep that began a week earlier with the election of Walter George as senator, Clifford Walker as governor, and Eugene Thomas as Superior Court judge. Several weeks later the ban on masked parades was lifted.[21]

The Atlanta klavern's success in the election was capped by the contest for the Georgia legislature. Among the Fulton County candidates was James O. Wood, editor of the *Searchlight* and a member of the city council. Calling for the abolition of capital punishment and more rigorous inspection of convents and religious orders, Wood boasted at campaign rallies, "I am the original Ku Klux Klansman, and I am proud of it. I belong to everything anti-Catholic I know of. I have always stood for the laboring man and for organized labor." With such an appeal, the editor of the *Searchlight* ran almost a thousand votes ahead of the twelve-man field. On the other hand, the most vigorous anti-Klan candidate, A. A. Baumstark, finished tenth and received less than two thousand votes.

Shortly after the 1922 primary, the Invisible Empire stood at the apogee of its power and leverage in Atlanta. Three months later, however, cracks began to appear in its armor. Nathan Bedford Forrest Klan No. 1, which had a long and close association with William Joseph Simmons, was sorely distressed when he was removed as Imperial Wizard in the November coup. Local Klansmen only temporarily acquiesced in the selection of Hiram Wesley Evans, whom the *Searchlight* initially described as exemplifying, "the highest in ideals, integrity and brotherly love. In honoring Dr. Evans, the Klonvokation no less honored itself and every member of the Invisible Empire."

The honeymoon was brief. Unlike the affable Simmons, the businesslike Dallas dentist was cold to local Knights and regarded the

Atlanta klavern as worthy of no special consideration. Charging that Klan No. 1 had long enjoyed unwarranted privileges because of its proximity to headquarters, Evans prevented the chapter's continued use of the Imperial Palace as a hangout and meeting place. The new arrangement was not kindly received by Atlanta members, who well remembered when they were the backbone of the national organization. Their disloyalty did not become general until early in 1923, when the new Imperial Wizard terminated the lucrative propagation contract of E. Y. Clarke and broke publicly with William Joseph Simmons over the issue of a female branch of the Klan. Atlanta members promptly offered support to the old officials, and the *Searchlight* declared, "There is only one Klan and Simmons is its head." In April local Knights forcibly took control of the Imperial Palace while the Imperial Wizard was out of the city. As we have seen, the complicated legal battle which ensued between Evans and Simmons ended with the former emerging victorious on May 1, 1923.[22]

With Simmons and Clarke out of the way, the national administration on Peachtree Road moved quickly to eliminate the threat posed by the Atlanta chapter. In July 1923, the charter of Nathan Bedford Forrest Klan No. 1 was suspended for non-payment of imperial taxes, and it was forbidden to act as a klavern except to receive dues. A pro-Evans Klan was organized in Kirkwood as John B. Gordon Klan No. 91, and another in College Park as Copaga Klan No. 96. Because *Searchlight* editor J. O. Wood had supported Simmons in the crisis, a new and official national magazine, *The Imperial Night-Hawk*, was published from March 28, 1923, to November 19, 1924, and distributed free by the Imperial Palace. The final anti-insurgent blow was struck on January 8, 1924, when the charter of the mother Klan of the Invisible Empire was revoked for "insubordinations, disloyalty, treason, and other acts inimical to the best interests of the Knights of the Ku Klux Klan."

Many Atlanta insurgents answered the call in 1923 of E. Y. Clarke for a national congress to launch the Knights of the Mystic Clan, and his anti-administration newspaper, the *Fiery Summons*, enjoyed temporary popularity in the city. Exalted Cyclops Henry J.

Norton refused the edicts of Hiram Wesley Evans and initiated more than seven hundred persons into Klan No. 1 in defiance of a court order. But the local chapter was no match for the national organization, and by 1924 the *frondeur* movement was defeated. Even the *Searchlight*, which had led the attack on Evans, crawled back into the administration camp. After labeling Simmons's supporters "Bolshevik Klansmen," the newspaper was rewarded with official recognition as the Klan organ for Georgia, North Carolina, South Carolina, and Florida.

The year-long struggle for control of the Invisible Empire so devastated the Atlanta Klan movement that the city had to be treated as an untapped territory. Special Klan lecturers spoke on the principles of Kluxism at free public meetings in Taft Hall, and Klan No. 1 was reorganized and rechartered under the over-all direction of Georgia Grand Dragon Nathan Bedford Forrest, who sent a letter to the state's exalted cyclops on January 12, 1924. Addressing himself to the problem of building and maintaining functioning Klans, Forrest asked for a real and conscientious effort on the part of the local Klan officers "to keep your Klan alive and make it valuable to our organization and to your community."

The revival of Atlanta klankraft was signaled on March 2, 1924, when the reorganized Nathan Bedford Forrest Klan No. 1 was host to Klan chapters from Fulton and Dekalb counties at a religious ceremony in the city auditorium. John B. Gordon Klan No. 91, which met on Thursday evenings at Red Man's Wigwam, also contributed to the resurgence by staging an open-air rally and initiation at Piedmont Park on April 3, 1924. Four hundred robed Knights were on hand as well as three hundred unaffiliated spectators who remained behind a Klan picket line. Meanwhile, East Point Klan No. 51 paraded through the business section of that suburban community. Publicity was eagerly sought by the secret order, and a Klan baseball team was organized to compete in the city's amateur leagues. Playing with crosses over the left breast of their uniforms, Klan sluggers earned newspaper recognition when they blasted the Baptist Tabernacle to win the 1924 Dixie League championship.

Reorganization and baseball victories did not return the Atlanta Klan to its former position of power and influence, however. Most members simply ceased to pay dues or attend meetings, while retaining nominal allegiance to the Invisible Empire. As a result, its local strength could not be measured, and politicians were reluctant either to defend or to denounce it. In the 1924 Democratic primary, for example, Klansmen Walter Sims and J. O. Wood won re-election as mayor and state legislator without mentioning the secret order.[23]

The only 1924 race in which the Klan was an issue was the contest for Superior Court judge, which ranged incumbent Gus H. Howard, an acknowledged Klansman, against L. F. McClelland. Declaring that he was not a Klansman and never had been a member, McClelland expressed the hope that former "one hundred per cent Americans," who had joined the Invisible Empire as a fraternity, would agree that its "recent active entry into the political arena removes it from the realm of fraternal organizations to that of a political party." But Howard turned back his anti-Klan challenger in a close race, winning 7728 votes to McClelland's 7143.

The national office abandoned Atlanta late in 1925, when Evans took most of his staff to Seventh and I Streets in Washington, D. C., in order that the Klan might take a more active political role and function as a more effective national pressure group. Locally, the Invisible Empire faded slowly, never quite disappearing or regaining its former status. In November 1924, southern Klansmen gathered in the Georgia capital for a Thanksgiving Day parade and an initiation ceremony on Stone Mountain. It was the last big Atlanta Klan celebration. Thereafter, local Knights had very little to cheer. In 1926 they sought to elect Richard Russell to the Senate and J. O. Wood to the governor's mansion. The results were disastrous, and every Klan-supported candidate was defeated. Even more damaging was the 1928 presidential election, which resulted in the resignation or banishment of many Atlanta Klansmen who refused to pledge against Al Smith. The only encouraging development was the chartering of Grand Klan No. 285 on January 10, 1928, with

Nathan Bedford Forrest, III, as exalted cyclops and future Governor E. D. Rivers as klokard.

Although there was a residue of Klan support in Atlanta throughout the 1930's, the secret order was relatively quiescent in the city until the last years of the decade. At that time, several incidents served to besmirch further the Klan's already tarnished name. Imperial Wizard Evans was himself a major cause of the difficulty. He was charged, along with Governor Rivers and the purchasing agent of the Georgia Highway Board, with having conspired to control the sale of emulsified asphalt in the state. During the three years of litigation which followed (ending in a mistrial), numerous irregularities were disclosed, and the moralistic Evans was made to appear somewhat hypocritical.

More serious than the personal indiscretions of the Imperial Wizard were the vigilante activities of suburban East Point Klan No. 61. Led by Deputy Sheriff W. W. Scarbrough, the masked floggers left a tragic trail of violence. In the summer of 1939, two men were abducted by hooded assailants, taken to a garbage dump, and severely whipped for "immorality"; several months later a similar fate befell the white proprietor of a Negro movie theater. The night riding continued into 1940. On March 2, a young man and woman were beaten to death in a lovers' lane for violating the accepted sexual code; two weeks later East Point barber Ike Gaston was whipped with a long cleated belt and left to die of exposure in an isolated glade. An investigation by the grand jury linked the Klan with at least fifty local floggings in a two-year period; eventually eight Knights were sentenced to prison terms.[24] Largely as a result of the adverse publicity, there were fewer than five hundred active Klansmen in the Georgia capital at the beginning of World War II.

The Invisible Empire's national office had meanwhile returned to Atlanta in 1929. For seven years the thinned-out imperial staff maintained the big headquarters mansion on Peachtree; in 1936 a deteriorating financial situation forced its sale. Ironically, the purchaser subsequently sold the building and grounds to the Catholic

Church, which since 1939 has maintained the structure as the official residence of the Archbishop of Atlanta. The Klan's new quarters were not so lavish. The Invisible Empire moved first to downtown Atlanta, then to an office building at 3155 Roswell Road, N. E., and finally to a shabby upstairs location at 278 East Pace's Ferry Road in Buckhead. The cycle was then complete in the imperial city.

4

Memphis: Capital of the Mid-South

Protected from floods by steep bluffs along the eastern shore of the Mississippi River, Memphis was a commercial rather than industrial center in 1920. The city was the largest inland cotton and hardwood lumber market in the world and derived its importance from a vast and fertile delta hinterland in Arkansas, Mississippi, and Tennessee. Both white-collar and blue-collar wages were low, and organized labor was weak in a social and economic environment dominated by the conservative business community; the C.I.O's first attempt to organize city workers in the 1930's was branded "communistic" and physically smashed by the police. Significant also was the Bluff City's strong tradition of vice and violence; in 1917 one of the most vicious lynchings in American history occurred on Macon Road.[1] Frequently referred to as the murder capital of the world in the 1920's, Memphis became a national disgrace when its homicide rate exceeded fifty per one hundred thousand in 1919. Despite national prohibition, liquor was readily available in all forms, and houses of prostitution flourished in a police-sanctioned red-light district.

But Memphis was also extremely moralistic and much given to censorship in the realm of the arts. Fundamentalists were responsible for most of the blue laws, but Presbyterians and Episcopalians were also numerous among the city's 162,000 inhabitants, of whom only 10,000 were Catholic and 10,000 Jewish. Regardless of religious affiliation, most inhabitants were not lifelong residents. According to a 1918 census of the National Bureau of Education, only 2 per cent of the white parents in Memphis had been born there. Of the remaining 98 per cent, three-fourths were from the rural South, mostly from the surrounding tri-state area.

Negroes represented by far the largest minority group in the Bluff City. Beale Street, made famous by W. C. Handy's "Memphis Blues," had long been a powerful lure for the field hands and share-croppers of the nearby black belt. In 1920, two Memphians out of five were colored, and their votes helped Boss Edward Hull Crump fashion a political organization that dominated Tennessee politics for a third of a century. But the civil and economic status of the Negro remained decidedly inferior.[2]

The first kleagles arrived in the river city early in 1921, and by late spring the Memphis Klan had a membership sufficient to qual-ify for the third charter issued in the Realm of Tennessee. Its first recorded activities took place in November, when local Knights marched in the Armistice Day Parade behind a banner reading, "One Hundred Per Cent American." In subsequent weeks Klans-men donated one hundred dollars to the Red Cross and five hun-dred dollars to Negro victims of a local explosion.

Unlike the situation in Atlanta, where the daily press was usually silent on the Klan issue, the Memphis klavern early incurred the active enmity of *The Commercial-Appeal* and remained under at-tack from the region's largest newspaper for more than three years. Editor C. P. J. Mooney first began to censure the Invisible Em-pire early in 1922, and by early summer was regularly finding fault with its operation. Acts of violence were particularly offensive to the editor, who noted in July that "Law and order have not yet gotten to the point where they must hide behind closed doors and mask their faces."[3] Even more effective than editorials were the scathing front-page cartoons of J. P. Alley, who conceived of Klans-men as vultures, criminals, and cowards using hoods to prey upon the rights of others. A typical cartoon depicted a Klansman, ordered to unmask, revealing an ugly, distorted face. The caption was: "No wonder he puts a sack over that mug." Cartoonist Alley also reveled in the internal struggles for control of the Imperial Palace.

The anti-Klan thundering of Mooney and Alley enlisted others in the campaign against bigotry in Memphis. On December 23, 1922, Judge John W. Ross advocated the enforcement of a conspiracy statute making it a crime for two or more persons to disguise themselves for the purpose of oppressing any citizen. Three days later, at a Hotel Gayoso luncheon meeting of the Lions Club, Episcopal Bishop Thomas F. Gailor denounced the Klan as "the curse of the country and an anti-society organization."

Throughout the winter and spring of 1923, *The Commercial-Appeal* continued to attack the Invisible Empire. The attitude of "Old Reliable" on the Klan question, however, did not derive from any progressive or generally enlightened world view. Even while taking up the cudgel against the Klan, the newspaper bestowed its blessing upon the anti-evolutionists and refused to support a much needed federal anti-lynching law. *The Commercial-Appeal* probably opposed the secret order either because its editor was a Catholic or because it feared that the Klan might stir up the Negroes and therefore threaten a comfortable status quo. An editorial of April 21, 1923, proclaimed:

> The "emperor's" fulminations regarding the east may amuse without doing harm, but when he veers to the south, and attempts to raise a race issue it is different. Ordinarily the white people and the negro get along very well. It's only when an "emperor" or a labor agent or something similar butts in that trouble ensues.

Whatever the motives of the anti-Klan campaign, however, *The Commercial-Appeal* was awarded the 1923 Pulitzer Prize for "its courageous attitude in the publication of cartoons and the handling of news in reference to the operation of the Ku Klux Klan." Apparently the prize reflected the view of the Invisible Empire as well, because several years later the *Kourier* listed *The Commercial-*

Appeal as one of "the three most vicious anti-Klan newspapers in the country."

If the newspaper attack had any debilitating influence on hooded Americanism, the secret order was not prepared to admit it. In April 1923, the Arkansas Klan's *Krowley Kridge Kronicle* declared:

> Every week the *Commercial-Appeal* proceeds to kill the Klan, but from the rumblings which have been heard from over across the "big muddy" during the past months or six weeks, that paper will no doubt have its hands full if it takes care of the local situation from the reputed strength which the Ku Klux are gaining in the Bluff City where the goal set by the workers for the immediate future is a membership of 10,000.

Memphis Klan No. 3 very likely approached its goal of ten thousand members in the summer of 1923. Klavern headquarters were established in the downtown Goodbar Building. Initiations, however, were more generally held just beyond the city limits in Bethel Grove, where the Klan took a one-year lease on a wooded area. After the first torchlit klonklave there on March 16, 1923, when speakers from Atlanta, Mississippi, and Arkansas addressed almost one thousand initiates, Memphians often whispered about secret Klan rites and noticed the heavy traffic going out Pigeon Roost Road (now Lamar Avenue) toward Bethel Grove. As in Atlanta, white supremacy was a basic belief, but anti-Catholicism was perhaps the more important incentive for growth. As early as 1890 Memphis was a center of anti-Catholic literature, and with the rise of the Klan the Knights of Columbus complained that scurrilous religious pamphlets and bogus K. of C. oaths were being circulated around the city. So large and potentially powerful had Memphis Klan No. 3 become by 1923 that the post of exalted cyclops was eagerly sought by no fewer than three candidates, with E. E. Bolin winning a narrow victory over County Coroner N. T. Ingram and B. Carroll.

Basically, Memphis Klansmen were concentrated in three sections of the city.[4] The first area of Klan strength was in South Memphis between McLemore Avenue and South Parkway East.

With some exceptions this area was relatively new and made up of modest one-story frame houses. It was threatened from several directions by Negroes.

A second important area of Klan strength lay west of the Fairgrounds to Barksdale Street and included the adjacent Lenox neighborhood. Although the famed Negro community of Orange Mound lay immediately to the southeast, there was no imminent racial threat to this section of small, deteriorating frame and brick houses. The third important Klan concentration was in Binghampton, a rough, working-class neighborhood in what was then the northeastern fringe of the city. Close to large cotton oil companies, this area was relatively new, with small frame homes that were not always well kept. A sizable Negro community lay just east of Binghampton in the Tillman-Scott area.

In addition to the above neighborhoods, there was scattered Klan strength in three other areas: (1) in the general vicinity of Chelsea and Vollentine Streets in North Memphis, (2) in an isolated white community along Vance Avenue in the central city, and (3) just north of McLemore Street in South Memphis. Basically, these lower-middle-class neighborhoods were similar to the areas of prime Klan strength, and serve only to substantiate the Memphis pattern. The Invisible Empire was quite weak in the better residential areas of the city. Clearly, the Memphis Klansmen did not represent a cross section of the local populace. Most members were poorly paid white-collar workers or semi-skilled employees of such large enterprises as the American Cotton Oil Company. Although official records are not available, it can logically be presumed that they were predominantly Fundamentalist in religion.

One result of Memphis Klan growth in 1923 was the establishment of the weekly newspaper *Tri-State American,* published locally but designed to serve a wider area. In the fall of 1923 mid-South Klan officials seriously considered issuing the newspaper on a daily basis in order to compete with *The Commercial-Appeal.* Twelve directors, four each from Tennessee, Mississippi, and Arkansas, were appointed for the proposed $1,250,000 Klan publication. The Tennessee directors, all from Memphis and listed with

"their full consent," included a candidate for city judge, the head of
an insurance company, a local attorney, and the southern representative for American Type Founders. Employment and stock
subscriptions were to be limited to Klansmen, although "Jews and
others would buy instantly." The limitations were apparently too
great, however, bcause the necessary stock was never subscribed
and daily publication was never begun. The weekly *Tri-State
American* itself encountered difficulty in 1924 when it was taken
over by the Empire Publishing Company, which printed in Memphis the Klan newspapers of Tennessee, Arkansas, and Mississippi.
This enterprise failed also, and by 1925 the area was without any
sort of Klan newspaper.

Political warfare meanwhile replaced journalistic skirmishing as
the primary concern of the Memphis Klan. In June 1923, rumors
enveloped the city that the secret order was sympathetic to the
administration of Mayor Rowlett Paine and was supporting the
candidacy of his secretary, Clifford Davis, for city judge. When it
was learned publicly that Davis had spoken at several Klan meetings and was himself a Klansman, Mayor Paine came under fire
from other commissioners who resented the implication that the
city government was favorable to the Ku Klux Klan.

The issue remained in abeyance until early September when a
member of the water commission became the first announced candidate for the mayoralty. Thomas Stratton rated the Invisible Empire as the most important issue in the election and charged that
Mayor Paine had "played hands from beginning to end with the
Klan." [5] When this challenge was made, Mayor Paine acted
quickly, and late in September he and the incumbent commissioners announced their candidacies for re-election. On October 1 he
fired Cliff Davis as his personal secretary, ostensibly because Davis
was running for city judge. Davis immediately declared that the
overriding issue was his close association with the Ku Klux Klan,
and he accused the mayor of "yielding to his big friends." Both
Mayor Paine and Vice Mayor Allen had previously rejected invitations to join the Invisible Empire, and after October 1, both were
enthusiastic in their denunciation of the Klan.

At full-dress night rallies in Bethel Grove, the secret order re-acted angrily to the hostility of the city administration. Klansmen decided to nominate their own slate of candidates in the November municipal election with W. Joe Wood for mayor, Clifford Davis for city judge, H. A. Roynon for tax assessor, and Met Selden, Charles Divine, Putnam Dye, and John Fitzhugh for the city commission.

The situation was clouded considerably by indecision within the powerful political machine of Edward Hull Crump, who was op-posed to both Mayor Paine and the Ku Klux Klan, and who report-edly favored a third slate. Charles W. Thompson was expected to head the Crump ticket, but he withdrew from the campaign after a barrage of criticism from his wife. Former City Judge Lewis T. Fitzhugh then announced his candidacy for mayor at the head of a third ticket, which he obviously hoped would be backed by Crump.

Dubbing itself the "anti-Klan ticket," the Fitzhugh group charged that 70 per cent of Memphis policemen were members of the Invisible Empire and that the Klan in politics was a dangerous menace to American institutions.[6] Unfortunately for the Fitzhugh camp, however, it was soon learned that two candidates on the "anti-Klan ticket" were themselves Klansmen. C. W. Miller and E. B. Hanson admitted "naturalization" into the Invisible Empire, but both said they had resigned after attending several meetings. They withdrew from the campaign, but the Fitzhugh ticket had been damaged severely.

Emphasizing the slogan "A Bigger and Better Memphis," the Klan launched its campaign in Gaston Park on October 11, exactly one week before Mayor Paine gave his initial speech from the same platform. Bolstered by a large turnout of Kluxers, Klan campaign manager Clyde Koen had local Knights out on the streets distribut-ing political literature the next day. Wood headquarters were estab-lished across the street from the despised Commercial-Appeal and a convenient half block from Klan headquarters (at 128 Court Street). Special Klan lecturers Otis L. Spurgeon, William McDou-gal, and a Dr. Hopkins were brought to Memphis for the struggle.

Because the local klavern had no voice in the selection of ward and precinct officials, the Tri-State American referred to the election commissioners as "low-browed, sullen, putrid, insignificant skunks and parasites." Aware that Memphis elections were not noted for their honesty, the Invisible Empire proposed to rectify the situation. On October 31, more than two thousand Klansmen marched through downtown streets to the courthouse and lodged a complaint with Election Commissioner John Brown. Exalted Cyclops Gene Bolin, at the head of the Klan column, demanded that Brown replace some election officials in order "to preserve some semblance of fairness." No changes were made.

Although the Wood ticket held occasional rallies in private homes and public parks, the Klan campaign was basically an exclusive, almost private, affair. Night after night the hooded order held boisterous meetings at the Lyric Theater, where Klansmen and their families packed the seats and lobbies to hear speakers talk about the menace of Rome or the international Jew. Considerable enthusiasm was generated at the clamorous meetings, and every mention of the Klan brought forth applause, whistles, and stamping of feet. But the nightly appearances of members of the Klan ticket were directed toward voters already firmly committed to their cause. While members of the Paine and Fitzhugh tickets were campaigning in all parts of the city, members of the Wood slate were typically on the Lyric Theater stage on either side of a white floral cross. Oblivious to the mismanagement of the campaign, Cyclops Bolin boasted of the Klan espionage system and predicted that his organization would poll 16,000 of the 26,000 votes cast. On November 7, the *Tri-State American* nevertheless cautioned Memphis Klansmen:

> If you fail to fulfill the duty you owe to your family the Ku Klux Klan will banish you and report your negligence to the duly constituted authorities. If you fail to fulfill the duty you owe to your country, then you lie when you call this your country.

While the Klan held exclusive rallies, Paine and Fitzhugh vied for the honor of being the more anti-Klan. Supported by the *Memphis Press*, Fitzhugh campaigned heavily among the many Negro voters who had paid the requisite poll tax of three dollars and thirty-five cents, but his anti-Klan boasts were weakened by the presence of his brother John on the Klan ticket. Mayor Paine also worked for the colored vote, but his great strength lay in the better residential wards. He labeled the Fitzhugh ticket the "most monumental fraud" in Memphis political history and asserted that the Ku Klux Klan was "THE ISSUE" in the election. Crosses were burned in his yard, but Paine carried his message to the enemy, promising Klan stronghold Binghampton a much needed neighborhood fire station.

The imponderable element in the election was Boss Crump, who declared on November 1: "I have nothing to do with either the Paine or Fitzhugh tickets and I have not been waiting to jump either way." In the face of obvious Klan strength, however, Crump realized that Fitzhugh and Paine would probably split the anti-Klan vote and open the way for a victory by Klansman Wood. He disliked Mayor Paine, but he abhorred the Klan and realized that Fitzhugh had no chance of winning. Two days before the election Crump made his eleventh hour decision. When his cohorts Frank Rice, Dave Wells, Will Logan, and Joe Boyle appeared at Paine headquarters and went quietly to work, every informed Memphian recognized the implication.

"The turmoil was without a parallel in the political history of Memphis" on election day. Female Kluxers were everywhere in South Memphis, and throughout the city Klansmen distributed Wood literature outside the voting places. Riot alarms went out from at least fifteen precincts, and *The Commercial-Appeal* called it, "the worst situation with which the police ever had to combat." Fist fights erupted frequently in the bitterly contested ninth ward in North Memphis, and Klansmen B. Carroll and J. H. Yarbrough were thrown out of a downtown precinct for "crowding the election officers." [7]

More serious disturbances took place while the ballots were being counted. Shortly before midnight hundreds of excited Klansmen threatened to storm the precinct at Second and Mill Streets because they suspected dishonesty in tabulating the returns. Less than one half hour later an even more alarming condition developed at 608 East Trigg Street, where Klansmen charged that Twenty-fifth

ward officials had temporarily ousted everyone from the voting
area so that an election steal could be perpetrated. The Invisible
Empire was very strong in the Trigg neighborhood, but additional
members rushed by automobile from downtown Klan headquarters
to the scene. Led by the Reverend J. Ralph Roberts, the Klan mob
demanded that the votes of the disputed precinct be counted in
public. Three riots alarms asking for "all available reserves" went
out to police headquarters. Meanwhile the election officials had
been forced outside the Trigg voting place, where they were encir-
cled by four hundred Klansmen and compelled to count votes before a large bonfire. When the police arrived, they ordered that the
controversial ballot box be taken to the courthouse in a riot car, but
a Klan leader was allowed to ride with the votes, and dozens of
Klan-laden automobiles followed behind.

Despite their efforts, Memphis Klansmen were defeated, at least
officially. Crump support was decisive, and Mayor Paine won re-
election along with his entire commission. In addition, H. G. Scar-
borough, candidate for re-election as city tax assessor, far outdistanced H. A. Roynon, his Klan opponent. *The New York Times*
hailed the result as, "the biggest black eye the Klan has yet received
in Southern territory east of the Mississippi," and *The Commercial-
Appeal* remarked that the election had unmasked the Memphis
group as "an ambitious political machine and nothing else." Suffer-
ing from an unimaginative campaign that was directed inwardly
rather than toward uncommitted white voters, the secret order was
woefully weak in the large central residential wards of the city. All
Klan candidates except one received only between eight and nine
thousand votes.[8]

The single successful Klansman was Clifford Davis, candidate for
city judge. His victory has generally been attributed to the good
fortune of having three opponents split the anti-Klan vote, thereby
allowing him to eke out a narrow victory. Actually, Davis was a
bright and ambitious lawyer, who earned his success by refusing to
rely solely upon Klan support and by actively campaigning among
non-Klan elements. Promising to dispense justice "without regard

to influence, station, faction, or creed," Davis built up a large personal following and polled 2700 votes more than any other Klan candidate. His 1923 victory marked the beginning of a long and successful political career; he represented Memphis in Congress for twenty-four years and was for decades the only local figure to enjoy a popularity approaching that of Crump himself.

Refusing to accept the defeat of W. Joe Wood, Memphis Klan No. 3 charged that the election should be voided for fraud. John A. Steel, counsel for the secret order, produced voting totals ward by ward and compared them with the official results.[9] Before a court-room crowded with male and female Kluxers, Steel charged the opposition with fraudulent registration, wholesale Negro "voting," and tampering with ballot boxes, and he declared that the Invisible Empire had unlimited manpower with which to investigate his assertions. He claimed that in certain small wards fifty to one hundred votes had been switched, and that the result of the ward had been changed. Unfortunately for the Klan, however, the paper votes had been destroyed on November 12, several hours before Judge Patterson issued an injunction against "tampering with, molesting or destroying the ballots."[10]

The 1923 election was not to be the last time that the Memphis Klan felt cheated by local officials. Early in 1924, the city commission changed the boundaries of many wards and precincts, particularly in areas where the secret order had previously demonstrated strength. More naked, however, was the blackballing of Coroner N. T. Ingram, a prominent Klansman, a member of the county court, and the legal heir to the post of Sheriff Perry, who had died on January 7, 1924. On January 21, the county court removed Ingram from the office of coroner by a vote of 20 to 7, along Klan-anti-Klan lines. Justification for the removal resided in the absence of an official record of his unopposed election as coroner in October 1922. At a stormy session, the county clerk apologized that his "memorandum was misplaced," and that he had failed to record Klansman Ingram's election in the county court minutes. The distraught Ingram was hysterical with rage: "I'm the coroner, I was elected in

October, 1922, and every member of this court knows it. Look at
my bond. That will show that I was elected." [11] His protest availed
him nothing.

The most serious blow to the Memphis Klan, however, was internal in character. Bitterness over the July selection of Gene Bolin as
exalted cyclops intensified five months later when he was tried in
criminal court on a charge of driving Negro laborers from the farm
of a political opponent. Although Bolin was allowed to go free because the prosecution was refused permission to demonstrate that
he had beaten Negroes on previous occasions, the trial brought the
Klan much unfavorable publicity and damaged its contention that
it stood for law and order. In addition to factionalism over Bolin,
there was another internal division concerning the Simmons-Evans
contest for control of the national body. When sentiment generally
seemed to favor Simmons, Hiram Wesley Evans revoked the charter of Memphis Klan No. 3 on February 9, 1924. The official announcement tersely declared that "the Imperial Wizard became advised of unfavorable conditions existing in the local organization."

For three months in 1924, the city was technically without a
functioning klavern. The only bright spot in the otherwise dismal
Klan winter involved the purchase of hats by the Memphis firm of
Wood, Wilson, and Moose. A minor official of the New York company from which the hats were ordered recognized the name of W.
Joe Wood was that of the Klan candidate for mayor. He dictated a
letter to Wood, Wilson, and Moose suggesting that it place its order
elsewhere because, "a member of your firm ran for mayor on the
Ku Klux ticket." The Memphis company forwarded the letter to the
Klan's Imperial Palace in Atlanta, which printed it on the rear
cover of its nationally circulated *Imperial Night-Hawk* and suggested that all Klansmen take notice. Within a week the president
of the New York hat firm wrote a letter of apology to Memphis
Klansmen, informing them that he had not known of the transaction, and that the guilty subordinate had been dismissed.

On April 26, 1924, at a large meeting on Summer Avenue near
Binghampton, the local group was reorganized and rechartered as
Shelby County Klan No. 50. The new exalted cyclops, W. A. Blank-

enship, sought to rekindle the spirit of the previous year by organizing a thirty-man drum and bugle corps to participate in the Confederate Reunion to be held in Memphis in 1924. But after practicing for weeks, the musicians of the Memphis klavern were disappointed. They were already in line for the grand parade when Mayor Paine ordered that the hooded Klansmen not be allowed to participate. Disgusted and defiant, the drum and bugle corps followed the parade with covered drums.

Weary of shabby treatment by Memphis politicians, the Klan promised to turn them all out of office in the 1924 Democratic primary. The most important race was for sheriff, and the Klan chose Squire Will Taylor as the man to unseat Sheriff Will Knight, who had the united support of both Crump and administration forces. There was concern over the Klan threat, however, because administration leaders estimated that four thousand of their voters were on vacation, while "the Klan constituency for the most part is staying home for the summer and they will vote." Ominous also, were the Will Taylor campaign stickers that appeared with alarming frequency on the windshields of automobiles. T. Galen Tate made it a two-man contest when he withdrew from the sheriff's race because he was, "running squarely between two well-organized contending forces, the machine and the Klan."

But the Klan failed pitifully on election day. Hundreds of local members had dropped out after the charter was revoked or when internal dissension replaced once exciting meetings. No candidate supported by the secret order emerged victorious, and no gains were registered in the county court. Although Klan strength was still apparent in South Memphis, Binghampton, and the Fairgrounds neighborhood, Squire Will Taylor could garner only one third of the total vote for sheriff. The Invisible Empire was clearly a spent political force in the city of Memphis.[12]

The *coup de grâce* for Shelby County Klan No. 50 came shortly after the 1924 primary. On August 18, several shots were fired during a scuffle for Klan records in the Goodbar Building. J. D. Jones, a Klan deputy sheriff from Birmingham, was charged with shooting with intent to kill, and three prominent Memphis Klansmen; Ex-

alted Cyclops Blankenship, the Reverend Otis L. Spurgeon, and a
salesman, H. M. (Manley) Folson, were arrested for disorderly
conduct.[13] The sorry spectacle was followed the next evening by a
boisterous outdoor klonklave. Factionalism was in the air. Klansmen were disgusted with court litigation that was tying up their
newspaper (*Tennessee Kourier*), with the election results, and
finally with the shooting and resulting bad publicity. Blankenship
was voted out as exalted cyclops and banished from the Invisible
Empire along with Folson for "conduct unbecoming a Klansman."
At the same time the local group again split into warring factions.

Matt Grantham was elected as the new exalted cyclops, but the
stricken Memphis Klan had already suffered too long and too
much. No effort was made to fulfill the promise of a Klan ticket in
November. Although a few Knights heard Billy Sunday speak at
the Auditorium on February 18, 1925, the membership rapidly
dwindled. A small group of faithful Klansmen continued to meet in
Woodman Hall as late as 1930, and in 1939, I. D. Deaton sought to
lead a revival of "one hundred per cent Americanism" in the Bluff
City. But the Invisible Empire was never again a threat in Memphis.

5

Knoxville: Industrial Appalachia

Two decades ago John Gunther described Knoxville as "the ugliest city I ever saw in America." His comment was acrid, but nevertheless indicative of the mountain city's grimy and uninspiring appearance. Economically dependent upon manufacturing in 1920, Knoxville contained over three hundred and fifty plants and was an important producer of textiles, marble, and finished furniture. In addition, both the Southern and Louisville and Nashville Railroads maintained extensive car repair shops in the city. The home of the University of Tennessee and a Fundamentalist stronghold where both Sunday baseball and movies were prohibited, it counted fewer than two thousand Catholics among its 78,000 citizens (Knox County: 113,000). Negroes numbered a substantial 13,000, but declined from 21 per cent to 15 per cent of the total population between 1910 and 1920. A center of Klan strength in southern Appalachia, Knoxville is one of the few communities for which actual records of the Invisible Empire are available.[1]

The first Knoxville Klansmen were initiated in the spring of 1921, when Kleagle Henry P. Fry, a World War I infantry captain, was operating out of the city and recruiting new members in Bristol, Johnson City, and other East Tennessee communities. The Knoxville klavern grew steadily and reached a membership of five hundred in the fall of 1921, when it was chartered as Knox County Klan No. 14.[2]

Traditional methods of propagation and publicity were followed in Knoxville. Sunday morning church services were interrupted by white-hooded men interested in informing parishioners of the Klan's financial and moral support of Protestant Christianity. Well-publicized activities included donations to the widow of a murder victim and to a World War veteran wounded by a "midnight marauder."[3] Useful also were professional Klan lecturers. On September 23, 1923, Dr. Harold Bullard spoke to four hundred persons at Market Hall on the principles and tenets of the Invisible Empire. Advocating the death penalty for any white person caught cohabiting with a person of any other race, Bullard boasted that the Klan was responsible for eliminating the iniquitous doctrine of evolution from Tennessee public schools and for passage of the national immigration restriction act.

Regular meetings were held on Monday evenings at the klavern at King Street and West Fourth Avenue, but special gatherings took place on Sharp's Ridge, a mountain just northwest of the city. On May 28, 1922, L. W. Miller and two other reporters from the *Knoxville News* were allowed to witness an initiation there. Parking in a pasture crowded with hundreds of automobiles, they climbed to the flickering fires at the top of the ridge. As a band hidden in a wood played "America," eight hundred men talked quietly in small knots on the broad hillside. Ordered to "cover your faces," the robed figures lowered their masks or tied handkerchiefs around their faces and formed a semi-circle about a little stand draped with an American flag. A large cross was set ablaze, and one hundred and forty candidates for initiation knelt and began reciting the necessary oaths of allegiance. Piercing yells signaled the end of the ceremony, the band played "Dixie" and hungry patriots disposed of barbecue sandwiches, ice cream, and "near beer."

Similar outdoor initiations later in 1922 and in the following summer raised Knox County Klan No. 14 to a strength of more than two thousand by the fall of 1923.[4] Surprisingly, it did not become obsessed with politics. Although C. Lewis Fowler declared that the Klan was in the City Hall and on the police force and would prevent Negroes from holding public office, the Knoxville Klan did not become a campaign issue. It did profess a strong interest in clean elections, a goal it hoped to further by stationing fifty Klansmen at voting precincts and by placing placards in the downtown area reading, "The Knights of the Ku Klux Klan Expect a Clean Election."

Following several large demonstrations, the meridian of Knoxville Klanishness came on September 29, 1923, designated Ku Klux Klan Day at the East Tennessee Division of the State Fair. Advertised extensively in midwestern and southern Klan publications, the event was billed as a four-state convention of Klansmen from Kentucky, Alabama, Georgia, and Tennessee. Fair officials tolerated the arrangement because the Klan ceremonies might stimulate attendance on the worst day of the exposition. Knoxville Klansmen advertised their program by scattering thousands of posters over the fairgrounds and the city. Three days before the event Tennessee Attorney General R. A. Mynatt forbade the wearing of masks at the demonstration, but expectations remained high that the rally would be the most successful ever held in the state.[5]

More than thirty-five thousand Knights of the Invisible Empire and their families passed through the gates of the fair for Klan Day. Female Kluxers and Junior Klansmen were very much in evidence at the festivities, which included a barbecue dinner and a fireworks demonstration. At the much heralded evening initiation, fifteen hundred men and eight hundred women were added to Klan rolls.

Following the success of Klan Day, the Knoxville klavern slowly faded from public view and began a long decline. In an effort to offset numerous resignations Exalted Cyclopes Howard Stawford and R. A. Brown reduced the initiation fee first to five and later to three dollars.[6] But the hoped-for renaissance never came and occasional parades were not sufficient to bolster sagging morale.[7] Heavy losses pared Knox County Klan to only 406 members in 1927, and to 191 members in 1928.[8]

Table 3*

OCCUPATIONAL DISTRIBUTION OF MEMBERS OF
KNOX COUNTY KLAN NO. 14, KNOXVILLE, TENNESSEE

White-Collar Workers	No.	Percentage of Klan Membership	Blue-Collar Workers	No.	Percentage of Klan Membership
Businessmen	27	6.9	Railroad employees	52	13.1
Salesmen	23	5.9	Unskilled workers	31	7.9
Ministers	21	5.2	Carpenters	22	5.5
Clerks	20	5.0	Textile-workers	20	5.0
Managers	5	1.3	Veneer workers	16	4.1
Lawyers	5	1.3	Marble workers	15	3.9
Contractors	3	0.8	Mechanics	12	3.0
Teachers	3	0.8	Foremen	11	2.8
Engineers	2	0.5	Painters	12	3.0
Druggists	1	0.3	Truck drivers	10	2.5
Prohibition Agents	1	0.3	Farmers	11	2.8
Dentists	1	0.3	Machinists	11	2.8
Undertakers	1	0.3	Skilled workers	9	2.3
Physicians	1	0.3	Telephone workers	7	1.8
Realtors	1	0.3	Electricians	7	1.8
Collectors	1	0.3	City employees	6	1.5
	116	29.1	Butchers	5	1.3
			Policemen	4	1.0
			Plasterers	4	1.0
			Military recruiters	2	0.5
			Soda jerks	3	0.8
			Cooks	3	0.8
			Barbers	2	0.5
			Bakers	2	0.5
			Postmen	2	0.5
			Laundrymen	2	0.5
			State employees	1	0.5
			Retirees	1	0.3
				283	70.9

* Knox County Klan No. 14 Papers, Emory University.

Table 4*

RELIGIOUS DISTRIBUTION OF MEMBERS OF KNOX COUNTY
KLAN NO. 14, KNOXVILLE, TENNESSEE

Denomination	Churches†	Number of Klan Members	Percentage of Klan Membership
Baptist	51	210	71.2
Methodist	25	73	24.4
Presbyterian	3	7	2.4
United Brethren	1	2	0.7
Episcopalian	1	1	0.3
Lutheran	1	1	0.3
Church of God	1	1	0.3
Christian	1	1	0.3
	84	296	99.9

Baptist Membership		Methodist Membership	
Bell Avenue	12	Second	4
Euclid	12	Lincoln Park	3
First Baptist	10	Roseberry	3
Lawndale	8	Whistle Springs	3
Dedrick Avenue	8	Fountain City	3
Detroit Avenue	8	First	3
Washington Pike	8	Washington Pike	2
Broadway	8	East Hill Ave.	2
Oakwood	8	Church Street	2
Calvary	7	Central	2
Elm Street	6	Vestal	2
Emmanuel	5	One each	14
Clyde Street	5	Unassigned	30
Mount Olive	4		73
Powell Street	3		
Grove City	3		
Free Will	3		
Central Street	3		
Burlington	3		
Lincoln Park	2		
Sugarland	2		
Mountain View	2		
Third	2		
A.B.C.	2		
Corrytown	2		
One each	26		
Unassigned	48		
	210		

* Knox County Klan No. 14 Papers, Emory University.
† Number of churches that had at least one Klansman in the congregation.

Fortunately, the dues records and chapter correspondence of the Kligrapp (secretary) of Klan No. 14 as well as 288 membership applications, have been partially preserved. The required application forms included the candidate's age, birthplace, home address, occupation, religion, height, weight, and number of years of residence in Knoxville. In most instances the date of initiation was stamped on the form.

The typical Klansman in the city of Knoxville was thirty-five years of age, 157 pounds in weight, and Fundamentalist in religion. Two out of three local members regarded themselves as Southern Baptists (for the city as a whole about one adult in three was a member of this church), although many misspelled it. One "minister of the gospel" twice recorded his religious affiliation as "Babtist," while a carpenter noted that he was a "Jentile" and a "Baptis." As might be expected, the average educational level was not high and stood at about seven years of schooling, although many applicants simply listed their academic achievement as, "free school," "public school," "common school," "country school," "very little," or "none." Only one member in fifteen boasted of a high school education.[9]

Knoxville Klansmen were not newcomers to an urban environment. Although the city more than doubled in population between 1910 and 1920, only one Klansman in three had lived in the city for less than ten years. Almost 40 per cent of local Knights were lifelong Knoxville residents, and well over half had resided in the community for fifteen years or more. Considering only those Klansmen who were not born in Knoxville, the average number of years a member of Klan No. 14 had lived in the city was 9.1. Significantly, Knoxville furnished 79 per cent of county Klansmen, but only 69 per cent of the county population as a whole.

The occupational and economic status of Klan No. 14 members varied considerably. White-collar workers accounted for about one-third of the total and included primarily salesmen, clerks, and small businessmen. Included also were many "Sunday preachers," who listed their occupation as minister in order to take advantage of the Klan's offer of free membership to men of the cloth. More than two-thirds of Knoxville Klansmen were laborers or blue-collar workers, most of them employed by such relatively large concerns as the Southern Railroad, the Foreign and Domestic Veneer Company, Appalachian Mills, or the Knoxville Power and Light Company. Fear of Negro economic equality, an abundance of low cost labor, and public antipathy against "radical" measures were sufficient to prevent unionization, so their wages were low. Unsuccessful financially and socially, they turned to the Ku Klux Klan in an attempt to regain their sense of dignity and importance.

6

Dallas: Dynamo of the Southwest

In Dallas on May 21, 1921, at precisely nine o'clock, street lights in the vicinity of Elm and Main Streets were inexplicably extinguished. From the old Majestic Theater hundreds of white-robed figures began to emerge, marching behind an American flag and a burning cross. Through heavy traffic and Saturday night crowds, the paraders moved down Main Street carrying black and white placards which proclaimed: "Pure Womanhood," "Our Little Girls Must Be Protected," "All Native Born," "The Invisible Empire," or any of a dozen other Klan slogans. Knots of onlookers cheered the signs, but the masked marchers were mute, and within forty-five minutes all 789 demonstrators had marched back up Elm Street and into the theater.[1]

The Sunday *Morning News* gave front page coverage to the nocturnal parade, terming it a "slanderous exhibition and a fit subject for the consideration of the grand jury." On the same page was a Klan proclamation addressed to the citizens of Dallas County:

> Be it known and hereby proclaimed, . . .
> That no innocent person of any color, creed, or lienage [sic] has just cause to fear or condemn this body of men.
> That our creed is opposed to violence, lynchings, etc., but that

we are even more strongly opposed to the things that cause lynchings and mob rule.

That this organization does not countenance and it will not stand for the cohabitation of blacks and whites of either sex. . . . It is equally opposed to the gambler, the trickster, the moral degenerate, and the man who lives by his wits and is without visible means of support.

The eye of the unknown hath seen and doth constantly observe all white or black, who disregard this warning. Whatever thou sowest, that shall ye also reap. Regardless of official, social, or financial position, this warning applies to all living within the jurisdiction of this Klan.

Your sins will find you out. Be not deceived. You cannot deceive us and we will not be mocked.

This warning will not be repeated.

The object of the Klan's warning was a cosmopolitan commercial and industrial beehive in 1920. The financial and fashion capital of the Southwest, Dallas lay in the midst of vast cotton and oil fields and harbored few of the Wild West traditions of neighboring Fort Worth. Its population of 158,000 (up 73 per cent from 1910) was relatively heterogeneous, and included 24,000 Negroes and 8800 foreign-born immigrants.

Against this backdrop, Bertram Christie initially organized the Dallas Klan late in 1920. Enrollment followed a familiar pattern. The prospective recruit would be presented at work or church with copies of the United States Constitution and the Ten Commandments and invited to a private dinner gathering at Woodman Hall. Only after arrival did the prospect learn that the meeting was that of the Ku Klux Klan. Although many indignantly departed, others remained and formed the nucleus of mighty Klan No. 66.[2]

At first, the Dallas klavern chose secrecy and under Exalted Cyclops Hiram Wesley Evans occasionally ventured outside the law to enforce its earlier warning to "the citizens of Dallas County." The first reported incident came on April 1, 1921, when Alexander Johnson, a Negro bell boy at the swank Adolphus Hotel, was accosted at work and dragged by masked men into a waiting car. Accused of associating with white women, he was whipped severely and branded on the forehead with acid. The New York *World* reported

that within a year at least sixty other persons were flogged in the
county, but not one of the perpetrators was apprehended.[3] Apparently the power of the Dallas Klan lay not so much in the willingness of Klansmen to regulate society as it lay in the willingness of
the larger group to let them regulate. The sentiments contained in a
letter to the Dallas *Morning News* on May 31, 1921, were perhaps
typical:

> The limitations and technicalities that hamper the enforcement
> of the law are the best excuses I can give for the order. . . . .
> The advantage of the protection afforded by the K.K.K. is that it
> can rid the community of undesirables before they commit some
> serious offense.

In March 1922, the grand jury finally decided to consider the
problem of vigilante justice. The specific issue involved the floggings of restaurateur Phillip Rothblum and lumberman F. H. Etheridge, both of whom positively identified three Dallas policemen as
being among their tormentors. Unexplainably, no indictments were
returned and the accused policemen suffered only a temporary suspension. Police Commissioner Louis Turley, himself a prominent
Klansman, immediately displayed his own lack of concern with the
inquiry by advising his officers to "forget all about the charges
brought against any member of the force."

Amid rumors that Texas Rangers might be sent to Dallas to suppress violence, bootlegging and gambling, twenty-five responsible
business and church leaders (twenty-three Protestants, one Catholic and one Jew) were called together by Judge C. M. Smithdeal to
discuss methods of combating marauders who "insolently exalt
themselves over all constituted authority." Arguing that there was
no middle ground for a good citizen to take if the "Dallas spirit"
was to be recaptured, they called for a public meeting at the auditorium on April 4, 1922. The proposal won the support of scores of
well-known citizens and the endorsement of the *Morning News*,
which recommended it as one device to "lift the disgrace that has
been brought on Dallas" by the Invisible Empire.[4]

The response to the anti-Klan appeal was encouraging; five thousand persons packed the auditorium and spilled over to Harwood Street outside. White supremacy was not questioned by the speakers, but religious tolerance and "freedom of conscience" were vigorously endorsed. They adopted the title of "Dallas County Citizens League" and the purpose of excluding from public office all members of the Ku Klux Klan. Their task was formidable; the secret order already claimed the allegiance of the sheriff of Dallas County, his chief deputies, the police commissioners, the chief of police, and the district attorney. Acutely aware of the swirling controversy, Mayor Shawnie R. Aldredge endorsed the Citizens League in an official proclamation on April 6, 1922. Appealing to the community spirit of Dallas Klansmen, he asked them to dissolve an organization which had brought discord to a peaceful city. Finally, he ordered Klan members employed by the city of Dallas to resign immediately from the Invisible Empire.

The Citizens League, the Dallas *Morning News,* and such locally prominent citizens as former attorney general Martin M. Crane, Judge Joseph Cockrell, Judge Robert B. Seay, Professor C. A. Nichols of Southern Methodist University, and the Reverend Charles S. Field echoed the mayor's appeal. Particularly significant was the sermon of the Reverend Charles E. DeBow of the First Methodist Church, who told his congregation that the Klan was totally un-American because "all Americanism worthy of the name is based upon equal rights to all men." The Dallas American Legion Post was also hostile. When presented by the Klan with a silk American flag, Commander Royal R. Watkins accepted the gift with brief thanks and the observation that "the only masks the American Legion has any use for are gas masks."

Some Klansmen did yield to the pressure to disband, among them Police Chief Henry Tanner, who explained that he had joined the Invisible Empire in 1921 after being advised that its sole purpose was to assist officers in law enforcement. Most Klansmen, however, remained loyal to the secret order and issued their official answer to the mayor at a mass meeting in the coliseum of Fair Park. A reported 2842 candidates were initiated in a ceremony which began at eight o'clock, when all the lights in the building and

park were extinguished for five minutes. Lusty cheers and pound-
ing band music reverberated through the coliseum for the next four
hours as a procession of speakers denied any involvement in acts of
violence and asserted that there was no valid reason for Klan No.
66 to disband. The only concession made by the assembly was a
resolution "to never again stage a parade in Dallas wearing the
regalia of the order."

With or without parades, Klan No. 66 continued its thrust in
1922. In a single year it amassed ninety-eight thousand dollars in
klectokens (initiation fees) and dues alone.[5] As membership approached ten thousand, the chapter outgrew its smaller meeting
halls on Elm Street (between Every and Ackard) and in Oak Cliff
at Tyler and Jefferson and began to gather regularly in the shell at
Fair Park.[6] On special occasions contingents from Dallas journeyed
to other Texas cities for hooded celebrations or remained at home
to attend en masse the repeat engagements of *The Birth of a Nation* at the Old Mill. As befitted its size and reputation, Klan No. 66
distributed food baskets at Christmas, financed a seventy-five-piece
drum and bugle corps, and supported a weekly newspaper, *The
Texas 100 Per Cent American*. In 1923 a chapter of the Women of
the Ku Klux Klan was organized, and a local woman was chosen as
national vice commander. In 1924 the ladies held their annual
Kloreo (state convention) in the city.

The Klan's experiment in Dallas benefited in part from the free
publicity of the New York *World* exposé, which was syndicated by
the *Morning News*. The fear of the Catholic Church and immigrant
"hordes," common among southern Protestants, was also important
in Dallas, as was the favorable attitude of some of the local ministry. In 1921, the Reverend T. O. Perrin of Westminister Presbyterian Church hypothesized that "the hand of God is working in this
organization." In 1922, the Reverend W. H. Wynn of Forest Avenue Baptist Church eulogized the Klan as a force for good, and in
the same year, the Reverend Alonzo Monk of the First Methodist
Church in suburban Arlington bluntly stated that as far as he knew
"tar and feathers have never been put on an innocent man." The
Reverend J. T. Renfro went one step farther and abandoned his

Methodist ministry to become an itinerant lecturer for the Klan.
The chief architects of the Klan's early achievement in Dallas
were Hiram Wesley Evans, a small-time dentist with "a lot of
Negro trade," and Z. E. (Zeke) Marvin, the wealthy proprietor of a
chain of drug stores. Stocky, blue-eyed, and articulate, Evans was
born in Ashland, Alabama, in 1881 and had studied briefly at Vanderbilt University (without winning a degree) before moving to
Dallas in 1900.[7] He joined the secret order in 1920, rose rapidly to
the position of exalted cyclops, and in 1921 personally led the
masked band that brutally acid-branded Alex Johnson. In 1922, he
was summoned to Atlanta as national secretary, and in the coup of
November 1922, was chosen imperial wizard of the Invisible Empire. Marvin also attained high Klan position, first as great titan
(district director) of Province No. 2, and later as grand dragon of
Texas. That both men were spawned by the Dallas chapter lent
considerable prestige to Klan No. 66.[8]

When Evans first left Dallas on April 10, 1922, he asked Marvin
to act in his stead as exalted cyclops until new officers could be
elected. The future grand dragon served only until May when A. C.
Parker was elected exalted cyclops and D. C. McCord was chosen
as klaliff (vice president). Parker was a forty-five-year-old evangelist who worked as a businessmen through the week and as pastor
of Forest Avenue or Rosemont Christian Churches on the Sabbath.
Pompous and brash, he never made a secret of his Klan affiliation.
Among his moments of grandeur was that of July 15, 1922, when he
stood on a spotlighted platform in the center of the stadium and
addressed 25,000 spectators, 3500 masked Klansmen, and 500 flag-
bearing women and girls of the female auxiliary. A pouring rain
and a faulty loudspeaker amplifier cut short the performance, and
the resulting traffic jam required the efforts of twenty policemen for
more than an hour.

On July 22, 1922, came the first major political test for Dallas
Klan No. 66. The focus of attention in the all-important Democratic
primary was on the contest for United States Senator. Charles Cul-
berson was seeking a fifth term, but the aged incumbent was in
poor health and had six enthusiastic challengers, including three

Klansmen: Dallas attorney Sterling P. Strong, Robert L. Henry of
Waco, and Railroad Commissioner Earle B. Mayfield. Strong
boasted of his membership in the secret order and publicly declared that Klan leaders were "incapable of doing an unlawful act."
Equally proud was "natural born Klansman" Robert Henry, who
reported that he could always be found "with the fiery cross in one
hand and the United States flag in the other." Although the third
member of the Klan triumvirate said nothing about his private affiliations, Mayfield was endorsed by the realm hierarchy and given a
vote of confidence by the potent Dallas klavern, which in a special
Klan runoff election lined up 1400 for Mayfield, 700 for Henry, and
400 for Strong. After it became clear that state Klan support would
go to Mayfield, Strong withdrew from the campaign, while Henry
remained as an active, but hopeless, independent candidate.

In Dallas itself as many as twenty county contests developed
into measures of strength between the Invisible Empire and the
Citizens League. Highest Klan priority went to the election of incumbent Dan Harston as sheriff, Shelby S. Cox as district attorney,
and Felix D. Robertson as criminal court judge. To support its endorsements, Klan campaign manager W. L. Thornton appointed a
Committee of One Hundred to raise the necessary ten thousand
dollars, and he secured official permission to station Klan supervi-
sors in each of the county's one hundred and four precincts.[9]

The Dallas County Citizens League welcomed the issue of invisible government and distributed a questionnaire to all candidates,
asking for a statement of personal belief on the Klan. The League
then endorsed open opponents of the Klan, such as District Attorney Maury Hughes. Relevant also in the anti-Klan struggle was the
Dallas *Morning News*, which decried Dan Harston as a "bedsheet
sheriff" and referred to Shelby Cox as a "river bottom advocate"
unqualified to administer justice in "daylight courts." On the day
before the election the influential daily made a final plea:

> For the children of evil work in darkness rather than in light
> because their deeds are evil. Shall not Texas vote in the light and
> only for men without a masked loyalty to a secret aim? Tomorrow
> we shall know.

Triumph on July 22, 1922, went to the Ku Klux Klan, which just three months earlier had been described as a "pitiful minority" that was "politically impotent." Earle B. Mayfield polled 27 per cent of the statewide vote to lead the six-man field for senator and qualify for the runoff with ex-Governor James E. Ferguson. Significantly, his greatest support came from Dallas County, where he won 42 per cent of the total vote and eclipsed his nearest competitors by a two to one margin. In local contests, eighteen of nineteen Klan-supported candidates were victorious. Sheriff Dan Harston was easily re-elected and Felix D. Robertson was nominated for criminal court judge. (In Texas in 1920 the Democratic nomination was tantamount to election.) In the race for district attorney, a runoff was necessary between Klansman Shelby Cox, who had a fifteen-hundred-vote plurality, and incumbent Maury Hughes.

When the election trend became evident, several thousand gloating Klansmen, unmasked and wearing street clothes, filed behind Exalted Cyclops Parker, Great Titan Zeke Marvin, Kligrapp George Butcher, and Judge Felix Robertson in a parade through downtown Dallas. They paused first at the *News* Building on Lamar to taunt the "dirty, slimy, Catholic-owned sheet." (In truth, the *News* had no Catholic owners or administrators.) Gathering momentum, they moved on to the *Times-Herald* Building, jammed around a truck set up for impromptu speech-making, and sang freely as the Klan band played the "Star Spangled Banner." Parker was the first to speak. He asked if everyone in the crowd knew him, but without hesitating for an answer shouted: "I am the cyclops of Dallas Klan No. 66." District Attorney candidate Shelby Cox came next to the platform and told the cheering crowd that he had marched "with the ranks of the Klan in Dallas and other North Texas cities." The demonstration lasted for well over an hour, and it was after midnight when the exhausted Klansmen dispersed.

But the question was not settled in those contests where no candidate received a majority of the total vote; therefore the Dallas klavern concentrated on the second primary five weeks distant. The battle for senator was one of the most intemperate in Texas history. Mayfield's opponent was Jim Ferguson, a Temple County farmer who had been impeached as governor by the 1917 legislature and defeated in an independent race for president in 1920. He favored a change in the Prohibition law and described himself as a man who would much prefer to "be out on the plains in a tent than to live in luxury in a flat in Chicago." Most importantly, Jim Ferguson aligned himself against the Invisible Empire. He charged that Mayfield was the pawn of a "hydra-headed monster," and he argued that "in Dallas, the Ku Klux is in the saddle. It has elected nearly all the county officials, and the law, therefore, can be violated with impunity." [10]

Meanwhile, in Dallas, the fight for district attorney also revolved about the Ku Klux Klan. Campaigning on an excellent public record, Maury Hughes denounced prejudice and hatred and labeled Exalted Cyclops Parker a "political preacher," who had transformed the admonition "repent, ye sinners" to "vote, ye suckers." But Hughes was hampered by the revelation that he had himself been an early member of the Invisible Empire and had resigned only when Klan No. 66 fell under the domination of "dirty handed politicians." For his part Shelby Cox admitted Klan membership and argued that the secret order required no defense. During an election rally at the auditorium he listened approvingly as Klan orators promised to bury Hughes "so deep he will never be heard of again in this county."

The Dallas Klan made good its threats on August 26, 1922. Shelby Cox ousted Maury Hughes as district attorney (14,000 to 10,000), Klan favorite George Purl won election to the legislature, and every candidate endorsed by Klan No. 66 was victorious. In the state contests only one of four Klan candidates received the nomination, but all ran better in Dallas than in Texas as a whole. Earle B. Mayfield received 52 per cent of the state vote and 69 per cent of the Dallas total. Klansman George C. Garrett won easily in Dallas, but lost the race for state treasurer, and Billie Mayfield (no relation to Earle), a prominent Houston Klansman, received 36 per cent of the Texas vote, while carrying Dallas with 52 per cent. According to the *Morning News*, the election gave "striking evidence of the political strength of the Ku Klux Klan in Dallas County."

The campaign success of Klan No. 66 triggered the second boisterous victory parade in Dallas in five weeks. Gathering initially on
Akard Street, the Klansmen marched to the tune of "Onward,
Christian Soldiers" toward the offices of the hated daily press.
Parker, Butcher, Cox, and Purl were all present for the festivities,
but speech making was held to a minimum and within an hour the
two thousand celebrants had dispersed without incident.

The scene of the triumphal march included the very precincts
that prevented the Klan ticket from completely sweeping the election. In addition to the downtown contingent for Ferguson and
Hughes, Highland Park and the environs of Southern Methodist
University voted heavily for the Klan's opponents. The strength of
Cox and Mayfield, and perhaps that of the Klan, lay primarily in
Oak Cliff and the section surrounding Fair Park, taking in the
neighborhood between Randall Park and Buckner Park. There was
additional Klan support in North Dallas, particularly in the precincts near the high school, Cochran Park, and Greenwood Cemetery.

In the November general election Republicans joined with anti-
Klan Democrats to send George Peddy against Earle Mayfield, but
the Democratic regulars recorded an easy triumph. In April 1923,
Klan No. 66 again demonstrated its political prowess when Marvin
E. Martin of the Citizens Association and Democrat Louis Blaylock
faced each other in the Dallas mayoralty race. For fourteen years
the Citizens Association had dominated municipal elections, but in
1923 the opposition ticket was the Ku Klux ticket, and Blaylock
was a friend, if not a member, of Klan No. 66. Expectedly, the issue
of invisible government was important; unexpectedly, the campaign was unusually quiet and failed to excite the enthusiasm of an
electorate apparently more interested in the efforts of several Texas
women to establish new world records for marathon dancing.
Fewer than 20,000 persons bothered to cast ballots, and of those
Blaylock received 13,500. The entire Klan slate was elected to the
city commission. Another easy victory was thus recorded by the big
Dallas klavern.

After the 1923 municipal election, local Knights increasingly turned their attention toward civic affairs with the proposed establishment of an institution for homeless children. In May, they staged an elaborate blackface minstrel show to benefit Hope Cottage, and in the summer, when construction began, they searched their own pockets for individual contributions. The entire $80,000 goal had been raised when the North Dallas orphanage was completed in early fall.

The dedication of Hope Cottage was held on October 24, 1923, in order to coincide with "Klan Day" at the Texas State Fair. The occasion could hardly have been more auspicious. Imperial Wizard Hiram Wesley Evans, together with an official entourage of fifty persons, was in Dallas for the festivities, joined by thousands of rank and file Klansmen who arrived on special trains from Houston, San Antonio, Oklahoma City, and a half dozen other communities. Here was an opportunity to demonstrate to Dallas and the nation that the Invisible Empire had abandoned violence and had found respectability in charitable and fraternal activities.

The Wednesday morning grand opening of the orphanage attracted two dozen high Klan and local officials as well as two visiting Klan bands. On the platform with the Imperial Wizard sat Congressman George C. Purl, Mayor Louis Blaylock, Judge Felix D. Robertson, City Commissioners Louis Turley, R. A. Wylie, and H. H. Gowins, Great Titan Z. E. Marvin, and the Reverend A. C. Parker. Exalted Cyclops J. D. Van Winkle welcomed the fifteen hundred spectators, and Mayor Blaylock spoke briefly on "Charity." The featured address was delivered by Zeke Marvin, who declared that the Dallas Klan built Hope Cottage not for vainglory or ostentatious show, but as a work of Christian service to benefit the helpless. He discounted the occasional improprieties of individual Klansmen and argued that the "great heart" of the Invisible Empire was sound. The high point of the ceremony came when Marvin presented the deed to the building, "free of any encumbrance," to the Hope Cottage Association representing the city of Dallas.

After the morning dedication, attention shifted to Fair Park and the activities of "Klan Day." [11] The setting was decidedly Klanish. Patriotic orators declaimed in booths and exhibit halls along the midway, rodeo performers appeared in Ku Klux regalia, and a large percentage of the patrons sported Klan badges on their shirts or coats. At one o'clock seventy-five thousand people gathered near the main plaza loudspeakers to hear the Imperial Wizard speak on "The Menace of Present Immigration Measures." Using statistics liberally, he labeled southern and eastern Europeans mentally inferior, called for congressional action to bar virtually all immigration, and urged that all forms of alienism be investigated promptly by government officials. Significantly, Evans took note of the lower-middle-class status of his followers and proposed a national system of universal medicare. "Just as education should be free, so should each and every agency of health be available without cost to every human being within our borders. Health ought to be regarded as a public function from beginning to end, with hospitals, doctors, and nurses available to all, rich and poor."

Predictably, the featured event of "Klan Day" came after dark. Exploding fireworks signaled the beginning of a mass initiation in the stadium, and a two-hour parade of bands and Klan patrols in the middle of the race track. Included among the seven thousand marchers were 68 elaborately dressed Klan war veterans, who adopted the title "Minutemen." Earle H. Silvan directed the cross burning and initiation before twenty-five thousand on-lookers in a spectacle described by the *Morning News* as "the most colorful and unique event ever seen in the city of Dallas."

Klan Day was an unqualified success. The Wednesday celebration attracted 151,192 persons to the State Fair (versus 22,763 on Confederate Day on Tuesday). Easily the largest weekday crowd of the exposition, it brought national publicity to the secret order. Indeed, the Hope Cottage project gave new respectability to the Dallas klavern, and Exalted Cyclops Van Winkle promised to maintain support for the institution. In March 1924, the local chapter sponsored a seven-day "Kolossal Klan Karnival" to benefit the orphanage. The exposition featured industrial exhibits, magicians, "aerial acts," and the giving away of a new Ford.

As summer approached, Klan interest reverted once again to realm politics. Two active members of the Dallas Klan, Judge Felix

D. Robertson and attorney A. V. Collins, a former state senator, sought the Klan nomination in the pivotal contest for governor. Both were enthusiastic Prohibitionists. Collins won the support of Houston Klansman Billie Mayfield, the editor of *Col. Mayfield's Weekly* and an unsuccessful candidate for lieutenant governor in 1922, but Robertson was endorsed by Grand Dragon Marvin and most of the state's three hundred local klaverns. The nod went to Robertson, a decision which disillusioned Collins, who remained in the race, and brought dissension to a previously united Dallas Klan.

From the beginning the chief issue of the 1924 Democratic "white" primary for governor was Robertson's admitted membership in the Dallas Klan. The judge cagily sought to capitalize on the Fundamentalist orientation of Lone Star voters by boasting that he cared not one whit whether his being a Knight of the Invisible Empire "suits the Pope in Rome or not." Never dodging the KKK issue, Robertson appropriately closed his campaign at an election eve rally before thousands of cheering members of Klan No. 66.

The Dallas judge piled up a two to one majority in his home city and led the six-man gubernatorial field with 193,000 votes, 50,000 more than his runoff opponent, Mrs. Miriam (Ma) Ferguson. The wife of fiery demagogue James E. Ferguson, who was ineligible because of his previous impeachment, Mrs. Ferguson was endorsed by all the defeated gubernatorial candidates of the first primary as well as by most of the state's daily newspapers. Wisely she and her husband never allowed the campaign to shift far from the issue of invisible government. Promising legislation to rid Texas of the secret order, she referred to her opponent as the "Crown Prince of Hate." But the Fergusons were almost as bigoted as Robertson, and in a campaign that was bitter even by Texas standards, each candidate accused the other of seeking the "nigger vote." By August 23, the anti-Klan coalition had hardened, and the Fergusons won an easy 443,120 to 345,911 victory over Judge Robertson.

In 1924 Texas was a typically Southern one-party state, where Democratic nomination was tantamount to election. The Klan sought vengeance, however, and joined with the Republicans behind Dr. George Butte, a diminutive University of Texas professor who repudiated the secret order but was nevertheless regarded as the Klan candidate. He was an energetic campaigner and forced the Fergusons to resume their anti-Klan crusade. Although he eventually received three times the normal Republican vote, Butte was trounced 422,558 to 294,970. The vote was interpreted throughout the nation as a crushing defeat for the Ku Klux Klan.

The Dallas voting results were not responsible for any of the Klan's 1924 political defeats, and in fact gave the Republicans a 24,187 to 16,005 vote margin. But the statewide loss sapped the enthusiasm of local Klansmen. Thereafter, losses exceeded gains and average attendance at meetings slipped from a peak of three thousand. The most influential of Dallas Klansmen, Zeke Marvin, resigned as grand dragon in December 1924, and after a dispute with local leaders, was banished from the Invisible Empire the following year. Meanwhile his successor, Marvin A. Childers, had moved realm headquarters from Dallas to San Antonio.

The Texas legislature made good the Ferguson campaign pledge by approving an anti-mask law 84 to 22 in the House and 25 to 1 in the Senate. It provided fines ranging from one hundred to five hundred dollars and imprisonment from six months to ten years for going near public places disguised, committing masked assault, or parading masked. To add to the woes of Klan No. 66, financial irregularities were discovered in the chapter's accounts late in 1925. An imperial inquiry found klavern records to be in chaotic condition, with dues lagging, expenditures unitemized, and funds withheld from the national treasury. The national headquarters then took charge of the Klan's accounts and placed a supervisor with the autority of receiver in complete control. A demoralized and weakened Dallas chapter found itself unable to continue its support of Hope Cottage. In 1925 the orphanage was renamed Klanhaven and taken over by the state organization. The transfer of responsibility solved none of the problems, however, and the institution was declared bankrupt later in the decade.

Early in 1926, former Grand Dragon Zeke Marvin told *The New York Times* that since 1924 Dallas membership had fallen from 13,-000 to 1200 and that of Texas from 97,000 to 18,000.[12] The Klan

organization continued to function in both the city and the state for
several more years; in March 1931 fourteen armed Knights abducted and flogged two Communist organizers in Dallas for making speeches against Jim Crow (segregation) laws and the lynching of Negroes. But Governor Dan Moody had been essentially
correct in 1926 when he proclaimed the Texas Klan "as dead as the
proverbial doornail."

7

The Urban South

Atlanta, Memphis, Knoxville, and Dallas were not unusual instances of Klan success in southern cities; their experience was typical rather than exceptional. As early as July 1921 no fewer than seventy full-time kleagles were scouring the Southeast and Southwest from their bases in Atlanta and Houston. They soon surmised that where there were more people, there also could be found more recruits and more dollars.

In North Carolina, the Raleigh Klan spearheaded a local clean-up campaign and was instrumental in the selection of the chief of police. In Virginia, Robert E. Lee Klan No. 4 of Roanoke and Richmond Klan No. 1 vied for recognition as the largest and most active klavern in the state. The Roanoke unit met in a white-porticoed mansion on Day Street and sponsored military training for its zealots. Meanwhile the two-thousand-member Richmond organization distributed food baskets at Christmas, donated to the Afro-American Old Folks Home, defeated the re-election attempt of a Catholic commissioner of revenue, attended en masse a showing of *The Birth of a Nation*, and planned a Chickahominy River recreational resort complete with 320 homesites and a centrally located klavern. F. E. Maxey was the principal Klan organizer in the Virginia capital, where the local unit temporarily broke away from the national body under the guise of the Anglo-Saxon Clubs of America. In Norfolk, the exalted cyclops boasted of the initiation of the chief of police, and in Newport News, the secret order claimed that the commonwealth attorney, the postmaster, the police court judge, several members of the city council, and the police chief were among its members.[1] West Virginia's Klan development was led by Wheeling Klan No. 1 and Charleston Klan No. 2. In North Florida, Jacksonville and Tampa were centers of Klan strength, and Miami's John B. Gordon Klan No. 24 held initiations on the golf links of the Miami Country Club.[2]

In Tennessee, Chattanooga Klan No. 4 warred on bootleggers, immorality, and crime, published *The Weekly American,* and led the revolt against Imperial Kleagle Edward Young Clarke. Strongest among industrial workers, the Chattanooga klavern was led by a well-known physician and came within a few hundred votes of electing its own city commission, failing only because "the colored wards had an unprecedented vote, Jews and Catholics stuck together for the first time, and liberal Protestants . . . feared the mask more than the Pope."[3] Nashville was the headquarters of Tennessee Grand Dragons J. R. Ozier and M. S. Ross and the scene of large initiations on historic Fort Morgan Hill.[4]

Perhaps the most powerful klavern in the Southeast was Birmingham's ten-thousand-member Robert E. Lee Klan No. 1, which was organized in 1916 as the second oldest chapter in the nation. It established an orphanage known as Klanhaven, published the weekly *American Sentinel,* and sponsored several Alabama-wide klonklaves. Because the big chapter was thought to control roughly one half the city's electorate, Hugo Black, later an associate justice of the United States Supreme Court, was only one of many ambitious Birmingham politicians who took the oath of allegiance to the Invisible Empire. The city council was pressured into defeating an anti-mask ordinance, and when Police Chief Thomas J. Shirley, a prominent Klansman and a member of the Imperial Kloncilium (national executive council), was discharged, he promptly launched a successful campaign for Sheriff of Jefferson County.

The Birmingham klavern remained active at least until 1932, when it routed Negro crowds and warned "Communists" against agitation in connection with the Scottsboro rape case. To the south, the Mobile Klan was almost equally powerful and claimed twenty-five-hundred members as early as 1921.

As in the Southeast, urban Klansmen were dominant in the Southwest. Seventy-eight hundred of Arkansas's 25,000 Knights were members of Little Rock Klan No. 1, which met weekly at Fourth and Main Streets. Led first by Exalted Cyclops James A. Comer and later by Robert A. Cook, the chapter was sufficiently affluent to serve barbecued beef and lamb at initiations and influential enough to gain political control of Pulaski County and the city of Little Rock. Election endorsements were determined by intra-Klan elimination primaries, and in 1924, almost ten thousand persons marched in a "Komme-moration" parade. In addition to being the home of Grand Dragon Comer, Little Rock was also national headquarters of the Women of the Ku Klux Klan. However, in November 1925, both the men's and women's organizations voted to secede from the Invisible Empire because of an internal conflict with Comer. By early 1926 the movement was almost dead in the Arkansas capital.[5]

In Texas, Sam Houston Klan No. 1 was established in 1920 as the first Lone Star unit. Led by Grand Titan H. C. McCall, the chapter counted Houston Mayor Oscar J. Holcomb and Police Chief Gordon Murphy among its earliest members. Mayor Holcomb soon resigned, but Murphy remained loyal, allowing fellow Knights to tap the telephone wires of Catholics, intercept messages at the telegraph offices, and maintain spies at the city post office. The coercive activities of the klavern were less subtle. On March 3, 1921, the castration of Negro dentist J. L. Cockrell for alleged association with white women was personally superintended by McCall, who argued that a little bit of violence was good for the Klan. His advice was apparently heeded, because beatings were administered to an automobile salesman, an attorney, and a merchant for such crimes as "annoying high school girls" and "too close fraternization with Negroes." The active Houston klavern initiated dozens of policemen, staged mass meetings with five thousand in attendance, and remained a potent force in community life until 1924, when declining membership forced Exalted Cyclops Sam McClure to sell the Klan meeting hall to the city.[6]

Although the Fort Worth and San Antonio Klans never achieved the strength and influence of their Dallas and Houston counterparts, both generated controversy. The bailiwick of Exalted Cyclops Julian C. Hyer's Klan No. 101, Fort Worth became Texas Klan headquarters in 1922 during the administration of Grand Dragon Brown Harwood. Klan No. 101 tarred and feathered a local gambler, demonstrated openly in the business district, established firm control over the city government, and sponsored Klan Day at the Southwestern Exposition and Livestock Show. Early in 1924 the Fort Worth chapter reached its pinnacle with the dedication of a magnificent, $100,000 "Ku Klux Klan Hall," featuring a four-thousand-seat auditorium. Six months later two mysterious explosions and a fire completely destroyed the structure.

Incendiaries were also a problem in San Antonio, where Klan No. 31's rented headquarters in Beethoven Hall was threatened three times. The local chapter featured "aeroplane maneuvers" and spectacular cross burnings at its Speedway Race Track initiations, and on one occasion five hundred special police were sworn in to prevent riots during a Klan celebration. Klan No. 31 was particularly hampered by an aggressive internal split over the Simmons-Evans issue, and after Grand Dragon Marvin A. Childers of San Antonio was replaced in 1925, the Invisible Empire ceased to be a factor in the life of the city.

The Realm of Oklahoma was smaller in size but equal in activity and influence to the Texas organization. Grand Dragon N. Clay Jewett's home, business, and headquarters were in Oklahoma City, where the county attorney, a district judge, the mayor, and the sheriff were among those with sheets in their closets.[7] The local chapter met in the courthouse, Convention Hall, the Congregational Church, and the old Epworth University building. Larger gatherings were held at the fairgrounds, where in 1924 a crowd of thirty thousand at a Klan ceremony cheered as an airplane with a crimson cross outlined on its wings circled above. A women's branch and a junior Klan were also established in the capital city. On one occasion the female Kluxers garbed themselves in flowing blue robes and captured a still four miles from the city.

Ranking even higher than its neighbor as a center of "one hundred per cent Americanism" was Tulsa, a city with a rather sordid history of violence. It was the scene of a public lynching in 1919, and in 1921 the Negro district was burned after a race riot in which more than thirty Negroes were killed. Governor B. A. Robertson declared martial law and blamed the debacle on a cowardly chief of police, who was suspended from office by a Tulsa jury. The Klan probably had nothing to do with the tragedy, but it was able to take advantage of the community's vigilante tradition of law enforcement. In one four-month period, no fewer than twelve persons were whipped by masked bands in Tulsa County. One year later, after the city was placed under martial law, military authorities charged thirty-one admitted Klansmen with night riding and assault.

Perhaps the best estimates of the influence of the Invisible Empire in Tulsa was that of the president of the Chamber of Commerce. In 1923 he spoke of Tulsa's shame and disgrace because "our courthouse and our city hall are practically filled with members of the Klan elected to office with Klan support." Meeting in the city auditorium or out on Broken Arrow Road prior to establishing headquarters in Beno Hall on the edge of town, Exalted Cyclops William Shelley Rogers' powerful Klan No. 2 made a practice of parading on horseback through city streets. It counted the publisher of the *Tulsa Tribune* among its many members, and in 1924 established a Junior Klan for boys twelve to eighteen years old. Female Kluxers were also active in the city; at a two-day Kamelia convention in 1923, several thousand representatives of pure womanhood marched nineteen blocks through the central business district.[8]

The chief antagonist of the Invisible Empire in Oklahoma was John Calloway "Jack" Walton, a heavy-set, middle-aged native of Indiana. As mayor of Oklahoma City, he pioneered in naming Negroes to the police force, posed as the poor man's friend, and allied himself politically with the Farmer-Labor party. When the Klan was organized in Oklahoma City, Walton warned policemen that Klan membership would not be tolerated, and he investigated KKK use of the fairgrounds. Elected to the governorship in 1923 over strong Klan opposition in both the primary and general elections, Walton managed to alienate his friends with a series of inept political maneuvers, and his legislative program was unsuccessful in the legislature. The governor then attempted to shift voter attention from the failures of his administration to the admittedly macabre activities of the Ku Klux Klan. Placing first Tulsa and then the entire state under martial law, Walton used national guardsmen in a vain attempt to foul a special election called to reduce the powers of the governor. He suspended habeas corpus and threatened the lives of dissident lawmakers. His actions were far more extreme than the situation warranted, and as Charles Alexander has noted, he forced people who did not like the Klan to choose between a despotic governor and the KKK. They chose the Klan. Walton was impeached in 1923 and removed from office. When he attempted a political comeback by winning the 1924 Democratic senatorial nomination, the Klan vote shifted to the Republican camp and Walton was humiliated by 339,646 to 196,412.[9]

The only big southern cities to resist effectively the encroachments of "one hundred per cent Americanism" were New Orleans and Louisville. The seaport metropolis was the first headquarters of the Realm of Louisiana and was the home of Old Hickory Klan No. 1, Algiers Klan No. 45, and Al-Gre-Har Klan No. 50. Meetings were held in rented Shalimar Grotto Hall on Dauphine Street, and initiations were often staged in a field opposite the Algiers Naval Station. Members of Klan No. 1 gave a lecture at Carrollton Presbyterian Church, and State Representative Thomas Depaoli, a great titan in the realm of Louisiana, argued that "some of the best citizens of New Orleans" were Klansmen. But opposition to the Invisible Empire quickly coalesced in both the city and the state. The catalyst was the heinous August 1922 murder of two young men in Mer Rouge, Louisiana. Filmore Watt Daniels and Thomas F. Richards had made no secret of their contempt for "one hundred per cent Americanism." While returning from a picnic, they were abducted by masked men. Four months later their decomposed bodies floated to the surface of nearby Lake Lafourche. Although the Morehouse Parish grand jury refused to indict the suspected Klansmen, the incident was publicized throughout the nation, and Louisiana Governor John M. Parker embarked upon a personal crusade to rid his state of the cancer of invisible government. In stable and predominantly Catholic New Orleans, Old Hickory Klan No. 1 shriveled in shame, and by 1924 the Crescent City was without an active chapter.[10]

The Klan entered Louisville in 1921 and eventually enrolled three thousand local citizens. But Mayor George Smith promised early to use "every lawful means to prevent and suppress its growth in our community," and he made good his threat. The street sale of Klan literature was forbidden, and meetings often had to be held across the river in Jeffersonville. The local chapter never gained wide community support, and in 1925 it suffered public humiliation after the Democratic party had to eliminate from its ticket a mayoral candidate accused of being a former Klansman. Perhaps foreseeing difficulty, the secret order in 1921 established Kentucky propagation headquarters in more congenial Covington, just across the Ohio River from Cincinnati. The exceptions only prove the rule, however, that the Ku Klux Klan was active and successful in the urban South.

III

THE NORTH

Experts say the Negro exodus has slowed up. But 500 milling, sweating, pushing blacks belied the statement in a decisive fashion last night when they tried to concertedly shove their way past the gateman at Central Station to get on Illinois Central train No. 4, bound for Chicago.

Memphis *Commercial-Appeal*,
September 2, 1923

After its initial achievement in the South, the Ku Klux Klan bridged the Ohio River at Cincinnati late in 1920. Ahead lay the populous Northeast, but the immediate objective was the Midwest—a ten-state agricultural and industrial colossus widely regarded as the most typically American of all sections. As the Invisible Empire spread northward, its leaders may have reflected upon the midwestern character and pondered their chances for success.

At first glance, the Midwest would seem to have presented more of an obstacle than an opportunity to bigotry's champions. In almost every respect it contrasted sharply with the South of William Joseph Simmons and Edward Hull Crump. The Corn Belt was perhaps the world's most prosperous agricultural region, an area where independent farmers were far more common than sharecroppers and Negro field hands. Early leaders in adult education, the lake states had many cultural institutions and boasted of distinguished universities and well-regarded symphony orchestras. Most importantly, the Midwest had a long tradition of religious tolerance. In the nineteenth century the region had been dotted with utopian, socialistic, and abolitionist societies, and Ohio, Indiana, and Illinois had formed a vital link in the underground railroad.

89

But despite prosperity and tradition, the Midwest became a showcase for the Ku Klux Klan and furnished the Invisible Empire with more than one-third of its total national membership. David C. Stephenson, the flamboyant "old man" of Indiana politics and the accused rapist of Madge Oberholtzer, was only the most infamous of mid-America's super patriots. Illinois, Indiana, and Ohio alone contributed well over five hundred thousand Knights and together they represented the heaviest concentration of Klan strength in the United States.

To what can we attribute such extraordinary acceptance of "one hundred per cent Americanism?" John Moffatt Mecklin, and those who have accepted his interpretation, would of course argue that the secret order found fortune in the small town, and particularly in the drabness of its daily routine. To be sure, the Ku Klux Klan was active and effective in such places as Racine, Kokomo, Muncie, and Valparaiso. Moreover, the essential emptiness of small-town life at that time has been depicted by a succession of authors. Edgar Lee Master's *Spoon River Anthology*, Sherwood Anderson's *Winesburg, Ohio*, Sinclair Lewis's *Main Street*, and Robert and Helen Lynd's *Middletown* revealed the mid-American town as shallow, unreflective, uninspiring, and monotonous.[1]

However, it was not the decaying town that provided the basis for Klan growth. The Midwest contained thirteen of the nation's fifty largest cities, and it was here, where the keynote was growth, change, and social unrest, that the kleagles found their finest potential for success. World War I had encouraged many southern Negroes to move northward to work in war industries. The resulting Negro economic and political competition was resented by white workers, as was the threat of neighborhood integration. In 1917, forty-seven persons were killed in an East St. Louis race riot, and in 1919, a similar incident in Chicago claimed thirty-six lives. Early in 1925, Frank Bohn wrote in the *American Journal of Sociology*, "There is at present more bitterness toward the Negro in the Middle West than there has been anywhere in the South since the days of Reconstruction."[2]

Negroes represented only part of the difficulty, however. Of equal or perhaps greater importance to white urban Protestants was the threat of ethnic and religious minorities—the hyphenated Americans who played a vital role in almost every major city. Chicago was crowded with Italians, Russians, Irish, Poles, and Germans; Detroit with Italians, and Poles; and St. Louis with Bohemians and Czechs. Even Indianapolis, perhaps the most homogeneous midwestern metropolis, had sizable German and Irish neighborhoods and a growing Negro population. In reaction against these "un-American" influences, the Ku Klux Klan took root and prospered in the urban Midwest.

8

Chicago: Goliath of Mid-America

Few cities should have been more unreceptive to the Klan of John Moffatt Mecklin than Chicago. Long a mecca for newcomers from eastern and southern Europe, the midwestern colossus in 1920 was the home of well over 1,000,000 Catholics, 800,000 foreign-born immigrants, 125,000 Jews, and 110,000 Negroes. Moreover, life there was hardly dull in the Prohibition era, when fifteen breweries, 20,-000 speakeasies, and such underworld racketeers as Dion O'Banion, Johnny Torrio, and Al Capone lent color to the urban scene. The Windy City's reputation for vice and corruption, its apparent disregard of Volsteadism, its boss-run government, and its numerous foreign-language newspapers seemed to make it the very antithesis of everything for which the Invisible Empire stood.[1] But the kleagles came to Chicago, and they found there no shortage of patriots eager to advance the cause of "one hundred per cent Americanism." Klan and anti-Klan met head on, and the extensive use by both sides of spies and intrigue made the long struggle unique in the United States.[2]

The first Klansman to appear on the south shore of Lake Michigan was probably C. W. Love, grand goblin (regional commander) of the Domain of the Great Lakes. Arriving from Indian-

93

apolis on June 1, 1921, Love directed the efforts of forty-one lesser
midwestern recruiters from his Clark Street headquarters in Chicago. King Kleagle Elmer Hockaday and seventeen regular kleagles were responsible for Illinois propagation, which was well
under way by mid-summer 1921.

The first public indication of Ku Klux Klan activity in Chicago
came at an initiation on the evening of August 16, 1921.[3] Some ten
thousand local Klansmen began gathering late in the afternoon on
North Central Park Avenue, where they were assigned to a long
caravan of automobiles. Departing from the city shortly before
sundown, the men were excited by the news that the Imperial Wizard himself had come from Atlanta to take part in the ceremony.
They arrived at a large meadow six miles south of Lake Zurich and
began a torchlight parade around a huge bonfire. Klan pickets kept
away curious spectators as 2376 candidates were "naturalized" into
the Invisible Empire. A steady rain cut short the ceremony, but the
initiates kissed the American flag and cheered as Simmons described their objective as, "the perpetuation of law, order, peace,
and justice."

Headlines the following day proclaimed, "Ku Klux Rites Draw
12,000," prompting the United States District Attorney in Chicago
to order his assistant, Colonel John V. Clinnin, to investigate the
secret order. Working for several months, Clinnin inspected the
Klan's charter of incorporation, its constitution, and other relevant
literature and declared that, although the organization would foster
disorder and anarchy, he could find nothing on which to base legal
action.

The spectacular September exposé of the New York *World* was
not syndicated in Chicago, but many copies of the eastern newspaper were sold in the city, and some of its information was published
in the local press. Predictably, the reaction was hostile. Labeling
the Klan "a menace to this and any community," former Governor
Edward F. Dunne and attorney Clarence Darrow took the lead in
organizing a National Unity Council to seek legislation to crush the
secret order. At about the same time the National Equal Rights
League met in special session at the Pilgrim Baptist Church in Chi-

cago and sent a telegram to President Harding asking for an extraordinary message to Congress. Police Chief Charles Fitzmorris joined the chorus by announcing that the rumored Loop parade of local Klansmen would not be permitted, and the weekly conference of the city's Baptist ministers unanimously adopted a resolution "issuing a general warning of the dangers of the Ku Klux Klan." On September 17, 1921, three thousand persons watched near the stockyards as a white-sheeted Klansman was hanged in effigy from the Ragen Athletic Club.

Responding to the anti-Klan mood, the city council unanimously pledged on September 19, 1921, to rid Chicago of the Invisible Empire:

> WHEREAS, the traditions and odium attached to the Ku Klux Klan and the acts which have been attributable to it make it a menace to a city like Chicago, having a heterogeneous population and different religious creeds; now therefore be it
> Resolved, that the City Council of Chicago officially condemns the presence of the Ku Klux Klan in Chicago and pledges its services to the proper authorities to rid the community of this organization.[4]

But resolutions and demonstrations did not have the desired effect. Anti-Klan activity was offered by enterprising kleagles as proof positive that alien elements were gaining control of American life, and that immediate action was necessary by white Protestants to protect the nation's heritage. The appeal to patriotism was heeded, and klectokens were soon pouring into the Chicago Klan office. Masons joined the organization by the hundreds, and Masonic halls were frequently utilized for Klan meetings. At one October meeting five hundred new members were inducted, and by January 1922 the eight local units gave Chicago "the largest membership of any city in the United States." [5] In June, Imperial Kleagle Edward Young Clarke, in the city to deliver a charter to a neighborhood chapter, declared that the rapidly growing Chicago Klan had thirty thousand members. He surmised that had the Klan been fully and thoroughly organized earlier, the recent increase in the crime rate could have been prevented "because the Knights of the

Ku Klux Klan would have been on the job behind the officers on their respective beats." Strangely enough, the Imperial Kleagle's sentiments were later echoed by Municipal Judge Henry M. Walker of the East Chicago Avenue Court. While considering a bootlegging charge against Mrs. Katie Lawkoski, he remarked: "Some of these foreigners come here to make money, and find moonshining the easiest way of doing it. I will say that we need the Ku Klux to put a stop to some of these practices. And I'm not a member of the Klan either. I couldn't be, because I'm not a native."

Typical Klan procedure was to charter only one chapter in any given city or town, but because of its size Chicago eventually claimed more than twenty neighborhood Klan units. Although each chapter was virtually autonomous in its particular district, joint central control was exercised by an executive committee composed of the exalted cyclops of each Klan. Among the earliest Illinois groups to be chartered were Englewood Klan No. 2, Woodlawn Klan No. 4, and Kenwood Klan No. 33, all located in south side neighborhoods threatened by the expanding Negro ghetto.[6] But the Klan also established healthy chapters in areas threatened ethnically rather than racially, such as Irving Park, South Shore, Logan Square, Austin, Windsor Park, Hermosa, Garfield, and Morgan Park. There was even a "Daylight Klan" for the benefit of night workers who could not attend the regular evening meetings.[7]

Although the Klan was larger and more active in the city than in the suburbs, white robes and fiery crosses were familiar sights in many of Chicago's satellite communities. South suburban Harvey's Klan No. 64 appeared publicly at the austere First Methodist Church and sponsored at least two area-wide Klan rallies. In nearby Blue Island and Chicago Heights the local chapters took great pride in their bands, while in Joliet and Tinley Park several initiations were held. To the west of Chicago, an active Aurora chapter included many successful businessmen (see Table 6), and Berwyn-Cicero and Oak Park Klans won charters in 1923. Wilmette and Waukegan represented the Invisible Empire on the north shore, where the Klan was relatively weak.

The heavily industrial Indiana harbor cities in the Chicago area were even more Klan ridden than the Illinois suburbs. As early as 1921, the secret order was said to have five hundred members in Gary, and two thousand five hundred in Lake County. It reportedly held several meetings in East Chicago churches and dominated the city administration of Michigan City. In Hammond, Lake Klan No. 72 rallied often in public parks, staged parades on Sibley Boulevard, donated substantially to the First Presbyterian Church, and reportedly listed the mayor, the police chief, and a city judge among its members.[8]

The rapid growth of the Invisible Empire in Chicago in the summer of 1922 was punctuated by two far south side demonstrations, the first near Joliet at Van Horn's Bridge on the DuPage River on June 4, and the second near Oaklawn at 91st and Harlem on August 19.[9] The latter demonstration was the more auspicious because it featured the initiation of 4650 persons, one of the largest groups in the history of the Invisible Empire. Representing the eighteen Klans then operating in Chicago and the twelve outside in Cook County, Klansmen began arriving at the huge field in late afternoon. They parked their "machines" in a large circle around a twenty-foot wooden cross, which was wrapped in cotton. After dusk, the twenty-five thousand Klansmen in attendance donned their white robes, mingled, chatted, and ate while the headlights of hundreds of automobiles illuminated the field. Long before midnight, the entrance of a silent procession from the south end of the roped-off area signaled the beginning of the ceremony.

At the head of the column marched short, heavy-set Imperial Representative Bertram G. Christie, who had taken charge of the Chicago District in June 1921. Next came Illinois Grand Dragon Charles G. Palmer, an attorney with offices in the First National Bank Building. As the two potentates reached the cross at the center of the field, the white robed throng formed a huge circle. Candidates for initiation lined up in squads and shuffled around the silent circle, "while searching eyes inspected them to make certain at the last minute that none should enter 'not fit' for the Klan." Torches were lit, and soon an eerie red glare was reflected from the faces of the assembly, who began to sing the familiar "Onward, Christian

Soldiers." The candidates then knelt on one knee, raised their right arms, and repeated the long secret oath of allegiance to the Invisible Empire. After the new members had been duly congratulated, the patriots motored home, secure in the knowledge that a beachhead had been established in alien Chicago.[10]

Less than twenty-four hours after the well-publicized event, the Klan appeared before a distressed inner city Protestant congregation at 23rd and Michigan Avenue. The spire of Immanuel Baptist Church had been torn away in a recent storm, and services were being held in the basement pending an appeal for funds. The Reverend Johnston Myers was delivering the Sunday evening sermon to about six hundred parishoners, when a dozen white-robed figures entered unannounced from the rear. Marching to the front of the sanctuary, their leader proclaimed, "The Knights of the Ku Klux Klan have come to do their part in this cause." Immediately, the front door swung open and five hundred additional Klansmen began to file silently past the minister, dropping contributions in a large basket. Twelve hundred dollars was deposited before the visitors turned, saluted, and hurried outside. Not a Klansman was in sight several minutes later.[11]

Although never again so well publicized, visitations to churches became a frequent activity of Chicago Klansmen. In a five-month period between November 1922 and March 1923, robed Knights made open donations to the Douglas Park Christian Church, the Pacific Congregational Church, the Third Congregational Church, the Southfield Community Church, and the Nazareth Evangelical Church. Not all the presentations were without incident. When a south side chapter gathered at Hegewisch Methodist Church in May 1923 to hear a sermon favorable to "one hundred per cent Americanism," the building was surrounded by several hundred "hoodlums." Fortunately for the Klan, six of its members were armed, and they dispersed their assailants with a "display of revolvers."

Among the Klan's more enthusiastic ministerial supporters was the Reverend John H. Williamson, whose Normal Park Methodist Church received a "substantial donation" from Englewood Klan

No. 2. A former law enforcement commissioner in Chicago, the Reverend Mr. Williamson declared, "Speaking for myself I could very readily state why a Protestant minister would stand with the K.K.K." [12] His sentiments were shared by few of his calling, however, most of whom rejected "one hundred per cent Americanism" at a special meeting of the city's Protestant ministers at the Y.M.C.A. in 1923.

Although financial support of selected churches may have been sincere on the part of most Klansmen, it was used as a publicity device by cyclopes and kleagles interested both in attracting new members and in presenting a more favorable public image of the order. Another method of recruitment was the payment of school children to collect the names and addresses of Protestant classmates, whose mothers were then sent the following circular:

> The Knights of the Ku Klux Klan, as a patriotic, fraternal, benevolent order, does not discriminate against a man on account of his religious or political creed so long as it does not antagonize the sacred right guaranteed by our civil government or conflict with Christian ideals and institutions.
>
> The Klan asks the support of churchmen everywhere in the great work of uniting into one organization, under one banner, all native born Protestant Gentile Americans.
>
> Although, as a woman you are not eligible for membership, you will, we are sure, if you sympathize with the aims of this order, not take it amiss if we venture to suggest that you might send us on a slip of paper a list of a few Protestant gentlemen who you think would be intei)sted to hear about the organization. We assure you in advance of our appreciation.

The most consistent method of propagation was the professional lecturer sent out from the national headquarters. A notable example was "the eminent Baptist minister of Atlanta," Samuel H. Campbell, who told an audience at Central Presbyterian Church that the Klan was "only composed of true, one hundred per cent, law abiding Americans." Appearing frequently in Chicago, Campbell also spoke at the Irving Park Klavern on October 16, 1922, and at the Masonic Hall on the occasion of the official chartering of the South Shore Klan. Occasionally, the endless recruitment was broken by social activity. On October 21, 1922, ambitious Austin Klan No. 6 welcomed three hundred new members at a "Harvest Jubilee and Rube Party," where "dancing predominated the evening."

Wisely, the Chicago Klan did not follow the example of Tulsa, Dallas, and Los Angeles klaverns in the occasional use of violence to accomplish desired goals. It warned floggers not to attempt to shield themselves behind the anonymity of the Klan and emphasized that Klansmen engaging in acts of violence would be found guilty before both the state and the Invisible Empire. Only one reported instance marred an otherwise clean record. On June 15, 1922, three Klansmen were arrested for speeding on Western Avenue and found to be in possession of two revolvers, a cat-o'-nine-tails, and a Klan membership receipt. William W. Newman, an officer in a Chicago klavern, admitted that the trio had driven to Morris, Illinois, and flogged a chiropractor for mistreating a teen-aged girl.[13]

In another much-publicized event involving violence the Chicago Klan emerged with clean hands. On February 7, 1923, police found a twenty-six-year-old girl on a south side street, almost unconscious and bleeding profusely. Miss Mildred Erick told of being threatened by the Klan because of her recent conversion to Catholicism and related the details of a harrowing ride with hooded men who cut crosses into her legs, back, and arms. Two days later, however, she retracted the story, explaining that she had forged the threatening letter and inflicted the wounds upon herself in order to impress upon her father, Klansman Henry Erick, "what a bad organization the Klan is":

> Recently I changed my religion. I understood my father joined the Klan, and I wanted to let him know they opposed my new religion. I cut a cross in each of my palms, one on each of my thighs, front and rear, and one on my back, all with a safety razor blade.
>
> I wrote myself the letter in red ink which was pretended to be an order from the K.K.K. to change my religion. Then I invented the whole story of how the Klan seized me, stripped me, and branded me.[14]

In October 1922, the Chicago Klan began publication of *Dawn: A Journal for True American Patriots,* one of the most influential of the Invisible Empire's many periodicals. Edited by Edwin J. Parke and published by the Forcum Press, the forty thousand dollar magazine proclaimed its aim to be, "a medium for acquainting the public with the noble principles, high ideals, and patriotic achievements of the Knights of the Ku Klux Klan." Names of members were not printed, thus circulation manager J. O. Barker, a tailor, felt free to offer the slick magazine for sale on Chicago newsstands at ten cents per copy. A major factor in *Dawn's* sixteen-month success was its attractiveness to advertisers, whose monetary support undoubtedly reflected a belief that the Klan was an important element in the city. The Hyde Park community, which borders the University of Chicago, was disproportionately represented among the advertisers, perhaps reflecting the fact that the magazine was originally published in the neighborhood.

By the summer of 1922, no informed individual could deny the existence of a significant Klan movement in Chicago. As early as September 1921, the *Chicago Tribune* denounced the secret order because of the "historical association of the name with mob law and night murder," and it ridiculed potential Klansmen with a front-page, six-part cartoon.[15] Primarily concerned lest the Klan become a major political issue and thereby weaken the *Tribune's* campaign to replace Mayor William "Big Bill" Thompson with another and more suitable Republican executive, the conservative newspaper was counseling only passive resistance to Kluxism by the fall of 1922:

It has been the American experience with such organizations as the K.K.K. that they ran their course without much disturbance if they were received with a smile. They have in their naive enthusiasms the elements of disintegration. If their acts take them outside the law they can be acted against according to the law. . . .

We'd be in the woods again if the K.K.K. and its opponents made that the chief issue at a time when we were trying to have a housecleaning and have fair prospects of getting one.[16]

The *Chicago Daily News* was more denunciatory, commenting on November 8, 1922, "Now that the Ku Klux have jumped into Chicago politics they can confidently be relied upon to make bad government worse, since they apply racial and religious tests and ignore tests of morality and efficiency." Catholic and foreign-language publications joined the Protestant *Northwestern Christian Advocate* and *Christian Century* in condemning the secret order, but the most vigorous anti-Klan newspaper among the regular press of the city's minority groups was the *Chicago Defender*. Recognizing the rapid growth of the Invisible Empire in Chicago in September 1922, it cautioned its readers not to take alarm, because the *Defender* claimed possession of the Klan's ritual, password, and signs, as well as the names and businesses of many recently initiated Klansmen.[17] Understandably, the spokesman of Chicago's Negro community saw the Klan not in the tradition of the Know-Nothing party and the American Protective Association, but rather as an extension of the Confederate spirit. In a front-page editorial captioned, "To Hell with the Ku Klux Klan," *Defender* editor Robert S. Abbott declared that Negroes "await the command of authority to join the field against the foe,—against sons of those who now try to win by signs and robes what their fathers lost by fire and sword."

Judicial denunciation of the Invisible Empire, advocated earlier by several groups, followed shortly thereafter. On September 18, 1922, Judge Joseph B. David, sitting in Superior Court, stated that because Klansmen had confirmed opinions they could not serve as jurors in his courtroom. Similar action was taken three months later by Chief Justice Michael L. McKinley of the Criminal Court, who prohibited Klansmen from serving on the December Grand Jury. Their actions were not universally admired. Although Methodist Bishop Edwin Hughes of Chicago was an implacable foe of the hooded order, the Methodist Ministers of Chicago characterized McKinley's decision as "virtually depriving Klansmen of their rights of citizenship, and in the nature of class legislation." [18]

The most potent manifestation of anti-Klan sentiment, however, was the formation of the American Unity League. Founded on

June 21, 1922, by Robert H. Shepherd, Grady K. Rutledge, and Joseph G. Keller, the A.U.L. was dedicated solely to the eradication of the Ku Klux Klan both in Chicago and in the nation.[19] The organization was designed to include all minority groups and Negro Bishop Samuel Fallows of the Reformed Episcopal Church was named honorary chairman. But the American Unity League neither sought nor received the full co-operation of Negroes and Jews, and its three most influential supporters were all priests: the Reverend William J. McNamee of St. Patrick's Church, the Reverend E. A. Kelly of St. Anne's Church, and the Reverend J. F. Noll, editor of *Our Sunday Visitor*. Predictably, the Klan accused the A.U.L. of being "an Irish, Roman Catholic clique." Its driving force was acting chairman (later president) Patrick H. O'Donnell, a dynamic criminal lawyer who made speeches all over Chicago and the Midwest on the subject of the Klan.[20] He estimated its strength in the Windy City at 27,000 in the summer of 1922, and as 50,000 in that same fall. The Klan meanwhile was claiming 100,000 Chicago and 100,000 suburban members.

The unique weapon of the American Unity League was a little weekly newspaper entitled *Tolerance*, which published the names, addresses, and occupations of thousands of Chicago area Klansmen. In its first issue on September 10, 1922, Chairman O'Donnell stated the policy of the periodical:

> We feel that the publication of the names of those who belong to the Klan will be a blow that the masked organization cannot survive. Many Klansmen are in business or the professions and are dependent largely upon patronage of those groups they classify as alien. We feel that it is only just that their attitude be made public.

Sold at newsstands, bus stops, and churches for a dime, *Tolerance* first listed the names of one hundred and fifty Chicago Klansmen on September 17, 1922. The entire supply of 2700 newspapers was quickly exhausted. Over 17,500 copies were published the following week, and by the end of the year, when the campaign to bring economic pressure to bear against Klan businessmen and em-

ployees reached high gear, the anti-Klan organ had a circulation of
150,000. "Distributed and sold widely among persons of the Roman
Catholic religious faith," *Tolerance* represented the only major attempt in the nation to publicize the names of rank and file Klansmen on a systematic basis.[21] The anti-Klan newspaper was itself
extremely vitriolic and, as Professor Mecklin noted, rivaled "the
most rabid Klan publications in its shrieking and hysterical con-
demnations of all things pertaining to the Klan."

The most prominent of many Klansmen who suffered from association with the Invisible Empire was Augustus E. Olsen, President
of the Washington Park National Bank and one of the best known
young businessmen of the south side. In the fifth issue of *Tolerance*
he was listed as a member of the Ku Klux Klan. Thereafter, Olsen
was bitterly assailed at anti-Klan meetings, and a concerted effort
was made to persuade depositors to remove their money from the
Washington Park Bank and redeposit it elsewhere. Many of the
bank's customers were of Irish or Jewish descent, and the with-
drawals soon totaled thousands of dollars.[22] At a meeting of the
firm's board of directors on October 31, 1922, it was determined
that Olsen should step aside as president. At the time of his resignation, the disheartened businessman declared, "I signed a petition
for membership in the Klan several months ago, but did not know
it was anything else than an ordinary fraternal order."

The experience of Augustus Olsen was not unique. A route salesman testified in court that after being listed in *Tolerance*, members
of minority groups "from thence hitherto wholly refused and still do
refuse to have any transaction, acquaintance or discourse with me
as they were before used and accustomed to have." [23] A grocer related that his "customers have ceased doing business with him and
have ceased to purchase meats and other provisions from him, since
and on account of said publication." A milkman employed by a
dairy of only five trucks reported that several Negro-owned estab-
lishments broke off business relations with his firm after his name
appeared in the weekly anti-Klan newspaper.[24] As a result many
Klansmen visited the office of *Tolerance*, expressing sorrow at having joined the secret order and fright at the prospect of being ex-

posed. At first the official position of the Invisible Empire was that the American Unity League held "no terror for the Ku Klux Klan"; eight months later, after *Tolerance's* revelations had taken a heavy toll, the secret order charged that the A.U.L. had resorted "to the tactics of the thug, the bribe giver, and the sneak to obtain information to which it was not rightfully entitled."

Labeling the boycott "a miserable weapon of cowards," the Klan retaliated by filing suit against the American Unity League for revealing its secrets.[25] Not intimidated, the A.U.L. declared that its anti-Klan campaign would proceed: "We propose to make the Invisible Empire visible in Chicago, and as far beyond as our influence can reach." Moreover, the American Unity League announced at a large Morrison Hotel luncheon gathering in December that four thousand women had already enrolled in a new female anti-Klan unit. On December 7, 1922, Grady K. Rutledge, editor of *Tolerance* and secretary of the A.U.L., optimistically declared: "Printing the names of its members has virtually broken up the Klan in Chicago," and four days later he estimated that the hooded order's membership in the city had fallen from 55,000 to 10,000 in the short space of four months.[26] By January 26, 1923, *Tolerance* had printed the names of four thousand Chicago Klansmen in twenty-one separate installments and was preparing to publish six thousand more. In the event that anyone had missed the early issues, the entire list of exposed Kluxers was published in the fifty-cent pamphlet, *Is Your Neighbor a Kluxer?* Advertised on light posts and trolley cars throughout Chicago, the little booklet concluded with a demand that the federal government take action against the Invisible Empire.[27]

The highlight of the American Unity League's visibility campaign came at an All-Nations Rally at the coliseum on February 26, 1923. Presided over by Judge Michael McKinley, the gathering was disappointingly small despite extensive local publicity before the event. The oratory featured two of the South's foremost anti-Klan veterans: Governor John Parker of Louisiana and former Senator Leroy Percy of Mississippi.[28] Governor Parker, in whose state were committed the infamous Mer Rouge murders of two young hecklers

who had ridiculed the KKK, told the audience that the American
Unity League had adopted the one method of fighting the Klan
that was sure to succeed. He reasoned that the secret order would
rather be abused than ignored and emphasized that it had thrived
and multiplied under attack from newspapers and magazines. But
turning the daylight on the individual members was quite another
matter; "Tell their neighbors just who these people are who seek to
lie hidden while they plot against the community and the nation,
and their neighbors will take care of them."

The task of uncovering the Invisible Empire was a sensitive one,
and the American Unity League won its success through a combination of diligence, good fortune, bribery, and intrigue. At one time
as many as seven investigators were on the A.U.L. payroll (at sixty
dollars per week plus expenses), but most of the pirated membership records came from disgruntled or banished former Klansmen.
The first list was furnished free of charge by Dr. Mortimer E. Emrick. A leader in Woodlawn Klan No. 4, Emrick had resigned in
disgust after being frustrated in an attempt to reorganize the south
side klaverns.

Another former Klansman who collaborated with the enemy was
tall, sandy-haired Dixie Shea, who usually posed as a representative
of the Atlanta-based Klan periodical *Searchlight* in order to gain
access to unsuspecting klaverns.[29] Still another co-operative informer was W. A. Hill, a youthful, small man who as secretary to
the grand goblin procured confidential literature and membership
lists for the anti-Klan group. Unfortunately, he faked some Klan
lists by placing on them the names of persons for whom he had a
personal dislike. The adventures of Louis D. Wisbrod, described by
the Klan as "a red-headed Jew," resembled those of a counterspy.
Working for both the Invisible Empire and the American Unity
League, Wisbrod kept the Loop streets hot between the two headquarters. He carried A.U.L. correspondence, an armful at a time, to
Bertram Christie to be photographed and brought back such gossip
and correspondence as he could surreptitiously gather in the Klan
office.[30]

But no one more seriously damaged the cause of the Klan in

Chicago than Marvin V. Hinshaw, a professional musician and a former king kleagle of the Domain of the Great Lakes. He was a popular and enthusiastic member, and in May 1922, he led the singing of "America" at the first provisional session of the Imperial Klonvokation in Atlanta. Falling from official favor that same summer, the Midwest's chief recruiter was banished from the Invisible Empire for "conduct unbecoming a Klansman." Anxious for revenge, he promptly let it be known to the A.U.L. that he had "a friend" in Chattanooga with the names of six thousand Windy City Klansmen. Demanding three dollars per name, or $18,000 for the entire list, the former kleagle spurned the league's initial offer of six hundred dollars. Hinshaw's avarice betrayed him, because the A.U.L. then resolved to take the list by trickery and force. Promising the former Klansman two thousand five hundred dollars, the A.U.L. invited Hinshaw to its headquarters at 127 North Dearborn, where the imposing stack of currency awaiting him actually totaled less than two hundred dollars. When Hinshaw produced the names, Grady Rutledge asked to compare them with anti-Klan records in an adjoining room. Following a prearranged plan, the *Tolerance* editor quickly exited by a rear door and, with list in hand, raced through downtown Chicago to the Ashland Block law office of fellow conspirator O'Donnell, where the Klan records were promptly locked away in a hidden vault. Meanwhile, back at the *Tolerance* office, Hinshaw soon discovered the deceit, but detested by both Klan and anti-Klan elements, he had little choice but to accept quietly the three hundred and fifty dollars the League eventually paid him.

While the American Unity League hacked away at Klan secrecy, the ethnically oriented Chicago City Council reviewed "one hundred per cent Americanism" as a possible local election issue. On December 4, 1922, Alderman Robert J. Mulcahy introduced a motion that the group consider a report that a city fire station in the west side Austin neighborhood had been used as a Klan initiation lodge. Five men all "of different nationality or descent" were appointed to the special committee to investigate Kluxism among city employees: "Ald. Mulcahy, Irish; Ald. Louis B. Henderson, colored; Ald. Oscar H. Olsen, Norwegian; Ald. S. S. Walkowiak, Polish; and Ald. U. S. Schwartz, a Jew." The diverse blue ribbon panel accepted the mandate enthusiastically, and after five days Mulcahy proudly announced, "I have seventy-five names of Klansmen who are city employees, at least fifteen of whom I can prove are Klansmen. I intend to call in these fifteen city employees and confront them with proof of their affiliations." More specific charges were forthcoming on December 13, when Captain William Hind and Firemen Joseph Cozdicke, Albert Peterson, and George W. Green were accused of being Klansmen. The aldermanic com-

Table 5

OCCUPATIONAL DISTRIBUTION OF MEMBERS OF THE KU KLUX KLAN IN CHICAGO, 1922-1923[*]

White-Collar Workers	No.	Percentage of Klan Membership	Blue-Collar Workers	No.	Percentage of Klan Membership
Businessmen	22	20.0	Foremen	8	7.3
Salesmen	13	11.8	R.R. workers	7	6.2
Clerks	10	9.1	Printers	4	3.7
Lawyers	5	4.6	Firemen	3	2.7
Physicians	2	1.8	Unskilled laborers	3	2.7
Dentists	2	1.8	Postmen	3	2.7
Buyers	2	1.8	Electricians	2	1.8
Store managers	2	1.8	Truck drivers	2	1.8
Realtors	2	1.8	Motormen	2	1.8
City employees	2	1.8	Policeman	1	0.9
Administrators	1	0.9	Guards	1	0.9
Undertakers	1	0.9	Factory workers	1	0.9
Office managers	1	0.9	Painters	1	0.9
Engineers	1	0.9	Carpenters	1	0.9
Musicians	1	0.9	Stage managers	1	0.9
			Steel workers	1	0.9
			Bakers	1	0.9
			Plumbers	1	0.9
	67	60.8		43	38.8

[*] Source: *Tolerance*, December 24, 1922, to February 4, 1923.

mittee further stated that the engine company at 816 North Laramie had been used for Klan initiations, probably by the very active Austin klavern. Fireman Green, who was reported to be a kleagle, was ordered to retire and the others were transferred to scattered locations.[31]

On January 17, the City Council suspended Fireman William H. Green, son of Kleagle Green, and preferred charges against him with the civil service commission on the grounds that he was an admitted Klansman. The vote for suspension was 56 to 2, and by the same vote the council also passed a resolution against having Kluxers on the municipal payroll. The only aldermen to defend the secret order were John P. Garner and Albert O. Anderson, both of whom represented the thirty-seventh Ward where the controversial Engine Company No. 117 was located. Garner, who was "often named as a Klansman in city hall rumors," accused the anti-Klan alderman of "playing politics." But the feeling of the majority of the council was summed up by Alderman Lyle, who declared, with no bows to accuracy, that "any organization which burns, murders, cuts out tongues and roasts human beings over red hot coals should be run out of the country." One week later, Fireman Otto Novotny of Engine Company 115 was suspended for alleged Klan activities. His only comment was, "Whether I am a Klansman or not is my own private affair."

It soon became apparent that the national headquarters of the Ku Klux Klan intended to dispute seriously the actions of the Chicago City Council. On January 25, 1923, Imperial Wizard Hiram Wesley Evans, Imperial Kleagle (recruiter) Edward Young Clarke, and Imperial Klonsel (attorney) Paul Etheridge arrived in Chicago from Atlanta, and that same evening were guests at a Klan dinner and dance at the Hotel Sisson attended by three hundred people.[32] According to the Imperial Wizard:

> The Klan hastens to join issue, and welcomes the test of strength before the people of Chicago and of the nation. No fair-minded, square-thinking lover of fair play in America is in sympathy with this action of the City Council, and the Klan claims that this action proves the absolute necessity for its existence.

Such statements buoyed the hopes of Klansman William H. Green, who appeared at the office of Fire Marshal Seyferlich and demanded to be formally accused before the Chicago Civil Service Commission. With support from national officers, Green argued that his case should be an example to the world "that the Ku Klux Klan is a law abiding and legal organization and prove that any city employee in any city has a perfect right to belong to it." Although the imperial officials left Chicago without waiting for a final decision, the secret order eventually won the point. The oath of allegiance was submitted in open hearings, and it was determined that Klan membership was no bar to city employment. The corporation counsel ordered the Fire Department to reinstate both Novotny and Green, and both returned to work on May 4. Novotny became a captain in 1939, and Green a lieutenant in 1940.[33]

Largely as a result of the city council investigation, Republican State Representative Adelbert H. Roberts of Chicago's Third District introduced an anti-mask bill in the Illinois Legislature on January 16, 1923. It passed overwhelmingly in both the House (110-2) and the Senate (26-1) and became law in the summer of 1923. The Chicago Klan was not accustomed to public demonstrations, however; thus the legal prohibition had little effect upon its activities.[34]

Perhaps irritated by the hostility of state and local lawmakers, the Klan made its Chicago election debut in the 1923 Republican primary for the soon to be vacated mayoral post of "Big Bill" Thompson. As expected, Postmaster Arthur C. Leuder, backed by the *Tribune* and a number of anti-city hall organizations, and Edward R. Litsinger, the representative of the powerful Lundin machine, were the strongest candidates for the G.O.P. nomination, with Leuder gaining a comfortable victory. Surprisingly, Arthur M. Millard, a political unknown and the president of the Masonic Bureau of Service and Employment, finished third, ahead of Municipal Court Judge Bernard P. Barassa, an avowed "beer and wine" aspirant, with majorities in the heavily Italian wards. Although not officially supported by the Ku Klux Klan, Millard was rumored to be the Klan candidate. His was a quiet, almost secret, campaign, and his 51,054 votes therefore offer some indication of the Invisible Empire's strength in Chicago early in 1923.[35] The primary was also important in other respects because it was the first in which the new fifty-ward configuration was used. A number of incumbents were defeated, including anti-Klan aldermen Walkowiak and Mulcahy.

The Democrats, led since the death of Roger Sullivan by the crafty George Brennan, meanwhile chose Superior Court Judge William E. Dever, son of a County Donegal man, as their standard bearer for mayor. Endorsed by organized labor and by former Progressives like Charles E. Merriam and Harold Ickes, Dever faced the April contest with Leuder confidently. The primary issue was the reputed corruption of "Big Bill" Thompson's G.O.P. administration, but as the election approached the Ku Klux Klan increasingly became the object of the political canards. In the final week of the electioneering, the religious issue seemed to overshadow all others and degenerated into what *The New World* referred to as a "whispering campaign of bigotry and Ku Kluxism." Dever was a Catholic, Leuder a Lutheran; the Democrats, therefore questioned the source and purpose of an inundation of scurrilous religious pamphlets against Catholicism. The Republicans vigorously denied any religious campaigning, and the Ku Klux Klan took no public position in the election. But the secret order was charged by various sources with having spent as much as $114,000 in the primary and general elections, and it was generally expected that the Klan vote would go to Leuder. Offsetting the anti-Catholic backlash, however, was the stand of the *Chicago Defender* and the city's Negroes, many of whom voted against the party of Lincoln for the first time in their lives because of the Klan issue. The election of Dever by a majority of 105,000 was thus interpreted as a decisive defeat for "one hundred per cent Americanism." [36]

The Invisible Empire fared no better in the aldermanic elections. In the Eighth Ward, Hjalmar Eckstromer, the manager of an electrical repair firm, lost his bid for election by two thousand votes, despite the united backing of the Ku Klux Klan. In the Thirty-ninth Ward, Democratic leader Frank J. Tomosak won an easy 9768 to 7407 victory over Klan-supported Charles Reuss. Kluxism was re-

portedly the main issue in the Fortieth Ward, the neighborhood of
the Irving Park Klan, where Alderman Christ Jensen was opposed
by Klansman Sophus E. Richards. Most of the candidates elimi-
nated in the February primary flocked to Jensen's standard in opposition to the Klan, and the incumbent won by nearly two thousand five hundred votes.[37]

Perhaps the most bitter aldermanic reverse for the Klan was the
defeat of Thirty-seventh Ward Alderman John P. Garner, who was
labeled an "apologizer and defender of the Klan" by the American
Unity League. The big issue in the Austin community was Garner's
"with the mayor, right or wrong" attitude, and a number of Thirty-
seventh Ward Republicans turned against their candidate and supported his Democratic opponent because of the alderman's close
connection with the "city hall machine." It was suggested that Garner knew that the Thompson issue would hurt him in the election,
and that he therefore turned to the Klan in an attempt to save
himself. His defeat by 11,943 to 9345, therefore, did little to en-
hance the Klan's political image in the city.[38]

The excitement of the campaign stimulated an outburst of violence in connection with the secret order. On April 1, a powerful
dynamite bomb exploded in the doorway of a meat market owned
by Harry Junker. Junker's name had been listed in *Tolerance* a
short time earlier, although his brother asserted, "He is not a member and so informed all his patrons after he was accused. If fact, he
is a Catholic. I don't know where they got his name or his purported signature."

Four days later the former publishing office of *Dawn* in Hyde
Park was practically demolished by a crudely made black powder
bomb. J. L. Forcum, the owner of the shop and an admitted Klansman,[39] ruefully remarked that the home of the Klan periodical had
been moved to the Loop in March. The police believed that the
bomb was hurled by members of the American Unity League, but
enraged *Dawn* editor Edwin J. Parke went one step farther and
openly accused the subscription editor of *Tolerance* of the crime.
Parke also declared that he had received numerous letters warning
him not to continue publication.

Shortly after the explosion at the Klan publishing office a second bomb was detonated at the shop of F. W. Gilliland, a roofer and recent advertiser in *Dawn*. Interpreted by police as a warning to prospective advertisers in the Klan periodical, it was only the first of several Klan-connected businesses to be bombed.[39]

Shaken by political defeat and discredited by the publication of the names of large numbers of its members in *Tolerance*, the Invisible Empire nevertheless held on in Chicago. *Dawn* heaped vituperation on the "traitors" who callously disregarded their sacred oaths and divulged Klan secrets to the American Unity League. Moreover, the A.U.L. exhausted its reservoir of Klan names in the summer of 1923, and was unable to secure others equally reliable.[40] In March, *Dawn* boasted that, "the total number of resignations since *Tolerance* began its attacks upon the Klan has not exceeded one hundred," and later in the month the Indianapolis Klan publication, *The Fiery Cross*, reported that growth in Chicago was "steady and satisfactory." Almost as optimistic was *The Imperial Night-Hawk*, which admitted that "a few men in Chicago have joined the ranks of those who fell away in former days," but argued that most remained "true to their obligations."

One clear indication of Klan vitality in the city in the summer and fall of 1923 was the continuing success of *Dawn*, which claimed it was "one of the strongest publications in the country supporting the Knights of the Ku Klux Klan and other all-American organizations." C. W. Paulsen took over as circulation manager in February, and by April was boasting that 50,000 copies were regularly sold, 35,000 of them in Chicago. In that same month the yearly subscription rate was raised from two to three dollars while the newsstand price remained ten cents. Advertising revenue increased 60 per cent in one year, enabling editor Parke to expand *Dawn* from sixteen to twenty-four pages. He provided readers with essays on patriotic topics, news of local and national Klan activities, and a classified advertising page. Among regular advertisements were those of a Woodlawn jewelry store offering miniature fiery crosses for three dollars and lapel buttons for seventy-five cents, the Quality Coffee Company, emphasizing "Kuality, Koffee, and Kour-

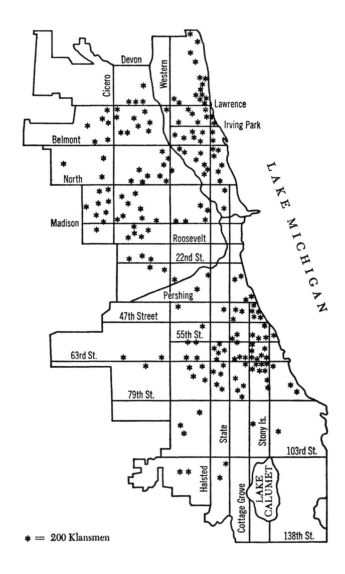

Figure 1. Distribution of Klan Strength in Chicago, 1923

tesy," Gilbert's Lunch Room, and, curiously, the J. S. Kobrzynski Loan Company.[41]

The Chicago Klan was further encouraged in 1923 by the numerous problems of its persistent adversary, the American Unity League. The A.U.L.'s basic difficulty was a barrage of law suits brought by outraged citizens who felt that they had been incorrectly identified in *Tolerance* as members of the Ku Klux Klan. The operator of a plumbing business and a physician each sued for twenty-five thousand dollars; and on March 15, 1923, J. William Brooks, an attorney and co-partner in an undertaking business, filed a one hundred thousand dollar slander suit in Superior Court after being listed in the March 11 issue.[42] Although Brooks said he was a life-long Catholic and, "naturally opposed to the Klan's purposes, doctrines, practices, and activities," he maintained that as a result of the publication of his name, "practically all his clients had deserted him, members of his parish church avoided him, and the undertaking business was nearly ruined." [43]

Easily the most important of the suits filed against the A.U.L., however, was that brought by William Wrigley, Jr., whose name and picture were printed in the New Year's Eve issue of *Tolerance*. The millionaire gum manufacturer issued a public denial to the charge that he was a Klansman, declaring that the signature on his alleged application was a "rank forgery and about as much like mine as the north pole like Vesuvius." Wrigley then filed a fifty thousand dollar suit against the American Unity League and offered fifty thousand dollars to any charitable organization that could prove he had signed an application for membership in the Ku Klux Klan. No one collected the reward because within the month, W. J. Winston, the Klansman who allegedly secured Wrigley's signature, admitted that the whole application was a forgery.[44]

The original decision to print the Wrigley name in *Tolerance* was a controversial one, and it triggered a long smoldering dispute among the leaders of the American Unity League which quickly wound up in the courts. Grady K. Rutledge, editor of *Tolerance* and secretary of the A.U.L., secured an injunction restraining co-workers Robert Shepherd and Patrick H. O'Donnell from interfering with the publication of the newspaper.[45] But ulitimate legal victory went to the Shepherd-O'Donnell faction, so the disgruntled Rutledge reversed himself and defected to the Ku Klux Klan. Noting that he was a Gentile and a Protestant and a lineal descendent of Edward Rutledge, signer of the Declaration of Independence, Rutledge began a long series of articles in *Dawn* exposing the inner workings of the A.U.L. and relating the names and methods of *Tolerance* informers. Summarizing his weekly *Dawn* installments, Rutledge published his version of the Chicago Klan–anti-Klan struggle in a short book entitled *The Flag Draped Skeleton.*[46]

A third serious setback for the American Unity League was the failure of its New York office, which was established in the fall of 1922. Unfortunately, the A.U.L. selected as the head man for the twenty-five state Eastern operation a paid spy of the Ku Klux Klan. Neufield T. Jones had been on the payroll of the Invisible Empire at least since 1921, when he had been an aid to Imperial Wizard Simmons during the congressional investigation. He arrived in Chicago on October 1, 1922, and appeared at A.U.L. headquarters at 127 North Dearborn Street with credentials indicating that he was thoroughly opposed to the principles and methods of "one hundred per cent Americanism." The ruse was successful, and the smooth-talking Klansman signed a contract with the anti-Klan organization less than three weeks later. His ostensible purpose in New York City was to duplicate the method used in Chicago by organizing a Unity League chapter and by publishing the names of New York Klansmen in a weekly newspaper. Jones mailed glowing reports back to Chicago while in reality he did nothing. The enterprise was a dismal failure, and Jones accordingly received an estimated thirty thousand dollars from the Ku Klux Klan.[47] Angry A.U.L. officials charged "misrepresentation and trickery," and filed suit against the secret order for a half million dollars. The New York fiasco brought to ignominious conclusion the sparkling achievements of the previous two years; by mid-1924 the American Unity League was bankrupt and *Tolerance* defunct. After the demise of the A.U.L. two Chicago newspapermen, Frank Poston and Thomas Shankle, organized the Let Live League as the leading anti-Klan group in the Windy City.

Greatly encouraged by the several difficulties of the A.U.L., the Klan was extremely active throughout 1923. Small suburban gatherings were held throughout the spring by local klaverns operating independently. The first major 1923 appearance came in May, when a sizable contingent from Chicago attended a Midwestern Klan gathering thirty miles southeast of the city in Valparaiso, Indiana. *Dawn* printed the schedules of the Nickle Plate and Grand Trunk Railroads to the Hoosier community and advised motorists to take the Lincoln Highway South. Jeweler George Penrose, a high officer in Woodlawn Klan No. 4, arranged with the Pennsylvania Railroad for a twenty-two car "Dawn Special" offering Chicago Klansmen round-trip transportation to Valparaiso for one dollar and twenty-five cents. More than two thousand Klansmen from the big city journeyed to the May 19 gathering, which featured a large fireworks display, a dozen bands, an address by Indiana Grand Dragon David C. Stephenson, the "naturalization" of 1500 "aliens," and the crowning of the "Queen of the Golden Mask."

Robert L. Duffus, one of the most perceptive contemporary students of the secret order, went to Valparaiso for the occasion and reported his observations in the popular monthly magazine *World's Work*. He detected a sharp distinction between city members and their country counterparts, the latter being, "bronzed, homely, good-natured persons who might have been selected at random from the farming populations of Indiana, Ohio, Illinois, Kansas, or Nebraska." Klansmen from Chicago, who wore badges and carried banners proclaiming their home city, were somewhat less impressive, and in fact, of "inferior type." Belonging to the less successful strata of the white-collar class, they were not "average American citizens" and neither did they represent organized labor. Rather, Duffus estimated Chicago Klansmen to be "small store-keepers, corporation employees, clerks, and clingers to the edges of the professions, with perhaps a sprinkling of more influential personages." [48]

After Valparaiso, the next large Chicago area Klan demonstration took place in Joliet, a steel-producing city slightly south of the suburban ring. Englewood Klan No. 2 performed the June 30 initiation rites for 612 new members, while an estimated 8000 Knights, who paid twenty-five cents per person to witness the ceremony, observed in silence. Mounted horsemen patrolled the perimeter of the South Chicago Street field and kept away more than a thousand curious spectators who were attracted by the fires and confusion of the spectacle less than two miles from the Joliet business district. This successful event was followed two weeks later by a Harvey Klan-sponsored initiation and picnic and by a mid-August "shindig" at the Fred Hammond farm near Oak Forest. The Joliet and Chicago Heights Klan bands were on hand for the latter event as were "25,000 Klansmen and 5468 autos at the most inspirational gathering yet staged by Chicago patriots."

As the summer drew to a close, the tempo of activity increased. On September 15, 1923, nearby Aurora was host to forty-five thousand people at a "Ku Klux Klan Home Koming," which featured "aeroplane maneuvers," fireworks, band music, and a "sensational parachute jump by a Klansman." The Midwest Pageant of Klankraft in more distant Rockford also attracted a large contingent from Chicago.

The final outdoor meeting of 1923 was designed to attract as many as two hundred thousand persons. Participants were advised to proceed to the western terminus of the Irving Park Boulevard streetcar line, and then to follow the signs directing them to the meeting place. But the night of the initiation was rainy, cold, and windy, and the field water-soaked. Attendance was disappointing, and the U. S. Grant Klan of Chicago could report only 576 new members for October 20, 1923.

When winter forced the curtailment of open air events, enthusiasm for God and country took other forms. The entire Chicago organization sponsored the presentation of a pro-Klan play, "The Invisible Empire," at the Aryan Grotto Temple. When *The Birth of a Nation,* was brought to the Auditorium Theater for a highly successful two-week engagement in early February 1924, hundreds of

Klansmen were in attendance.[49] Lectures on patriotic topics were frequent and presumably popular. The South Shore Klan met at the Masonic Temple at 75th and Coles for an October lecture on "Americanism"; later in the month, Dr. Norman B. Barr delivered a sermon on "Knights of the Ku Klux Klan, Save Us." Woodlawn Klan No. 4 remembered the Morgan Park Protestant Home and the Protestant Women's Orphan Home at Christmas, while the Oak Park Klan met the medical expenses of an impoverished widower. Grand Dragon Palmer established a Klan Legal Aid Bureau in his

Table 6

OCCUPATIONAL DISTRIBUTION OF KLANSMEN IN
AURORA, ILLINOIS, 1922-1923*

White-Collar Workers			Blue-Collar Workers		
	No.	Percentage of Klan Membership		No.	Percentage of Klan Membership
Dentists	7	9.6	Railroad workers	6	8.2
Realtors	5	6.9	Laborers	5	6.9
Salesmen	7	9.6	Foremen	3	4.1
Businessmen	6	8.2	Electricians	2	2.7
Office workers	4	5.5	Telephone		
Department			operators	2	2.7
managers	2	2.7	Purchasing agents	1	1.4
Lawyers	2	2.7	Shipping clerks	1	1.4
Bookkeepers	2	2.7	Factory workers	1	1.4
Bank tellers	2	2.7	Motormen	1	1.4
Superintendents	2	2.7	Draftsmen	1	1.4
Bankers	1	1.4	Printers	1	1.4
Hotel managers	1	1.4	Postmen	1	1.4
Engineers	1	1.4	Painters	1	1.4
Ministers	1	1.4			
Opticians	1	1.4			
Physicians	1	1.4			
Druggists	1	1.4			
Photographers	1	1.4			
	47	64.4		26	35.6

* Source: *Tolerance*, December 24 and 31, 1922.

Table 7

OCCUPATIONAL DISTRIBUTION OF MEMBERS OF
STEPHEN A. DOUGLAS KLAN NO. 72,
WINCHESTER, ILLINOIS*

White-Collar Workers			Blue-Collar Workers		
	No.	Percentage of Klan Membership		No.	Percentage of Klan Membership
Clerks	13	7.2	Farmers	74	41.1
Businessmen	7	3.9	Laborers	33	18.3
Ministers	6	3.3	Mechanics	6	3.3
Salesmen	3	1.7	Telephone		
Chiropractors	3	1.7	linesmen	5	2.8
Politicians	3	1.7	Carpenters	4	2.2
Teachers	3	1.7	Barbers	3	1.7
Physicians	2	1.1	Blacksmiths	2	1.1
Druggists	1	0.6	Miners	2	1.1
Undertakers	1	0.6	Painters	2	1.1
Dentists	1	0.6	Printers	1	0.6
Bookkeepers	1	0.6	Hodmen	1	0.6
Lawyers	1	0.6	Railroad workers	1	0.6
Professors	1	0.6			
	46	25.6		134	74.4

* Source: Dues records of Klan No. 72 in possession of the Anti-Defamation League.

Loop law office, and *Dawn* editor Edwin Parke organized a Chicago chapter of the Royal Riders of the Red Robe for foreign-born Protestants. Occasionally, the secret order participated in the funeral services of its departed members, as when twelve Klansmen and a fiery cross were present at the private interment of Murray J. Brady on December 18, 1923. Continuing to recruit on the northwest side, Logan Square Klan No. 9 reported that a large class of initiates, "took the noblest obligation mortal man can take," before 439 Klansmen at a regular meeting on December 12, 1923.

The Ku Klux Klan always maintained that it was a social organization, and it did not neglect revelry in Chicago. In 1923, Klansmen and their wives were urged to make reservations early for the "first dinner dance of the season, which is to be held on the evening of November 9, at the same place as those affairs that proved so successful last year." Even more important was the U. S. Grant Klan's "Ku Klux Mask Ball" at the Broadway Armory on George Washington's Birthday in 1924. The Friday night fete charmed three thousand persons and featured the unmasking of all Klansmen in attendance "at the mystic hour of midnight." Favors were peaked paper caps with drop visors for men and mardi gras masks for women. National guardsmen, Chicago police, and sheriff's deputies protected the guests and no disorders marred the evening.

Although the Invisible Empire had been politically inactive in the spring of 1923, it was enthusiastic about the November 6 election and particularly the struggle for judicial posts and for passage of a school bond issue. Dividing its tributes among Republicans and Democrats, the Klan claimed that twelve of nineteen acceptable candidates won election to the bench.[50] One of the unsuccessful Klan-backed candidates was William Legner, Democratic nominee for coroner, who led in Chicago by 5628 votes, "but the county, where the Klan is not so strong, piled up a majority for his opponent, Oscar Wolff." [51] The Windy City jingoists also credited themselves with "the tremendous victory for the school bonds, the heavy outpouring of voters, the order prevailing at the polling places and by the balloting in the judicial and other elections."

The unwarranted boastfulness of the Chicago Klan found fullest expression in *Dawn*, which issued a special forty-eight page anniversary edition on November 23, 1923. Featuring more than fifteen pages of advertising, the magazine included a giant two-page notice reading: "Chicago Klansmen Send Greetings to All Brothers Throughout the Nation." Five weeks later, *Dawn* announced the KKK program for Chicago and Cook County in 1924:

1. Development of an employment bureau and other agencies for solving the employment and allied problems.
2. Reviving the "Go to Church" movement.
3. Supporting officials in all phases of law enforcement.
4. Bringing about a more generous support of the Red Cross.

Beneath this thin veneer of optimism, however, lay the menace of internal dissension. As in other cities, the cause of difficulty was the struggle between Evans and Simmons for national Klan leadership. The deposed founder visited Chicago in July 1923 and succeeded in winning a vote of confidence from four of the city's largest and most influential chapters: William Joseph Simmons Klan No. 1, Garfield Park Klan No. 11, Chicago Klan No. 15, and Kenwood Klan No. 33. An alarmed national and realm hierarchy immediately suspended the charters of the four rebel klaverns. When Exalted Cyclopes Franklin C. Browne, James C. Stockwell, and Millard F. Roberts of the disgraced chapters attempted to hold a strategy session at the regular meeting hall of Klan No. 15 at 19 West Adams Street in the Loop, the meeting was soon broken up by deputy sheriffs acting under an injunction granted by Judge Walter P. Steffens. Meanwhile, Imperial Wizard Evans hastened to the city to quell the midwestern revolt. Arriving on August 15, the potentate and his staff were honored by Illinois Grand Dragon Palmer at a Hotel Sisson dinner party. The primary purpose of the visit was never in doubt, however, and Evans spoke on both the north and south sides to audiences restricted to card-carrying Klansmen. On Thursday evening, the Imperial Wizard appeared at the Broadway Armory, and the following night he spoke in the shadow of the University of Chicago at the spacious Midway Masonic Temple. On both occasions, he admonished his listeners to disregard the "self-seeking adherents" of Colonel Simmons and to unite behind the duly constituted authorities in Atlanta. But the wounds were already too deep, and the schism was not closed. Moreover, the situation was soon clouded further by charges of corruption in Garfield Park Klan No. 11, where the Kligrapp was arrested for the embezzlement of the "money, roster, charter, paraphernalia, and chattels," of the Klan.

At the center of the Chicago melee was autocratic Illinois Grand Dragon Palmer. On November 24, 1923, he declared: "I have known for some time that a small group of chronic revolutionists wished to disrupt the organization in Chicago so that they could step into the artificially created breach and grab control." One

week later Palmer began to "clean house" by removing from office
the chapter presidents of ten Chicago Klans, including the leaders
of the strong Englewood, Woodlawn, and Austin klaverns, for alleged loyalty to Colonel Simmons.[52]

Anti-Palmer sentiment began to balloon throughout the city and
state. The Grand Dragon tried to still criticism of his regime by
boasting that the Klan held the balance of power in Illinois and
could get what it wanted from the state administration. He was
unsuccessful, however, and continued to sit uneasily upon his
throne, particularly after he banished fourteen thousand Illinois
Klansmen, including the great titan of Southern Illinois, for disloyalty in the fall of 1924. Soon thereafter, outraged associates formally charged Palmer with "graft and despotism," and ordered him
to undergo a Klan trial. Meeting on November 9, three thousand
Klansmen, including one hundred and sixty exalted cyclopes from
throughout the state, gathered for the verdict at the Broadway Armory. Although many members charged that the Illinois Klan was
headed for ruin, Palmer won a narrow vote of confidence at a boisterous all-day session. Within the month, however, the Atlanta
office dismissed Palmer and designated Gail S. Carter Illinois grand
dragon.

The secret order even had trouble with the female Kluxers of
Chicago in 1924. Organized in Chicago in the summer of 1923 as
the National League of Protestant Women of America, they enjoyed only one year of peace before beginning to war among themselves. The chief protagonists were Mrs. Victoria B. Rogers and
Mrs. Ida P. Unangst, and their conflict involved most of the female
auxiliary and destroyed whatever hope the organization may have
had for local success.

The disintegration of the Windy City Klan was apparent as early
as February 1924, when the once-proud *Dawn* ceased publication.
In May came the revealing announcement that the twenty-six Chicago units had come together in a giant merger, clearly indicating
that the Klan's ranks were so decimated that local klaverns could
no longer operate efficiently as separate administrative units. The
Klan's national periodical *The Imperial Night-Hawk* attempted to

conceal the misfortune in Chicago with a series of optimistic pronouncements in 1924. In January, it announced the launching of a
new recruiting campaign and related that "every Klan organization
in the city reports the membership rolls growing rapidly." In February, *The Imperial Night-Hawk* told of the formation of a drill
team in the Great Lakes metropolis, and in July the bombastic pro-
nouncement was the creation of the world's largest band, a six-
hundred-member ensemble trained and outfitted by the "mammoth
Klan of Chicago." The most ludicrous announcement came in June,
however, when the magazine headlined, "Terrors of Chicago's
Giant Klan to Naturalize Ten Thousand." Beneath the caption was
a picture of thirteen lonely Klansmen standing around an American
flag.

By the fall of 1924, the Chicago Klan was clearly in its death
throes, and no amount of optimistic back-slapping could alter the
fact. It died down noiselessly, only rarely breaking into the news.
However, while the Leopold and Loeb murder trial was winning
national attention in August, a human head, a pair of withered
arms, and a single discolored leg were found opposite Richard
Loeb's home together with the warning:

> If the court don't hang them, we will.
> K.K.K.

Again, on October 17, 1924, when the Greater Bethel A.M.E.
Church, "the largest colored church in America," was almost com-
pletely consumed by flames, the Reverend Carl Tanner accused the
Klan of setting the one hundred thousand dollar fire, and one of the
church's trustees divulged: "For the last two months the Ku Klux
Klan had been sending threatening letters to the church. . . .
Nearly every night we would go down there and find a K.K.K.
sign tacked on the front door."

There were scattered references to Klansmen and Klan meetings
in the fall of 1924. In October, Imperial Wizard Evans and other
Klan officials gathered at Chicago's Blackstone Hotel for a national
political strategy session. One of the last reported activities of the

secret order in the area came on the evening of July 11, 1925, when several hundred men and women paraded in automobiles through the western suburbs. Demonstrating only three days after the chief investigator for the West Suburban Ministers and Citizens Association had been shot in Cicero following a dispute with Al Capone, the motorists admitted (or claimed) membership in the Ku Klux Klan, although none wore either robes or a mask. They drove through Berwyn, Stickney, LaGrange, and Cicero, visiting vice resorts and warning proprietors against law violations. Scarface Al was not intimidated.

The Invisible Empire was virtually inert in Chicago after 1925. Nevertheless, in 1926 the state grand dragons met in the city and reelected Hiram Wesley Evans as Imperial Wizard before journeying to Washington for the Imperial Klonvokation (convention). In 1927, three hundred Klansmen and their ladies dined in the elegant Red Lacquer Room of the Palmer House to hear an address by Judge Charles J. Orbison, a member of the Indianapolis Klan, and in 1928, the decaying empire held its national convention in Chicago's Eighth Street Theater.[53]

To some extent the Windy City organization owed its collapse to the same internal disputes that plagued the secret order elsewhere. But the Klan in Chicago suffered uniquely from the publication of the names of real or alleged Klansmen on a systematic basis by the American Unity League. The fear of exposure felt by men who had taken the oath of allegiance to the Imperial Wizard could not then and cannot now be measured, but it was doubtlessly sufficient to cause thousands of local men to rue the day they first donned a white robe. On a nationwide basis the Invisible Empire took great pride in the jealousy with which it guarded its membership rolls and ritual; indeed, the initiation ceremony consisted very largely of oaths pledging secrecy in one form or another. In Chicago the names of Klansmen were not only lost to the enemy, but also printed and distributed to the public.

Very substantial evidence indicates that the Klan movement in Chicago and its environs numbered at least forty thousand and perhaps as many as eighty thousand members. While this total represented only about 2 per cent of the city's population in 1923, it should be remembered that no more than 15 per cent of Chicagoans qualified as adult, white, native-born, Protestant males. The important factor is the relative attractiveness of the Ku Klux Klan to those who were eligible for membership. On that basis, Chicago ranked high as a national center of klankraft.

Beginning in the summer of 1921, the Invisible Empire found success for at least thirty months in the Windy City, with a precipitous decline dating from the early months of 1924. It drew its primary support from lower echelon white-collar workers, small businessmen, and semi-skilled laborers, many of whom resented the economic, social, and political pressure of the city's Catholics and second-generation immigrants, and were equally alarmed by the rapid influx of Negroes into an ever-expanding ghetto.[54] Strongest on the south side, particularly in Woodlawn, Englewood, Hyde Park, South Shore, and Kenwood, the Klan also found numerous adherents in the north and west in a broad belt around the city midway between the inner core and the outward fringe. In this "zone of emergence," the Klan profited from the fear and insecurity felt by white Protestants in the face of a continuing challenge which they only imperfectly understood and could not stop.[55] Thousands looked to the Invisible Empire as an instrument which might temporarily prevent change and allow a short respite. Unequal to the problem, the Klan could find no permanent function in the city of Chicago.

9

Detroit: The Write-in Challenge

The era of the Model T was a boom time in Detroit. Attracted by the relatively high wages of the automobile industry, Negroes, immigrants, and southern whites flocked to the city of Walter P. Chrysler, Henry Ford, John and Horace Dodge, William C. Durant, and the seven Fisher brothers. Between 1910 and 1930, the population of the motor capital tripled; in 1920 it stood at 993,000 and qualified Detroit as the fourth largest city of the United States. Housing, transportation, schools, and movies were overcrowded; jerry-built homes on business lots twenty feet wide were sold as rapidly as they could be constructed. Fully 25 per cent of the labor force worked at night, and census takers revealed that beds in all-male boarding houses were being rented in eight-hour shifts. Everything was in short supply; everything except alcohol. Because of its proximity to Canada, Detroit was an important center of the bootlegging industry. On the Canadian side of the river, speed-boats took on cargoes of whiskey and, avoiding the United States Customs Patrol, slipped back to the American side under cover of darkness.

Among the newcomers to Detroit, more than 25 per cent were foreign-born. Canadians, Italians, Poles, Scots, Hungarians, and

Yugoslavs were the most numerous, but practically every ethnic group was represented. They crowded into the lower east side ghetto or, if they were Polish, into Hamtramck, a city completely surrounded by Detroit. Of particular importance to "one hundred per cent Americanism" was the fact that most of the "aliens" were also Catholics.

Religious intolerance was not a new phenomenon in the Motor City. In the 1890's it had been the home of both the national president and national secretary of the anti-Catholic American Protective Association, as well as the location of a thriving chapter of that organization and the seat of publication of *The Patriotic American,* which created a sensation by printing a spurious document ascribed to Pope Leo XIII in which American Catholics were absolved from their allegiance to the United States government.[1] In 1920 when the city's Catholics numbered more than 350,000, traditional fear of the Pope took new form as a concentrated effort in Michigan to abolish parochial schools. However, this proposal, spearheaded by James A. Hamilton of Detroit, was defeated, 610,-699 to 353,817.

Although not so firmly rooted in the Detroit past, the "Negro problem" became increasingly important during and after World War I. In 1910, there were only 5741 colored persons in the city, but between 1915 and 1925 no city approached Detroit in the number of Negroes arriving to work and live.[2] Numbering 40,000 in 1920, the total skyrocketed to 80,000 in 1925, and to 125,000, in 1930. There was work for them in the foundries, mills, and factories, as garbage collectors, elevator operators, and laborers. But decent housing was denied them and tuberculosis was common in the segregated slums. Cramped into a tiny east-side ghetto, Negroes were forced by the crush of physical necessity to seek expansion in white neighborhoods.

The vast population influx dramatically affected the sedate homes and tree-lined streets of the older residents as well as the new because the pace of neighborhood transition accelerated, moving white to Negro, Protestant to Catholic, and German to Italian. Lower- and middle-income whites, jealous of such social status as was theirs, were disturbed at the resulting destruction of neighborhood tranquility. As a result, Detroit became the unquestioned center of Klan strength in Michigan.[3] Although the secret order had active chapters in Grand Rapids, Flint, Bay City, Jackson, Lansing, Kalamazoo, Saginaw, Pontiac, and Muskegon, approximately half the Wolverine state's 70,000 Klansmen resided in Detroit.[4]

The first kleagle in the Motor City was C. H. Norton. Arriving in the summer of 1921, he made little headway until the September exposé of the New York *World* publicized the Klan in the city. Copies of the eastern daily were snatched up at prices ranging up to fifty cents on Detroit newsstands. Norton saw his opportunity and placed an advertisement in *The Detroit Free Press* inviting white Protestant citizens to membership in the Invisible Empire. Local Negroes immediately called for an investigation by the United States District Attorney, and John C. Lodge, president of the city council, instructed the police department to regard Klan demonstrators as disturbers of the peace. The Invisible Empire chose not to challenge the city administration and canceled its scheduled Thanksgiving Day parade.

After attaining a membership of three thousand in the fall of 1921, Wayne County Provisional Klan experienced relatively slow growth in 1922. Kleagle Norton, who was not an adept salesman, was hampered by the regional Klan emphasis upon recruitment in Ohio and Indiana and a lack of interest in the Wolverine state. Such activities as the Detroit klavern undertook were usually secret, insignificant indoor affairs. Klanswoman Esther Tansel, who with her husband earned a living by distributing anti-Catholic literature in the metropolitan area, reported that she had to go through three sets of locked doors to get into the meeting hall. While speakers harangued the membership about Nordic superiority, men stood around the exits with revolvers in their belts.

The fortunes of the Wayne County Klan improved early in 1923, when Manly L. Caldwell became the chief Detroit organizer. In eighteen months he increased membership from 3000 to 22,000 and earned $76,000 in the process. His most effective confederate was

the Reverend Sam White, a Klan lecturer so devoted to the cause
that he returned payment for fifty special appearances (at ten dollars per speech) to the Invisible Empire "because I believed in it."
With the additional membership thus generated, the Detroit Klan
no longer felt impelled to schedule sessions behind locked doors.
Yet the membership was still hesitant to demonstrate publicly
within the city.

The first outdoor muster of the Ku Klux Klan in Detroit came in
a snow-covered wood a few miles from Royal Oak near the Wayne
County line on April 4, 1923. On the same Oakland County farm,
thirty-five miles northeast of downtown Detroit, a reporter from
the *Free Press* witnessed a similar cross burning on the evening of
June 13, and noted that "Sentries allowed no machine to pass unless
the countersign was given." Before dining on hot dogs and coffee,
eight thousand Knights listened to a diatribe by the grand goblin of
the Domain of the Great Lakes on the mental and physical superiority of Nordic peoples.[5]

The scene of the Detroit Klan's initiation ceremonies shifted the
following month to a farm adjacent to the Detroit Riding and Hunt
Club, a half mile west of the junction of Snyder and Seven Mile
roads. On July 12, 1923, "patrols of Klansmen" shielded the farm as
five thousand hooded Knights inducted eight hundred new members. More seldom used than the Seven Mile Road location was a
field near John R. Street and Fifteen Mile Road, where 792 prose-
lytes were initiated on August 18, 1923. That the initiations habit-
ually occurred in such rural and suburban locations obscured the
fact that most of the celebrants were city dwellers.

Probably typical of Klan propagation attempts in the Detroit
area was a meeting in suburban Royal Oak on September 21, 1923.
In response to notices of a public lecture by C. S. Townsend of
New Jersey, about two thousand persons gathered in a vacant lot
near the center of town. Three avowed Klansmen were present;
two on the platform and one passing out membership applications
and selling copies of Klan newspapers.

With the passage of the Burns Law in the summer of 1923, the
Michigan State Legislature prohibited public meetings of masked

men. At first the Detroit Klan failed to heed the legislation. On August 29, nine Wayne County deputy sheriffs accidentally stumbled upon an assembly of three thousand hooded Klansmen on Seven Mile Road, one hundred of whom were accepting congratulations for raiding two roadhouses. Although the law officers informed the Klansmen that their regalia violated the law, the white-hooded figures refused either to unmask or to leave the field. Because the deputies had no warrant, no action was taken. But the Detroit klavern did not always defy the Burns Law. On October 20, 1923, at a demonstration featuring an electric cross at the Seven Mile Road location, not one of five thousand Klansman was masked.

As the Klan blossomed in Detroit, public criticism of the secret order was persistent. At the Century Theater on January 22, 1923, Thomas Dixon, author of the novel on which *The Birth of a Nation* was based, praised Reconstruction Klansmen as "the bravest and noblest men of the South," but berated their modern counterparts as unprincipled marauders. In July prominent Detroit Methodist Lynn Harold Hough, a former president of Northwestern University, dubbed the secret order, "the most diabolical institution this country ever saw, an absolute contradiction of everything for which America stands, and the apotheosis of race and religious hatred." His words were echoed by the Detroit Conference of the Methodist Church, which unanimously condemned "any organization which would substitute lawless methods for the appeal to the Court and the ballot." The attitude of an unsympathetic metropolitan press was reflected by the *Detroit News:* "The Klan boasts no saving grace. No man operating behind a mask ever intended to effect any purpose save the violation of law."

Opposition to the Klan later focused on the street vending of the Michigan edition of *The Fiery Cross*. Detroit police confiscated the Klan newspaper, which specialized in the regional and state activities of the hooded order, but in October 1923 public sale of the propagandistic weekly was approved by the city corporation counsel. When the police continued to arrest and detain *Fiery Cross* newsboys, the Wayne County Klan secured an injunction from the

Circuit Court preventing further official interference with the newspaper's sale.[6]

Too weak to participate effectively in Detroit politics in 1922, the Invisible Empire took only slightly more interest in the 1923 municipal election. Its primary interest was removing from the city council Dr. Frank Broderick, who was denounced enthusiastically at a hymn singing Klan demonstration in rural Wayne County on October 29. Placing ninth in a field of eighteen, Broderick narrowly survived the Klan attack, and received fewer votes than any other successful candidate.[7] As the returns were being tabulated on the evening of November 6, a five-foot tall cross blazed on the lawn of the city hall before being quenched by the hastily summoned fire department.

The burning of crosses near public buildings developed into a favorite activity of the Detroit Klan in 1923. On Christmas Eve, a six-foot oil-soaked cross was set afire on the steps of the county building. A pre-arranged Klan rally followed. A masked Santa Claus opened the Cadillac Square ceremony by leading a huge throng, estimated by the *Detroit News* at 4000 and by the Klan at 25,000, in the Lord's Prayer. Further proceedings were interrupted by the arrival of police riot squads. Taunts and hoots met the policemen, but the area was quickly cleared by officers with drawn revolvers.

As was the case in other cities, a visit by the Imperial Wizard usually signaled dissension within the secret order. On February 8, 1924, Hiram Wesley Evans addressed eight thousand Knights at the Armory, the largest indoor meeting of the Klan in Detroit history. Interrupted six times by cheers, the former Dallas dentist dwelt upon public schools and good government, neglecting to discuss an issue sorely troubling Detroit officials: the Wayne County Klan had not been officially chartered in 1924 despite its large membership and was therefore provisional. Unlike chartered or numbered Klans, provisional klaverns could keep no part of the ten-dollar "klectoken" required of all new members. Money went to Atlanta, therefore, which would otherwise have been available for Detroit projects.

Because the charter was not forthcoming in 1924, local Klansmen technically broke away from the national office and formed the Symwa Club (Spend Your Money with Americans). The new organization superseded the local Klan chapter, but it continued to function as part of the Invisible Empire. Most important, it sent only five dollars of each initiation fee to the Imperial Palace in Atlanta. Symwa Club had the same officers, meeting places, dues, and goals as the Wayne County Provisional Klan, and the Symwa kleagle was the official representative of the Ku Klux Klan. Until recognized with a charter, however, the Detroit organization was determined to withhold some financial support from the national body.[8]

James A. Colescott, who was to become the Klan's imperial wizard in 1939, arrived in Detroit from Minnesota in 1924 and eased the unhappy situation. With the aid of Kleagles Daniel E. Rhoads and Charles E. Lewis, Colescott increased Detroit Klan strength to thirty-two thousand, a feat which *The Fiery Cross* labeled, "nothing short of phenomenal."[9] A Junior Klan for boys under eighteen and a local branch of the Women of the Ku Klux Klan were organized. The need for additional meeting halls was alleviated in late 1923, when the local order secured "two whole floors" and 40,000 square feet of floor space at 206 Hancock Avenue East, where the symbol of the cross was hung over the door.

Under new leadership, the demonstrations of the Detroit Klan became even more elaborate. Bands, quartets, and abundant refreshments were the usual ingredients of a successful initiation. At one 1924 gathering of fifteen thousand just north of the city in early May, a fireworks display featured exploding bombs of red, white, and blue and a band playing revival favorites.

With new muscle, the Detroit Klan enthusiastically entered the political lists in 1924. Among important projects were the election of a Klan sympathizer as Michigan governor and the passage of a state law outlawing parochial schools. The battle for governor was fought within the Republican primary, where both of the Klan favorites, James Hamilton of Detroit and the Reverend Frederick

Perry of Adrian, were defeated by incumbent Governor Alex J. Groesbeck. Having been condemned by virtually every daily and weekly newspaper in Michigan, the parochial school amendment was equally unsuccessful, losing by almost three to one.[10]

It was in a local contest, however, that the Detroit Klan made its influence most keenly felt. On September 9, 1924, a primary election was held to determine candidates for the remaining one year of the term of Mayor Frank E. Doremus, who had become seriously ill and could not continue in office. John W. Smith and Joseph A. Martin led the voting and were therefore certified for the runoff election in November. But the third-place finisher, attorney Charles S. Bowles, decided to disregard the primary election and run as a write-in candidate against the two successful campaigners. It was an unprecedented move, but with the active support of the Ku Klux Klan the "sticker candidate" almost accomplished a political miracle.

A lawyer trained at the University of Michigan, with offices in the Dime Bank Building, Charles Bowles was the first president of DeMolay (Masonic order for boys) in Detroit and held high office in several Masonic lodges. His platform emphasized subways, economy, and "strict law enforcement." Bowles's support by the Invisible Empire was blatantly expressed at an anti-Ku Klux Klan rally at the Arena Gardens, where Aldrich Blake of Oklahoma was scheduled to expose the "one hundred per cent American" movement. Hours before the October 21 event was to begin, a menacing crowd of six thousand men and boys gathered at the entrance to the Gardens. Police were unable to disperse the mob, which shaped itself into a column, three abreast and several blocks long. Marching up and down Woodward Avenue, the solid chain of humanity shouted, "Bowles, Bowles, Bowles," and effectively isolated the box offices from all who might wish to purchase a ticket to the anti-Klan rally. Several hundred Bowles supporters massed opposite the Public Library and forcibly posted Bowles stickers on the windows of passing cars as they slowed down.

Riot calls to police headquarters brought four squads of fifty men each to the area. Forming flying wedges, the police drove the mob in both directions on Woodward, hastening its retreat with tear gas bombs. Originally scheduled for eight o'clock, the rally was delayed for thirty-five minutes to allow four thousand five hundred persons to purchase tickets. Meanwhile the police lined both sides of the street to prevent any recurrence of the disorder.

Neither of the remaining mayoralty candidates chose to ignore such evidence of Klan influence in the Bowles campaign. Joseph A. Martin, a clean-government, business candidate with strong support in upper-income wards, charged that in the orgy of un-Americanism, the "Klan accidentally tore the night shirt and pillow case from its hero and revealed to the entire citizenship that Charles Bowles was the Ku Klux candidate for Mayor and general manager of Detroit." He added that in the "riotous demonstration to prevent an anti-Klan lecture, the Ku Klux Klan of Detroit pasted the symbols of the Klan and the symbols of the Bowles campaign side by side the length and breadth of Woodward Avenue from Antoinette Street to Palmer Avenue."

The Klan issue was seized upon even more eagerly by John W. Smith, whose primary support was among Catholics, Negroes, and recent immigrants. Referring to southern whites as "ignorant hill-billies," Smith concentrated his campaign in lower east side wards, where he spoke often of the alleged misdeeds of the Invisible Empire against minority groups. Typical of his approach was an appearance at St. Stanislaus Catholic Church two days before the election. Arguing that the question was not so much one of who was going to be Mayor of Detroit as it was whether the Klan was going to be allowed to say it elected the mayor, Smith stated that Klansmen "have robbed Catholic churches and have attempted to burn them. They have tortured and slain Negroes and Jews." At St. Hedwig's Catholic Church on the day before the election Smith called the Klan an ugly monster from the South, "which is going to the polls tomorrow to put over the parochial school amendment and its candidate for Mayor."

Realizing that he had the "one hundred per cent" vote in his pocket, Bowles was careful to avoid mention of the secret order despite persistent challenges by Martin and Smith. Martin's remark was typical: "If Charles Bowles is not the candidate of the Ku Klux Klan, as I have repeatedly charged, why does he not publicly give the Klan that condemnation which it so richly deserves?" But the "sticker candidate," well aware of the zeal of his hooded supporters, remained silent.

On the Saturday evening immediately prior to the election, the largest meeting of Klansmen in Detroit history congregated in a field in Dearborn Township. Hundreds of women were in the crowd, which began arriving as early as six o'clock under the glare of a huge flaming cross and the lights of thousands of automobiles. Estimates to the number, none of whom were hooded or cloaked, ranged from twenty-five thousand to fifty thousand. Because Klan pickets prevented non-members from entering the field, Bowles's appearance was not officially reported. However, he may well have attended the rally, and his name met the eye wherever it turned. Most of the automobiles were plastered with Bowles campaign labels and with instructions on how to vote for the "sticker candidate."

On the day of the election the *Detroit News* reaffirmed its endorsement of Joseph Martin, denounced John W. Smith as the machine candidate, and warned the citizenry: "If you want the City of Detroit to be advertised over the nation as a city controlled by the 'invisible empire' of the Ku Klux Klan . . . Vote for Charles Bowles." The vote for mayor was the heaviest in Detroit's history; there were several fights between Smith and Bowles supporters, but no major disturbances. When the returns began to come in, it was apparent that Bowles had cut heavily into Martin's strength. In most of the districts where Smith was strong, both Bowles and Martin were weak; but in districts where Martin was strong, Bowles was also strong and the Smith vote was light. Only in the most "respectable" districts of the city did Martin edge Bowles out, while in the lower-middle-class Protestant sections, Bowles fared the better of the two. Martin supporters felt, therefore, that had Bowles accepted his primary defeat and not entered the general election as a write-in candidate, then Martin would have won by a tremendous majority.

With the ballots counted Smith seemed the winner:

John W. Smith	116,807
Charles Bowles	106,679
Joseph Martin	84,929
	308,415

As was expected, Smith piled up big majorities in the Third, Fifth, Seventh, Ninth, Eleventh, and Thirteenth wards, showing great strength on the lower east side, where many predominantly Catholic or Negro precincts gave him more than 90 per cent of their total vote. Along the present Chrysler Freeway between Napoleon and Willis Streets, anti-Klan sentiment was particularly overwhelming. In one Third Ward polling place at the Ginsburg Library, Smith outdistanced Bowles 699 to 0; at Adelaide and Hastings Streets the vote was 792 to 1; at Russell and Watson Streets the tally was 806 to 1; at Medbury and DuBois, 578 to 0; and at Rivard and Livingston, 718 to 2.

Despite the fact that Bowles was unable to overcome such mountainous leads, he carried twice as many wards as Smith and won an absolute majority in the Twenty-second Ward. The Klan candidate's greatest support was in a triangular area bounded roughly by Grand River Avenue, Philadelphia Street, and the present John C. Lodge Freeway. Additional Bowles strength was noticeable along the Woodward Avenue side of Palmer Park, on the far east and west sides, and in the northwestern part of the city. In the absence of Klan membership records in Detroit, this voting pattern may be presumed a fair indication of the secret order's strength in the city.

The official canvass of the election revealed that while 325,678 votes had been cast, only 308,415 ballots were tabulated. According to the election commissioner most of the 17,000 discarded votes were for the write-in candidate and had been rejected for various mistakes. The placing of a period following the name or the use of the surname only was sufficient for disqualification. On November

7, the *Detroit News* listed 120 ways in which voters had invalidated Bowles ballots, including:

Chas. Bowles	Charlie Bowles
Charles Boles	Charles Bouls
Cha. Bowles	Bowles, Charles
Ch. Bowles	Bowles
Charles Bowls	Charles S. Bowles
Charles Bowels	Charles E. Bowles

Two days after the election Bowles announced that he would ask for a recount, "since unquestionably more persons attempted to vote for me than either of the other candidates." His attorneys argued that numerous precedents demonstrated that absolutely correct spelling was neither essential nor necessary, and that the presumptive intent of the elector was shown in many instances where the ballots were thrown out. Bowles argued for a liberal application of the rule of "idem sonans," or the spelling of a word by sound.

The request for a recount was granted, but the election commission refused to alter the original instructions, and write-in votes not absolutely perfect were again discarded. As a result Bowles found himself behind by more than 14,000 votes.[11] Although Bowles's supporters claimed that 15,545 disputed ballots should have given their man victory, the Board of Canvassers declared John W. Smith mayor. Because a request to the Michigan Supreme Court for a writ of certiorari would have required at least one year to complete, Bowles reluctantly withdrew from the struggle on November 20. Two days later the *Detroit News* commented: "No one will probably ever know whether more voters intended to vote for John W. Smith or Charles Bowles at the mayoralty election." [12]

Although the Motor City Klan suffered defeat, its near victory was a surprise to many. The liberal *Christian Century* expressed dismay and incredulity that, "In Detroit, a Klan write-in candidate, almost totally unknown in the city, whose name was not even printed on the ballot . . . came within a few thousand votes of being elected mayor of the fourth city in the United States." Perhaps the vote for A. J. Brodie, endorsed by the Klan for the city council, offers a better indication of the secret order's strength in Detroit. He polled only 68,887 votes against Robert G. Ewald's 180,618.

Wayne County Klan No. 68 was the new designation of the Detroit klavern when it finally received its charter early in 1925, but decline had already set in. The strenuous election campaign had sapped some of its strength, as did the ill-fated financial ventures of the Symwa Club. The most damaging was a scheme to buy, subdivide, and sell a tract of land on the Middle Belt Road, using the profits to build a temple "like Solomon's" for Detroit Klan headquarters. Known as the "gold brick deal" because contributors were given a pasteboard lapel button in the shape of a brick, the project failed to materialize. Fourteen thousand dollars were invested by Detroit Knights, but the klavern was never built, and the money was never returned. More amusing was a scheme to manufacture and sell Klan phonograph records throughout the country, but the Cross Music and Record Company of Detroit never produced a single record.[13]

As a result of such misadventures, the Wayne County Klan was in frequent financial difficulty. A judgment of $424.60, representing two months' rent, resulted in the temporary removal of furniture from the Klan office at 206 Hancock Avenue East in 1925, and late in 1926 the owner of the property sued the Klan for ten thousand dollars in damages to her building.[14] Apparently the Detroit Klan had very little money, and even that could not be properly accounted for. The Grundy Audit Company, employed to inventory the organization's books in 1925, refused to sign the audit after ninety days of work.

When the Detroit Klan seemed on the verge of collapse, the explosive and easily exploitable issue of neighborhood segregation breathed new life into the secret order. By 1925 the Negro population of Detroit had increased to 80,000, yet they were still confined to three small wards that had been apportioned to them in 1910. As fewer residences became available in the ghetto, many colored business and professional men looked for good houses outside the colored boundaries. The Ku Klux Klan reacted quickly. On July 11, 1925, the Invisible Empire staged a huge meeting on West Fort Street, a mile west of Lincoln Park Village. Standing on a platform illuminated by the red glare of fiery crosses, a speaker advocated laws to compel Negroes to live in certain sections of the city.[15]

The first racial incident in 1925 came when Dr. Alex Turner, a Negro surgeon on the staff of Grace Hospital, was forced by a Klan-inspired white mob to vacate his recently purchased home in the northern part of Detroit a short distance out of the colored section. Several weeks later a similar result accompanied the attempt of James Fletcher to escape the Negro ghetto.[16] Unquestionably, however, the major crisis came in September, when Dr. Ossian Sweet bought a two-story brick house in a white workingman's neighborhood on Detroit's East Side. According to his wife: "I had in mind only two things: first to find a house that was in itself desirable, and, second, to find one that would be within our pocketbook. I wanted a pretty home, and it made no difference to me whether it was in a white neighborhood or a colored neighborhood. Only I couldn't find such a house in the colored neighborhood."

Even before the young Negro physician took possession of his home, white neighbors, including many foreign-born Catholics, had formed the "Water Works Improvement Association" to preserve segregation. When the Sweet family moved in at 2905 Garland (at Chalevoix), mobs formed on the streets and threw bricks, bottles, and stones at the house. The tragic result came on September 9, when Dr. Sweet's brother Henry shot and killed Leon Breiner, a white neighbor demonstrating in the street. Although Detroit police had made no attempt to protect the Sweet home, the Negroes were promptly arrested and charged with first degree murder.[17]

The trial of Dr. Ossian Sweet and his brother attracted national attention. Chicago attorney Clarence Darrow agreed to defend the accused Negroes. He spent three weeks selecting a jury, carefully excluding known Klansmen. Darrow had to contend with an unsympathetic white population and with "law and order" advocates who demanded that an example be made of the Negroes. He based his defense upon the right of any man to protect his family and his home. In a celebrated decision, the Sweets were ultimately acquitted.

Although the Ku Klux Klan was not officially involved in the incident, it thrived upon and fed the racial hysteria that enveloped the city. Three days after the Sweet shooting, Mayor John W. Smith sent an open letter to Police Commissioner Frank H. Croul. Charging that the Ku Klux Klan was responsible for neighborhood violence and had capitalized on the disturbances, Mayor Smith suggested that the secret order was seeking to establish a "dictatorship" in Detroit. But the mayor, who had been elected with Negro votes, let it be known that he harbored no sympathy for their efforts to escape the ghetto:

> . . . I must say that I deprecate most strongly the moving of Negroes or other persons into districts in which they knew their presence may cause riot or bloodshed.
>
> I believe that any colored person who endangers life and property, simply to gratify his personal pride, is an enemy of his race as well as an incitant of riot and murder. These men who have permitted themselves to be tools of the Ku Klux Klan in its effort to fan the flames of racial hatred into murderous fire, have hurt the cause of their race in a degree that can not be measured.[18]

Mayor Smith's letter won him no new friends among Klansmen, who vowed to frustrate his attempt to win a full term in November 1925. Again the Klan favorite was Charles Bowles, but this time he sought broader support. Although he accepted the Klan endorsement with equanimity, he vigorously denied membership in it and even campaigned actively for the Negro vote.[19]

As evidence of its serious intentions, the Invisible Empire assessed its Detroit membership five dollars per man and brought in Kleagle Ira W. Stout to direct the campaign. Appealing to Protestant solidarity, Klan workers formed Bowles Clubs on most blocks and distributed pamphlets and handbills on the streets. One political observer labeled the secret order a "highly organized, fanatical group," and predicted that the Klan would defeat Mayor Smith unless a heavy vote was recorded.[20]

Two imponderable elements complicated the situation: (1)

Henry Ford's endorsement of Mayor Smith, an action which placed Jewish citizens in the position of either voting with the Ku Klux Klan or aligning themselves with the nation's most notorious anti-Semite; and (2) the Klan's endorsement of five candidates for the city council. Councilman Phillip A. Callahan was a former president of the Symwa Club and an obvious Klansman, but another endorsee, Councilman Robert G. Ewald, scorned hooded support: "I am not a Klansman, did not solicit their endorsement, and do not want it." A. J. Brodie and Sherman Littlefield said they were not Klansmen but accepted its endorsement.[21]

The final week of the campaign was predictably the most vitriolic. Both sides predicted victory. A 20-by-5-foot KKK banner was hung from the rotunda of the City Hall, and the secret order arranged for services in many churches. The wife of one minister declared in her husband's church that any woman not voting for Bowles should be tarred and feathered. Many Protestant clergymen objected to this sort of behavior, including Reinhold Niebuhr of Bethel Evangelical Church, who dubbed the Ku Klux Klan "one of the worst specific social phenomena which the religious pride of peoples has ever developed."

The 1925 Detroit election was a disaster for the Invisible Empire. Although Callahan won a place on the city council, Charles Bowles was defeated 140,000 to 111,000, and no face-saving charges of election fraud could be made. Bowles did well in the north end and northwest sections of the city, but could not crack Smith's strength among Catholics, Negroes, and immigrants.[22]

Failure in politics accelerated the demise of Wayne County Klan No. 68, which was down to less than half its peak strength by 1926, and to only a few hundred members in 1928. Its few activities were inoffensive. In 1926 and again in 1929, the secret order promoted indoor circuses, the first in Highland Park and the second at Danceland. Both were financial failures; the Danceland circus particularly so because the performers were stranded in Detroit when their checks were not honored by the bank.[23] Despite the efforts of Exalted Cyclopes W. F. Jackson and Charles Spare, the Detroit Klan had ceased to exist by 1934.[24]

More sinister and violent than the Ku Klux Klan was the Black Legion, which had a brief and infamous career in Detroit and parts of Ohio in the mid-thirties. Formed ostensibly to seek jobs for southern whites, the Legion was anti-Negro, anti-Semitic, and anti-union. Its power was broken in May 1936, when the body of Charles Poole, a young WPA worker, was found on a desolate suburban road near Detroit. Seven Black Legionnaires were convicted of the murder and the authoritarian secret organization soon lost most of its several thousand members.[25]

Between 1939 and 1941 a brief effort was made to revive the dormant Detroit Klan. Meetings were held in a variety of locations: Odd Fellows Halls, the Danish Brotherhood Hall, the Findlater Masonic Temple, and the Klan's two-story, frame headquarters on West Forest.[26] Recruiting was desperate and intense and unsuccessful. At a large banquet, on October 19, 1941, members were told by Klan officials: "Bring an eligible American and if we Klux him that night we will refund your dollar." [27] Even with such an uncritical admissions policy the Ku Klux Klan was dead in Detroit before news of Pearl Harbor offered patriots new enemies.

10

Indianapolis: Center of Klandom

On the edge of downtown Indianapolis stands an unwashed and unimpressive building known simply as Cadle Tabernacle. Several of its stucco entrances are boarded over, and except for an occasional convention, its cavernous auditorium is empty. A network of faded banners hangs from the barnlike ceiling, and the neat rows of hard-backed seats below face a raised platform and an unadorned baptistry. The creaking floors are now covered with dust; the air is musty. The ghostlike atmosphere is quite unlike that which prevailed in the 1920's, when the auditorium reverberated with the prayers and hymns of the faithful during appearances by local or traveling evengelists, or when thousands of Ku Klux Klansmen in hoods and robes sat enraptured by the oratorical wizardry of Grand Dragon David C. Stephenson.

From 1922 to 1925, Indianapolis was the unrivaled bastion of the Invisible Empire in Mid-America.[1] Not only was it the base of operations of the legendary Stephenson, but it was also the headquarters of the powerful Realm of Indiana and the home of its largest Klan. With 314,000 residents in 1920 the Hoosier capital was much smaller and less ethnically diverse than either Chicago or Detroit, but the threats to "one hundred per cent Americanism" were clearly

defined in Indianapolis. First and second generation immigrants in
the city, even though made up primarily of northern Europeans,
such as Germans and Irish, and numbering only sixty thousand,
were considered inferior almost by definition. Catholics, who comprised 12 per cent of the population, were regarded with hostility
and suspicion by Protestants nurtured from youth in the customary
fear of an authoritarian and inquisitorial Pope. Negroes, who increased from 22,000 to 44,000 in Indianapolis between 1910 and
1930, were classified as no better than home-grown aliens. Concentrated along Indiana Avenue immediately northwest of the downtown business area, Negroes moved north toward middle-class
white neighborhoods after World War I. In addition, a black
ghetto northeast of Monument Circle pushed east toward Sheldon
Avenue.[2] Predictably, racial tensions increased, and on at least one
occasion, noted southern integrationist Will Alexander was called
to Indianapolis to help ease an explosive situation.[3]

The Ku Klux Klan entered Indiana late in 1920, when Joe M.
Huffington organized a chapter in the Ohio River city of Evans-
ville. In March 1921, Indianapolis was invaded by Grand Goblin
C. W. Love and Kleagle J. S. Engleerth, who found a room in the
Lincoln Hotel and established an office at 447 Lemcke Annex
Street. Their solicitations were eminently successful and among
those contributing the requisite ten dollars in the summer of 1921
were Brandt C. Downey, president of the Commercial National
Bank, and Chester A. Jones, a veteran cashier at the National City
Bank. Grand Goblin Love meanwhile secured an Indiana state
charter for the secret order on August 13, 1921.

The early development of the Invisible Empire in Indianapolis
and the state was largely made under the auspices of the Horse
Thief Detective Association. In the 1870's the Indiana legislature
sanctioned by statute the organization of men in various counties
for the purpose of arresting horse thieves and other felons. A few
citizens could group themselves together, apply for a certificate to
the secretary of the state, then have this certificate approved by the
three commissioners of the county in which these sleuths were to
function. At once they obtained the powers of a constable, and,

unlike the average policeman, they were under no bond for the correct and faithful performance of their duties. Under Klan control, the H.T.D.A. functioned as a vigilante unit, stopping and searching automobiles on the highways, raiding vice dens, driving through the Negro district in Indianapolis with guns drawn, and protecting the privacy of Klan meetings.

The adoption of the Horse Thief Detective Association to the service of the Invisible Empire was largely the work of David C. Stephenson, the most dynamic and colorful Klan leader in the United States. Born in Texas in 1891, he married before the war, lived for a time in Oklahoma, became a father in 1916, and served in the Army during World War I. In 1920, he divorced his wife and moved to Evansville, Indiana, where he entered into a business partnership with L. G. Julian and became a successful coal dealer. Shrewd and personable, the powerfully-built Stephenson joined the Ku Klux Klan in 1921 and rose rapidly to high station. He was a natural orator with a Machiavellian approach to administration. As Grand Dragon of Indiana, he advanced his realm to first rank in the Invisible Empire; as director of recruiting for twenty-three eastern states he funneled millions of dollars into the Klan treasury, as well as a considerable sum to his own account. Among the accouterments of his position was a fine home in Irvington, a 98-foot yacht on Lake Huron, and a Kresge Building office that boasted the then phenomenal total of eight telephones (including one fake direct line to the White House). The young demagogue liked to compare himself to Napoleon and his expressed ambition was to become the President of the United States.[4]

Under the general direction of Stephenson the Indianapolis Klan made its appeal for members on two distinct levels. On the one hand it stressed law enforcement, motherhood, virtue, patriotism, and temperance. So effective was this method that a Catholic priest, respected in Indianapolis as few men were, explained: "If they had brought their pledge to me in the early days of the Klan, I declare that I would have signed it. It proclaimed what I have always held as an American citizen." Law enforcement and "quick" justice were particularly significant tenets. For instance, Dr. William Forney Harris, pastor of Grand Avenue Methodist Episcopal Church, told his congregation in February 1922 that he had always opposed mob violence, lynching, and clandestine coercion, "but when judges and other officials fail to demand redress for wrong through orderly process, then I welcome the Ku Klux Klan or any other Klan which will startle justice into action." [5]

But the Indianapolis Klan consorted also with bigotry. The chief enemy was the Pope, but attacks were also made on every minority group. The advice of Indiana Grand Dragon W. Lee Smith to one Klan speaker was: "You can't make it too strong against the Jew and the Catholic in a closed meeting—give them hell." Klan lecturer Charles H. Gunsolus articulated the typical hooded attitude from the pulpit of the First Congregational Church on a stormy July night. First denouncing immigration and the League of Nations, Gunsolus described the Negro as "a servant of humanity," and the Jew as an "un-American parasite." The last and most serious problem was the Catholic question because "they are a curse to humanity and the freedom of conscience." [6]

Utilizing such appeals to best advantage, the Indianapolis Klan attained a membership of about five thousand by the summer of 1922. An important element in its success was *The Fiery Cross*. Established in July by the Realm of Indiana, headquartered in the Century Building, and edited originally by Ernest W. Reichard, the weekly newspaper was sold on at least a dozen Indianapolis newsstands and was circulated by mail to approximately one-fourth of Indiana's Klansmen.[7] It reported on local, state, and national Klan news, as well as the menace of unrestricted immigration and the attempt by Catholics to impede construction of needed Indianapolis public schools.

Although *The Fiery Cross* was not technically a publication of the Marion County Klan, Indianapolis businessmen accounted for most of its advertising revenue. Tailors, cleaners, contractors, grocers, druggists, photographers, and restaurants placed notices in the weekly Klan organ, which boasted a circulation of 125,000 in August 1923. Although it was not necessary to be a Klansman in order to purchase space in *The Fiery Cross*, the wording of many advertisements doubtlessly reflected the sentiments of the firm involved. Typical instances would include Kaufman's Kampus Klothes, Washington Cleaners, which "Kleans Klothes Klean," the Kareful Klothes Kleaners, and Klean, Klinkerless Koal. The H. A. Weaver Furniture Company invited patrons to come in and listen to such recent Klan music and piano rolls as "The Cross in the Wildwood" and "Why I Am a Klansman." The Johnson Ford Company was even more emphatic: "We solicit the patronage of 100% Americans who prefer being served by 100% workmen." [8]

The confident nativists were threatened by Chicago's American Unity League in the spring of 1923. On April 1, an unidentified person pilfered a list of 12,208 Klansmen from Klan headquarters on the third floor of Buschman Hall at 11th and College Avenue, and placed it in the possession of the American Unity League. *The Fiery Cross* maintained that the document was only a "mimeographed poll of Protestant citizens available to membership in the Klan," [9] but the A.U.L. considered it an accurate list of Indianapolis Klansmen and scheduled it for publication in *Tolerance*.

Hysterical at the threatened exposure of the "poll of Protestant citizens," the Invisible Empire secured an injunction from Judge George A. Carpenter in United States District Court in Chicago preventing publication of the list in *Tolerance*. An involved legal battle ensued, but several copies of the list had already been made. The enraged *Fiery Cross* credited the thievery to former Klansman Lawrence Lyons, the Indiana Republican State Chairman. Describing him as "born in hell and inspired by Satan," the secret order promised to relegate Lyons "so far into political oblivion that there will be only a faint but hideous memory." [10]

An unfortunate result of the controversy was a further intensification of religious fanaticism in Indianapolis. Because Catholics reportedly boycotted Protestant merchants identified as Klansmen, Milton Elrod, the new editor of *The Fiery Cross*, published the names of local Catholic businessmen on April 27 and May 11, 1923.[11] The well-known Claypool Hotel was a center of dispute when its superintendent of service was discharged shortly after being listed in *Tolerance*. Responding quickly, Elrod declared that, "the Claypool is the headquarters of the Knights of Columbus, the Jewish B'nai B'rith and propagation headquarters for both."

Unlike the situation in heavily Catholic Chicago, where exposure as a Klansmen often brought disastrous economic consequences, the campaign of the American Unity League in Indianapolis was unsuccessful. Only 10,400 copies of the Hoosier list were printed and most of those were impounded by the United States District Court. In addition, many non-members in Indianapolis were likely to take the side of the Klan in a dispute with the Roman Catholic Church, so the effect of a Catholic boycott was rarely severe.

Guarding its rolls more closely, the Indianapolis chapter launched an unprecedented period of growth in the latter half of 1923, when it was chartered as Marion County Klan No. 3.[12] Under Kleagles Arie P. Renn and William M. Rogers, membership reached 28,000. Buschman Hall, Englewood Community Hall, and the Fairgrounds were popular Klan gathering places, but Cadle Tabernacle was the favorite haunt of local Knights, who also enjoyed motoring to regional Klan demonstrations in such places as Kokomo and Shelbyville. Emphasizing law enforcement, the suppression of bootlegging, and charitable activity, the Indianapolis Klan worked hard to promote its public image. On Christmas Day in 1922 and 1923, "bushel baskets of groceries, candies, shoes, and bedclothing," were loaded into twelve big trucks and distributed to more than one hundred homes, including "several colored and Catholic families." Particular attention was also devoted to properly observing the death of a fellow Klansman. Standard procedure called for flowers in the shape of a fiery cross decorated with a KKK streamer, but a few deceased members also received "ritualistic services" at the gravesite. So honored was Policeman Fred K. Russ, whose funeral cortege was followed by 316 marching Klansmen in full regalia.[13]

Like Klansmen everywhere, Indianapolis members spoke often of purity, chastity, and motherhood. It was only natural, therefore, that they gave every encouragement to the organization in 1923 of a local unit of the Women of the Ku Klux Klan. Designated Court No. 14 and led by Laura Foote, Clara Aldridge, and Char-

lotte Short, female Kluxers were recruited primarily among the
wives of Klansmen and numbered about ten thousand by the end
of the year. A persistent problem was the lack of an adequate
meeting place for the women, who sought unsuccessfully to use
Tomlinson Hall for that purpose. They rented the coliseum for special occasions, such as the visit of Imperial Wizard Evans on November 16, 1923.

Clergymen were important for the success of both male and female Klans in the Hoosier capital. Few ministers went so far as the
Reverend W. H. Brighmire of Wesley Chapel, who labeled the Invisible Empire, "the greatest secret organization in the world," but
many privately expressed support for "one hundred per cent Americanism." Klansman Clarence Wilhelm, pastor of Calvary Baptist
Church in West Indianapolis, admonished his congregation to
"come early if you desire to see the cross burn," and delivered a
sermon on, "The Reason for the Existence of the Fiery Cross." During Sunday evening services at Brightwood Methodist Episcopal
Church in July 1922, ten robed Klansmen quietly filed into the
sanctuary, knelt in silent prayer at the altar, and presented the Reverend Roy A. Ragsdale with one hundred dollars for the building
fund. Riverside Baptist Church, Wesleyan Methodist Church,
Windfall Christian Church, Hall Place Methodist Church, and Garfield Christian Church were locations of various Klan activities or
lectures, but Brightwood Congregational Church, where crosses
were frequently burned on the lawn, was known as "the center of
Klandom." [14]

Defiance of the Invisible Empire by the Protestant clergy was
also remembered. Klansmen sought to prevent the reappointment
of the Reverend Edward A. Robertson to the East Park Methodist
Church, and then persecuted and embarrassed him for refusing to
permit them to hold business meetings in the church. At the Seventh Christian Church, where all but four or five families were
members of the Klan, the Reverend Clay Trusty, Sr., was forced to
resign in favor of the Reverend Gerald L. K. Smith, who later distinguished himself as an anti-Semitic pamphleteer and professional
rabble-rouser.[15]

The mantle of leadership of the anti-Klan forces in Indianapolis was worn by Mayor Samuel Lewis Shank. Elected to a four-year term in 1921, before the secret order became powerful in the city, the ex-vaudevillian Republican executive frustrated the local klavern on several occasions. He prohibited masked parades in the city, refused the use of Tomlinson Hall for female Klan meetings, and ordered the arrest, on charges of inciting a riot, of newsdealers handling *The Fiery Cross*. In addition, he was determined to enforce a Board of Public Safety ruling against the burning of crosses within the city, an edict challenged by the Ku Klux Klan.

The first confrontation on the cross-burning question came on July 10, 1923, when the Westview Baptist Church in West Indianapolis sponsored a carnival and lawn social. The attendants at soft-drink stands, ice-cream counters, and concession booths wore red and white paper caps with white crosses printed upon the front, and similarly decorated balloons filled the air. A feature of the affair was an address by Klan lecturer Fred B. Griffith, who spoke from the rear of a truck to more than seven thousand persons. Almost the entire audience raised their hands when Griffith asked how many were "one hundred per cent Americans." An unlit cross was placed beside the truck, but a police detachment on the scene ordered that it not be ignited. Open antagonism swept across the crowd, but the Reverend J. Luther Jones leaped to the truck and appealed to them to "remember our pledge to uphold the laws." Hundreds of angry Klansmen then formed a caravan out West Morris Street to the city limits, where the cross was ceremoniously burned. But many Klansmen openly objected to their retreat.

A more serious test of the cross-burning prohibition came one week later. In the early evening of July 18 an electric cross was lit in West Indianapolis. One hour later five thousand persons gathered a block farther south and lit an oil-soaked wooden cross. Firemen rushing to the scene were met with a hail of rocks, and one was injured. Police entered the fray with drawn revolvers, arrested a truck repairman and a Fifteenth Ward Republican committeeman, both Klansmen, ending the disturbance. The challenge was repeated the following evening when the fire department had to extinguish an 8-by-4-foot cross in a school yard nearby. Mayor Shank responded by demanding the unqualified loyalty of every man in his cabinet, "regardless of their membership in secret organizations," and promising to continue the ban on cross-burning. Police Chief Herman F. Rikhoff supported the mayor: "I think preachers who advertise such meetings from their pulpits should be prosecuted."

The bitter controversy between the Ku Klux Klan and Mayor Shank continued throughout 1923. *The Fiery Cross* charged that "Limber Lunged Lew" was mayor as a result of a "miscarriage of justice," threatened him with impeachment, and accused him of giving aid and comfort to bootleggers and criminals. Not until May 1924, however, did the Invisible Empire have opportunity for revenge. Mayor Shank entered the Republican gubernatorial primary on an anti-Klan platform and collided with Indianapolis Klansman Edward Jackson.

Exalted Cyclops Grover Smith and Marion County Klan No. 3 went all out to ensure the defeat of the mayor. Local members distributed campaign literature and on the Friday before the election the Invisible Empire held a rally for Ed Jackson at Cadle Tabernacle. The vote on May 6 was the largest ever recorded in an Indianapolis primary and was extremely gratifying to hooded patriots. Klan-endorsed Omer Hawkins won the nomination for sheriff, and Ralph Updike defeated Congressman Merrill Moores 27,866 to 25,796 when the incumbent's early lead was wiped out by returns from heavily Klan precincts in the First, Fourth, Ninth, and Tenth Wards. Jackson easily won the nomination for governor, defeating "Limber Lunged Lew" by 38,668 votes to 20,306 in Marion County.[16] The county surveyor and county prosecutor were the only Republicans to break the Klan stranglehold. Insult was added to injury when the Invisible Empire won control of the Marion County Republican organization three days later by electing George Coffin as county chairman over the mayor's candidate. Samuel Lewis Shank conceded defeat, dismissed scores of city employees who worked against him either in the primary or the county Republican convention, and rescinded his ban on Indianap-

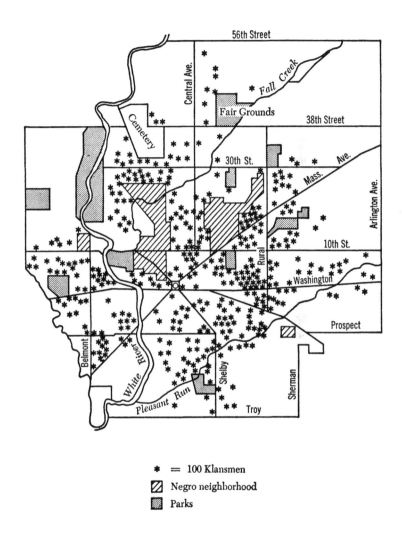

56th Street

Central Ave.

Fall Creek

Fair Grounds

38th Street

Cemetery

30th St.

Mass. Ave.

Arlington Ave.

10th St.

Rural

Washington

Prospect

Belmont

White River

Shelby

Sherman

Pleasant Run

Troy

＊ = 100 Klansmen

▨ Negro neighborhood

▦ Parks

Figure 2. Distribution of Klan Strength in Indianapolis, 1923

olis Klan parades: "The people around here seem to want that kind
of stuff, for they voted for the Kluckers last Tuesday. If they hold a
parade we will give them police protection."

Flushed with pride, the Indianapolis Klan was now at the peak
of its power, and in celebration a monster parade moved down
Indiana Avenue, in the heart of the Negro section, and then
through the business district. With a local membership of perhaps
40,000, the Invisible Empire was strong throughout the city, but
several areas were conspicuous for their concentrations of Knights.[17]
The neighborhood immediately east of the Indiana Women's Prison
to Dearborn between Michigan Street and the Baltimore and Ohio
Railroad was particularly infested, as were sections in the south-
eastern part of the city in the general vicinity of Fountain Square
and in the central city between College, North, Pennsylvania, and
Fifteenth Streets. West Indianapolis was particularly well represented; especially around New York and Elder Streets, and also
south of Rhodius Park and east and west of George Washington
High School. The expanding Negro ghetto drove many persons into
the Invisible Empire, and this doubtless explains Klan strength
north of Twenty-seventh Street toward Crown Hill Cemetery, east
of Sheldon Avenue at about Seventeenth Street, and east of Parker
Avenue near Twenty-fifth Street. Noticeable also is the fact that the
secret order was not strong in the best residential districts. The evidence clearly indicates that the Marion County Klan had broad
middle- and lower-middle-class support.[18]

The decline of the Indianapolis chapter dates from May 1924,
when internal dissension began to raise speculation about who actually spoke for the Klan and controlled its enormous vote.[19] At the
center of the controversy was Grand Dragon David C. Stephenson.
Known as "the old man" to Hoosier patriots, he resigned his post in
September 1923, but retained an active interest in the Klan and
disputed publicly with his replacement, Walter F. Bossert. On
April 7, 1924, Imperial Wizard Hiram Wesley Evans banished Stephenson from the Invisible Empire, whereupon "the old man" retaliated by suggesting the secession of northern Klans from Atlanta
domination:

They donated $100,000 to erecting a monument at Atlanta to the memory of the rebels who once tried to destroy America, yet they refused to give a single dollar for Valparaiso University to help educate the patriots of the north who saved the Union to posterity; unsullied from the contamination of southern traitors.

Stephenson called a statewide meeting on May 12, 1924, at Indianapolis's Cadle Tabernacle. Only four hundred delegates attended the convention, but they elected "the old man" as grand dragon (the first time any grand dragon had been chosen by the membership) and chose Earl Sigmon of the Sigmon Coal Company as grand klaliff (state vice commander), and Dr. M. L. White, a dentist with offices in the Bankers Trust Building, as grand nighthawk (investigator). The Imperial Palace in Atlanta naturally refused to recognize the new officials, and ordered Grand Dragon Bossert and Kleagle Grover A. Smith to call the first annual Kloreo (state convention) of the Realm of Indiana for September 5, 1924, at Cadle Tabernacle.[20] But Stephenson, like his idol Napoleon, seemed to command the loyalty of his troops. "The old man" was the most popular Klansman in the state, and as Senator James E. Watson succinctly put it: "All politicians in Indiana know Stephenson."[21] From his eight-room office on the third floor of the new Kresge Building, he moved in a powerful circle in the capital city. When the 1924 Republican State Convention met in Indianapolis, at least 500 of the approximately 1300 delegates were loyal to Stephenson. Most importantly, anti-Klan state chairman Lawrence Lyons was replaced by Clyde Walb, a short, stocky, and middle-aged crony of "the old man."

The power of D. C. Stephenson was tested in November 1924, when the general election was fought largely on Klan–anti-Klan lines. In Philadelphia, NAACP President James Weldon Johnson advised Indiana Negroes of their "plain duty to vote against the Republican candidate for Governor." Indeed, Democratic candidate Carleton B. McCulloch's "freedom and liberty" platform contrasted sharply with the Klan affiliations of his opponent, Ed Jackson. The anti-Klan campaigner decried efforts to make "religion, race, color, or accidental place of birth a political issue," and argued that the Republican party of Indiana had been "delivered into the hands of an organization which has no place in politics and which promulgates doctrines which tend to break down the safeguards which the Constitution throws around every citizen." [22]

Carleton McCulloch was correct in his assessment of Klan dominance within the Indiana Republican party, particularly since both factions of the secret order were united behind the candidacy of Ed Jackson for governor. In a mimeographed letter distributed throughout the realm less than two weeks before the election, Grand Dragon Bossert counseled his subjects:

> You must realize that we cannot win this fight with the Klan vote alone. We must secure all Protestant support and get the information to all Protestant people relative to our program and the men whom we will support. . . .
>
> Remember also that the amalgamated enemies of the organization are influencing the negro and foreigner to such an extent that practically the entire negro and foreign vote will be cast for anti-Klan candidates. . . .
>
> Let's establish Indiana as the Realm that can proudly boast of the most efficient and effective organization throughout the Nation. Let's let Indiana show Oklahoma and Texas how it can be done. We can do it.[23]

Such efforts were apparently successful, because the Klan claimed a great Protestant victory in the November Indiana and Indianapolis elections. Although there were marked defections among colored voters, and some Negro precincts reported Democratic majorities for the first time in history, the Klan elected the governor and a majority of the state legislature (including State Senator William T. Quillen of Indianapolis). Running slightly better in the capital city than in the state as a whole, Ed Jackson carried Marion County 85,740 to 71,876.[24]

The political grapevine soon spread the word that if you "wanted anything" in Indiana you went first to David C. Stephenson and afterward or not at all to those who had the official power to grant the request. His boast, "I am the law," was only slightly exaggerated, and his influence was well illustrated by the written pledge he extracted from John Duvall in 1925:

> In return for the political support of D. C. Stephenson, in the event I am elected mayor of Indianapolis, I promise not to appoint any person as a member of the Board of Public Works without [sic] they first have the endorsement of Stephenson.
> I fully agree and promise to appoint Claude Worley as Chief of Police and Earl Klinck as a Captain.

The wonderful world of David C. Stephenson shriveled in the spring of 1925, however. He was arrested and brought to trial for the rape and murder of twenty-eight-year-old Madge Oberholtzer, a frequent companion whom he forced to accompany him on an overnight train ride to Hammond. During the trip Stephenson repeatedly assaulted the buxom statehouse secretary and "chewed" on her body. When they stopped in Hammond, the hysterical Miss Oberholtzer took poison. Stephenson was frightened because the girl was in agony but refused to let her see a doctor until they returned to Indianapolis. She died several weeks later, and the State of Indiana charged that she had committed suicide "because she had lost that which she held dearer than her life—her chastity." Soon after Stephenson's arrest, a mysterious fire destroyed his home and many of his personal papers.

Although upset by the well-publicized scandal and subsequent murder trial, Klan No. 3 nevertheless concentrated its efforts in 1925 on the election of a suitable successor to the hated Mayor Shank. Marion County Treasurer John Duvall, a Klansman, easily won the Republican nomination in May and faced Walter Myers in the November election. The November general election was doubly important because the Marion County Klan supported a five-man United Protestant School Board ticket, which promised to clean up school affairs and see that the Bible and the American flag received foremost attention in the classroom.

Working independently of the Republican City Committee, the Klan established campaign headquarters in the City Trust Building, where policemen and firemen were prominent among hundreds of assistants and visitors. The primary effort of the Indianapolis Klan was a mass meeting at Cadle Tabernacle. Mayoral candidate John Duvall and former Superior Court Judge Charles J. Orbison were the chief speakers, but with one exception every member of the Republican city ticket and the United Protestant School Board ticket was there.[25] Although Exalted Cyclops George S. Elliot maintained that the meeting was not held in the interest of the Ku Klux Klan, admission was either by password or by an invitation card signed by the chapter leader. In the front rows youthful members of the Junior Klan went through well rehearsed cheers for the speakers, several of whom expressed pride in being supported by "the greatest Protestant organization in the world."

Largely because John Duvall was so closely associated with the Ku Klux Klan, all three Indianapolis newspapers editorially supported the Democratic candidate. Two days before the election former mayor John Holtzman declared that a Duvall victory would result in the "nourishing and strengthening of the D. C. Stephenson brand of politics." But November 3, 1925, brought victory for the Ku Klux Klan and its "clothespin" state. John Duvall was elected mayor by a vote of 53,250 to 43,276, and all five United Protestant School Board ticket members were elected. That evening thousands of Duvall supporters marched around Monument Circle while a band played Klan songs. The *Indianapolis News* noted sorrowfully that "the Klan made it a clean sweep by electing all its candidates for the school board, defeating by substantial majorities the citizens' nonpartisan ticket, and several other groups of candidates."

But the campaign did weaken the notion of Klan invincibility in Indianapolis. Republican officials complained of "the failure of the strong Klan precincts to show the strength expected," and Duvall's victory margin was the lowest of any Republican candidate in the election. Ironically, it was the return of the Negro voters to the G.O.P. column, encouraged by "organization and brains and money," that enabled Duvall to emerge the winner.[26]

Despite the narrowness of the victory, Duvall was a Klansman, and the Invisible Empire expected him to deliver. Prior to taking office on January 1, 1926, the mayor-elect went to Washington at Klan expense and conferred with Imperial Wizard Evans, who recommended Judge Orbison as Indianapolis Corporation Counsel. Initially, Duvall concurred with the recommendation, but he finally appointed Lafe Rucker, who was not a Klansman, to the post.[27] Nevertheless, the mayor's list of appointments reflected his obligation to the secret order, and the *Indianapolis News* reported that it "gives promise of being a Klan administration to a considerable extent." Orbison was named to the Park Board, as was Exalted Cyclops George Elliot of Klan No. 3. Orin E. Davis, an electrical contractor and Klan official, was appointed to the Board of Public Safety, and the first and second assistant fire chiefs were Klansmen. Arthur B. McGee was named inspector of police, but this selection was altered when colored voters pointed out that he had been arrested several times for assaulting and beating Negroes. The new man, Walter White, also had the Klan endorsement, however.

Neither Mayor Duvall nor the Invisible Empire could long savor their Indianapolis victory. Only two weeks after the election, David C. Stephenson, who did not take the stand in his own defense, was found guilty of second degree murder by a Hamilton County jury in Noblesville and sentenced to life imprisonment.[28]

Confidently expecting a pardon from Governor Jackson, the "old man" told reporters he had just begun to fight. But Stephenson quickly discovered how fleeting is political power; the official word never came. After waiting angrily for almost a year in the Michigan City penitentiary, he began to reveal some of the contents of his "little black box." The governor and the prison warden attempted to isolate Stephenson, but Vincennes publisher Thomas Adams induced the Marion County grand jury to investigate alleged political irregularities in Indiana. The resulting exposé of corruption astounded even those who had shared in the plunder. Mayor Duvall was sent to prison for violation of the Corrupt Practices Act, along with the sheriff of Marion County, a congressman, the city purchasing agent, the city controller, and many lesser officials. Governor Jackson was indicted for bribery, but escaped punishment by invoking the statute of limitations. Among other things he had accepted nineteen thousand dollars in connection with appointments to the Indiana Public Service Commission from Chicago's Insull utility interests, which owned the Indianapolis Street Railway Company.[29]

Indianapolis Klansmen were probably no less startled than the nation. Most members could not excuse the irrefutable evidence of hypocrisy and political preferment in the Indiana Klan movement and therefore never attended another meeting of the Invisible Empire. Several thousand Indianapolis Klansmen swallowed their pride, however, and remained active until 1926 when rancor developed over the Klan endorsement for senator. Most Indianapolis Klansmen favored Charles Orbison, a local judge and a vigorous Prohibitionist, but the national office ordered Indiana Knights to support the re-election effort of James E. Watson, a non-Klansman who was well liked by Imperial Wizard Evans. When Grand Dragon Walter Bossert protested the decision, he was removed from office, and W. Lee Smith was appointed to the position.[30] Disgusted Indianapolis Klansmen then resigned from the Invisible Empire almost as a body and formed the Order of the Red Star. Klan No. 3 quickly fell to pieces from non-support.[31] Some of its former associates, such as Congressman Ralph Updike and Sheriff Hawkins, continued to serve in elective office, but only by underplaying the role they had played earlier in the secret order.

The *Indianapolis Times* won a Pulitzer Prize in 1928 for its "savage campaign" against the Ku Klux Klan, which supposedly resulted in a net circulation loss of five thousand. But the campaign was almost unnecessary, for there were fewer than seven thousand paid-up members in the state of Indiana in 1928.[32]

11

The Midwestern Response

The experience of other midwestern cities with the Ku Klux Klan varied considerably. In Minneapolis, where North Star Klan No. 2 began operations in August 1921, the Invisible Empire never made much headway. Unable to gather at the Municipal Auditorium, the Klan held propagation meetings at Foss Memorial and Olivet Methodist Churches and quickly gained a membership of two thousand. Negroes were rarely seen in Minnesota's capital and largest city, but Catholics, particularly in neighboring St. Paul, were the object of growing concern. Most Minneapolis Klansmen were Masons, and the state leaders included many prominent Shriners.

The Minneapolis Klan floundered during the 1923 mayoralty election, when Exalted Cyclops Roy Miner of Klan No. 2 opposed incumbent George E. Leach, whose deeds as mayor had indicated a lack of sympathy with "one hundred per cent Americanism." Campaigning against gambling and vice, the Klan printed and distributed a story accusing the mayor of sexual intimacies with a local woman and of attendance at wild parties. Leach took his case to a grand jury, and five over-zealous Klansmen, including Exalted Cyclops Miner, were convicted of libel. The resulting publicity damaged severely the secret order's hopes for success in the Twin Cities.[1]

In heavily Irish, German, and Polish Milwaukee "one hundred per cent Americanism" capitalized upon the aggressive leadership of insurance man William Wieseman and fared much better than in Minneapolis. First organized in Wisconsin aboard a Coast Guard cutter anchored in the Milwaukee River, the Klan met originally over the Pabst Theater as the Milwaukee Businessman's Club. Advertising "Masons Preferred," the local chapter held its largest meeting at the Milwaukee Auditorium, where imperial official C. Lewis Fowler discussed patriotism before three thousand Knights. By 1924, the city's forty-four hundred Klansmen were sufficiently affluent to purchase a permanent home at 2424 Cedar Street. The location of the largest and most powerful Klan chapter in the state, Milwaukee served also as Realm of Wisconsin headquarters and as the seat of publication of its monthly organ, *The Badger-American*. Atlanta officialdom muffed its excellent Milwaukee opportunity, however, by refusing to grant the local klavern a charter when its membership reached five thousand. Belated recognition as Klan No. 1 came only after many local Knights had resigned from the Invisible Empire and filed suit against the national office for refusing to charter the local unit.[2]

The political situation in Milwaukee led to a curious alliance between the Socialist party and the Klan. Through the common bond of anti-Catholicism, the two groups supported John Kleist for the state supreme court as both a Socialist and a Klansman. The Klan had more Socialists on its rolls, Kleist told the party leaders, than they did. Although he lost, Kleist ran better than any other Socialist in Wisconsin history.

The Invisible Empire was noticeably weak in the Dakotas, Grand Forks being a notable exception, but the realms of Nebraska, Kansas, and Iowa were quite active between 1922 and 1925. An estimated six thousand Wichita Klansmen donated $8,500 for hospital construction and initiated publication of *The Jayhawker American*, while in Topeka the Invisible Empire staged at least two downtown parades and held open-air meetings on a field one mile west of the city limits. Statewide membership approached forty thousand and so alarmed William Allen White that the famed Emporia editor entered the 1924 gubernatorial campaign solely to dramatize the extent of hooded influence in Kansas.[3] In Omaha, where former Kleagle Edgar Fuller sought to organize the American Fascisti, Klan No. 1 set up offices, sponsored large out-door initiations, and spawned an active Junior Klan. In Des Moines, ministers led the recruiting effort, and the head of the local Klan was the pastor of the Capitol Hill Church of Christ. Although political success came rarely to Hawkeye state Klansmen, the secret order's unsuccessful gubernatorial candidate did carry the state's capital and largest city. Moreover, as Professor David Chalmers has pointed out, Klan voting strength in Des Moines tended to be slight in the silk stocking districts on the west side and strong on the east side, where Swedish, Negro, and Italian settlements were encroaching upon the homes of Anglo-Saxon office and factory workers.[4]

Despite the fact that St. Louis was the headquarters of Grand Goblin F. A. Crippen's Domain of the Mississippi Valley and of King Kleagles G. A. Glasscock and Casey Jones, the secret order never got off the ground in the Missouri metropolis. Organized as William Joseph Simmons Klan No. 7, the local klavern made the tactical error of pledging fifteen thousand dollars to a Boy Scout fund drive in 1922 and producing only a tenth of that amount. It remained insignificant and was publicly condemned by both the Democratic and Republican city committees. The St. Louis klavern's most notorious and active adherent was the Reverend Charles D. McGhee of Raven Street Methodist Church, who upon being criticized for his Klan activities, retorted: "If it comes to a choice between the Methodist Church and the Klan, then I shall choose the Klan." McGhee made good his promise and became a full-time Klan lecturer when Bishop McMurry removed the Klansman from his pulpit.

With a membership of five thousand, the Kansas City Klan was slightly stronger than its St. Louis counterpart. Led by John R. Jones, who was banished by his superiors in Atlanta after complaining about Klan political activity in 1924, the Kansas City klavern engaged in the usual patriotic pastimes and sponsored an emotional anti-Catholic demonstration at Convention Hall in 1922. Its greatest effort was put forth in connection with the 1924 national klonvokation, which was held in Kansas City in September. The natives remained unfriendly, however. A "Ku Klux Klan Shop," opened in 1923 to distribute patriotic and Klan publications and novelties, had been in business only three days when bricks were thrown through the windows, and the Maxwellton Inn, where the Klan had held an initiation, was bombed. The relative strength of the Klan was greater in stagnant St. Joseph than anywhere else in the state, but even there a Klansman was shot in a scuffle following a speech at the Klan's Crystal Theater.

The relative weakness of the secret order in Missouri was not characteristic of Ohio, which enrolled two hundred thousand Knights and ranked behind Indiana as the most populous realm of the Invisible Empire. Directed during its expansionist period by David Stephenson, the Buckeye organization took full advantage of latent feeling against the influx of Negroes and East European immigrants into Ohio. Much of the realm's strength was centered in the state's large cities, seven of which claimed more than 130,000 inhabitants in 1920.[5]

The Klan first entered Ohio at Cincinnati late in 1920, when propagation headquarters were established in the First National Bank Building and the first of nine klaverns was formed in populous Hamilton County. By 1922 the secret order was sponsoring a fifty-piece band, holding initiations at Carthage Fairgrounds and on nearby Mount Healthy, and claiming a Cincinnati membership of 12,181 and a metropolitan enrollment of 18,982. Cincinnati Klansmen were led by C. William Schmidt, but the most admired local member was Dan Caldwell, a lieutenant colonel in the Ohio National Guard's One Hundred and Forty-seventh Infantry and the exalted cyclops of one of the city's largest klaverns.[6]

Clerical support for the Klan was infrequent in Cincinnati, but the Reverend Orval W. Baylor of historic Richmond Street Christian Church helped alleviate the numerical imbalance. When two Paulist priests denounced the Invisible Empire shortly after a

Christmas Eve cross burning, Baylor retorted from his pulpit that "when Father Conway tells you that the Ku Klux Klan is neither American nor Christian, he not only utters a falsehood, but he insults approximately 40,000 native-born American Protestant men and women of Hamilton County." [6]

Reportedly the home of forty thousand citizens of the Invisible Empire, nearby Dayton was the scene of even more Klan activity than Cincinnati. "One hundred per cent Americanism" was particularly attractive to the skilled native-born artisans who manned the Gem City's precision industries. Montgomery County Klan No. 23, led by Frank Ramsey, O. B. Wolf, and Jim Sultz, published *The Kluxer*, donated five thousand dollars to the local Council of Religious Education, sponsored a military unit, and staged such large and frequent demonstrations that President Bernard P. O'Reilly of the Catholic University of Dayton protested that students "are losing sleep and getting behind in their studies, all because of the activities of the Ku Klux Klan in burning fiery crosses where they may be seen from the dormitories." [7]

The headquarters of the Realm of Ohio was appropriately located in Columbus, first at the State Street dental office of Grand Dragon Charles L. Harrod and later in the Yuster Building. The immediate objects of the Klan's concern were the capital city's Negro and foreign-born contingents, most of whom lived in segregated neighborhoods like Bronzeville and the Italian district northwest of the state capitol. Officially designated Buckeye Klan No. 8, the flourishing Columbus chapter engaged in frequent charitable activities, held occasional open meetings in churches (particularly the Church of Christ), published a monthly newspaper known as *The Pitchfork*, and sponsored public viewings of the Klan propaganda film *Toll of Justice*. On May 4, 1923, Buckeye Klan No. 8 planned a large ceremony in the Columbus Driving Park just east of the city limits, but its opponents secured a court injunction preventing Klan use of the public facility. Angry Knights then marched back and forth on High Street before driving two miles east of the city limits to "Smith's Forty Acres" and initiating fifteen hundred Franklin County men into the Invisible Empire. [8]

The Ohio Klan was impotent in the state's northernmost cities, Toledo and Cleveland, even though in Toledo the secret order got off to a fast start under the leadership of Exalted Cyclops C. K. Wilson, owner of the Wilson Chemical Company. When two radicals criticized President Harding at a street meeting, they were kidnapped and narrowly escaped lynching at the hands of the Klan. But the Toledo Klan faltered with the resignation of Wilson in 1922. In Cleveland, where in 1921 Mayor Fitzgerald ordered the police department "to suppress the Ku Klux Klan in this city," the Invisible Empire could claim only two thousand members.

Thirty miles south of Cleveland, a very different history was experienced by Fred W. Yoos's Akron Klan No. 27. Together with such active auxiliaries as the Royal Riders of the Red Robe, the Junior Klan, and the Women of the Ku Klux Klan it held large initiations in Tallmadge, Perkins Woods, the old Masonic Hall, Sherbondy Hill, and the Cuyahoga Street District. On one occasion the Rubber City chapter even blocked traffic for an hour for a hooded ceremony. At its peak in 1923 Klan No. 27 claimed 350 applications per day, suggested that the name of Summit County be changed to Ku Klux Kounty, and enrolled so many national guardsmen that the local artillery battery became known as the Grand Dragon's Guard. Among Akron's more prominent members were the mayor, a Common Pleas Court judge, a candidate for congress, a city councilman, the school board president, the sheriff, and a United States commissioner. The judge was later quoted as saying: "The Klan to me was just another club to join. I belonged to anything I could get in. Anybody with any political pretensions joined." [9]

The focal point of Akron Klan activity was the public school system, which seemed to Klansmen to be deficient in Bible reading and patriotism. To remedy the situation the local chapter lent strong support to a front organization entitled the South High Civic Association, and in November 1923, elected at least one Klansman to the Akron Board of Education. Shortly thereafter it made public donations of Bibles and flags to South Side High School and secured adoption of an elective course in Bible study. [10]

Financial irregularities resulting from heavy capital expenditures for a drill team and a costly lot for a proposed auditorium finally caused public quarreling within the mammoth Akron Chapter. The Reverend A. C. Henry was hastily appointed provisional exalted cyclops in the summer of 1925, but he was unable to ease the dissension and was removed from office in 1926. When Ohio Grand Dragon Gilbert Taylor then sent his personal representative, Frank Cox, to take charge of Summit County operations, a majority of Akron Klan members withdrew and formed the Buckeye Civic Association. A series of lawsuits immediately tied up Klan assets, and the dream of a Klan auditorium on Fir Hill vanished. The complete demise of the Rubber City Klan came in 1927.

Rivaling Akron, Dayton, and Columbus as the premier Klan city of Ohio was Youngstown, a bustling Mahoning Valley industrial center of 132,000 people in 1920.[11] The local chapter was established in 1921 by Kleagle D. E. Glosner, one of the most able and efficient Klan administrators in the nation. In 1922, the mantle of leadership fell to Colonel E. A. Gunder, who had directed the Klan's Horse Thief Detective Association (similar to that of Indiana) and who now transferred Klan headquarters to the Terminal Building. Youngstown klankraft crested in November 1923, with the election of Klansman Charles F. Scheible as mayor. Twenty-five thousand Knights marched through the streets to celebrate, and the Youngstown chapter hailed the election as "the biggest victory won by the Klan north of the Mason and Dixon line." Klansmen on the city council were so jubilant that they presented a resolution requesting the Invisible Empire to pay off the city debt of six hundred thousand dollars. The local klavern meanwhile continued its frequent picnics and dances and planned the creation of a Klan savings bank. Further evidence of Youngstown influence came in 1924, when Clyde W. Osborne, law director for the Klan mayor, was named Grand Dragon of Ohio.

As the home of large numbers of recent Catholic immigrants, the Youngstown area offered problems as well as opportunities to the purveyors of "one hundred per cent Americanism." Smoldering antagonism between the various ethnic and religious groups finally ignited on November 1, 1924. The occasion was a well-planned tri-state meeting of area Klansmen in Niles, a small Ohio community seven miles northwest of Youngstown. Mayor Harvey C. Kistler had granted permission for a robed parade, but the Niles executive could not speak for the anti-Klan Knights of the Flaming Circle. This predominantly immigrant and Catholic organization announced a counter demonstration for November 1 and warned its members to avoid bringing women and children. On the appointed day Klansmen began arriving in Niles by auto and train from every direction. It was soon obvious that Sheriff Thomas would be unable to contain the large and determined crowds which surged through the streets. Klansmen entering from the south were particularly unfortunate. Anti-Klan mobs met the visitors at the edge of the city, chased frightened Knights from their automobiles, and confiscated the robes of the invaders. Scores of persons were injured and Governor Donahey called out the National Guard to prevent a major confrontation. Miraculously, no one was killed, but the well-publicized incident and subsequent investigation revealed the extent of mistrust and hatred in the Mahoning Valley.

Unlike the similarly powerful realms of Texas, Indiana, Oregon, and Colorado, the Ohio organization never won statewide political success. Early in 1923 Klan influence was sufficiently great to crush an anti-mask bill by a vote of 81 to 26 in the lower house of the state legislature. The bill would have required secret organizations, other than those purely social, to file a list of officers with the state and to keep their membership rolls open for official inspection. Later in 1923, the *Cleveland Press* reported that only two of eighteen Ohio lawmakers interviewed would come out openly against the "bed sheet paraders," and early in 1925 Grand Dragon Osborne boasted that forty-five members of the Ohio House of Representatives were Klansmen.[12]

But the secret order fell short in its major 1924 effort to win the governor's mansion. The Democrats had taken a strong anti-Klan position, so the Klan lined up behind Joseph B. Sieber, an Akron Republican and a political unknown whose trademarks were two American flags which always hung from his automobile radiator.

While never openly admitting membership in the Invisible Empire, Sieber spoke frequently before Klan meetings and surprised political pundits by collecting one hundred thousand votes and finishing second rather than seventh in the primary. The victor was former Governor Harry L. Davis, a vigorous anti-Klan campaigner who expected to ride Calvin Coolidge's coattails into the state house. Grand Dragon Osborne resolved, however, to commit the Klan's predominantly G.O.P. membership to Democratic incumbent Vic Donahey, a popular governor who refused to endorse an Ohio Democratic party resolution denouncing the Klan by name. Significantly, while President Coolidge carried the Buckeye state by an overwhelming two to one margin in November, Donahey survived the Republican sweep and defeated Davis by a comfortable 170,000 votes. With considerable accuracy, Republican leaders traced Davis's demise to "religious and racial hatreds" and "that element which stands for bigotry." Not strong enough to win control for itself, the Klan nevertheless demonstrated its ability to deny success to its enemies.[13]

12

Seaboard Success

In September 1921, the Reverend T. F. Coakley of Old St. Patrick's Catholic Church in Pittsburgh reflected upon the growth of the Invisible Empire:

> That the Ku Klux Klan had its rise in Alabama and South Carolina, and now has its headquarters in Georgia, explains the whole movement. South Carolina is the most illiterate State in the Union, next comes Alabama. Georgia is 44th in the list of states where ignorance reigns. You don't hear of the K. K. K. in the territory influenced by Harvard, Yale, Princeton, Columbia, Cornell, or Chicago Universities.[1]

Father Coakley failed both as observer and prophet. Not only did the Klan thrive in the very shadow of the University of Chicago and establish chapters at Harvard and Princeton,[2] but it won hundreds of thousands of converts in the Northeast and was an important factor in community life from Portland, Maine, to Washington, D.C. To many native-born Protestants the threat of Catholic and Jewish immigration was greater than the menace of hooded Americanism.

The most important realm in the Domain of the Northeast was Pennsylvania, which was divided early at the Susquehanna River

170

into western and eastern provinces. Western headquarters were established in Pittsburgh, where Grand Dragon Sam Rich and Kleagle Arthur L. Cotton sought recruits from an "Advertising and Publicity" office at 4100 Jenkins Arcade Building.[3] In addition to the William Penn Klan, which held demonstrations on Monument Hill and initiated seventeen hundred in a single group in Soldier's Memorial Hall, Pittsburgh chapters were established in Homestead, Hazelwood, Duquesne Heights, Olympia Park, and Carnegie. In 1922, the Invisible Empire reported that "Pittsburgh, socially, morally, and politically, is on the upgrade since the 'Klan Kame Kloser.'" The *Searchlight* was sold regularly on the city's newsstands, and local knights boasted of the allegiance of several score local clergymen. The number obviously did not include the Reverend Ralph W. Urmy of Bellevue Methodist Church. When sixteen robed Klansmen interrupted Easter services in 1923, Mr. Urmy refused their donation, ordered the intruders from the church, and subsequently delivered a blistering anti-Klan sermon.[4]

The most publicized incident in Pittsburgh Klan history actually came in Carnegie, a heavily-Catholic, industrial community of twenty-five hundred just west of the metropolis. On the evening of August 25, 1923, ten thousand area Klansmen gathered on a hill overlooking Carnegie for an initiation and parade through the town. After assembling they were informed that the mayor of Carnegie, fearful of violence, had refused a parade permit. The news was received as a Catholic challenge. Imperial Wizard Hiram Wesley Evans, who was present for the occasion, suggested a parade in defiance of the mayor. Five thousand Klansmen promptly pushed aside several automobiles blocking their path and marched into the city. A shower of rocks and bricks met the column, and wild confusion ensued. A shot rang out; Klansman Thomas Abbott fell to the pavement and died with a bullet in his temple. The column retreated to the hill, and local Knights never again challenged authority in the Pittsburgh area.[5]

East of the Susquehanna River, realm headquarters were located in Philadelphia, where Grand Goblin F. W. Atkins established a six-man office at 5643 Walnut Street in May 1921. The first Klan initiation in the City of Brotherly Love came on August 25, 1921, when Atkins told his subjects that the purpose of the Klan was to rouse the spirit of "real Americanism" and to throttle the "devil's scheme" of native traitors or alien invaders. He concluded with the promise "We, the Ku Klux Klan; we, the Invisible Empire, rally to aid the faltering hands of our law—and to protect our homes, our lives, our people and our nation's future against a wave of living hell."

But Atkins himself later became a "native traitor," publicly denouncing Atlanta officialdom on December 2, 1921. Promptly banished from the Invisible Empire, he was succeeded in Philadelphia by Imperial Representative Paul Meres Winter and King Kleagle Joseph R. Shoemaker. With the aid of a Carnegie Hall address by Edward Young Clarke late in 1922, the new officials increased local membership to thirty thousand, and that of eastern Pennsylvania to one hundred thousand.[6] The Philadelphia and Chester County organizations were divided into a fourteen-hundred-member women's unit, and at least a dozen regular klaverns, including Liberty Bell Klan No. 1, Old Glory Klan No. 5, the William Penn Klan, and the Paul M. Winter Klan. Outdoor initiations were usually held near Oak Lane and the city limits, and local activities included such items as excursions on the Delaware River.

Because "one hundred per cent Americans" were themselves a minority group in Pittsburgh and Philadelphia, Pennsylvania's largest cities offered no examples of Klan political success. When W. T. McCullough, a pro-Klan Pittsburgh Republican, ran for the County Commission in 1923, he finished fourth with 39,097 votes. As a Pittsburgh exalted cyclops later recalled: "It would have been impossible to do much more than influence ward politics so we didn't try. The city was so large that nothing could be done about city politics by one group." Circumstances were basically similar in Philadelphia, although the Klan rejoiced over the election of a Protestant as mayor in 1923.

Usually avoiding politics, both the Pittsburgh and Philadelphia organizations remained active until 1926. When the secret order staged a parade in Washington on August 8, 1925, the Pittsburgh delegation was the largest in the nation, and that of Philadelphia exceeded one thousand.[7] Predictably, internal dissidence eventually ravaged the Invisible Empire in both cities. Philadelphia's 550-member Warren G. Harding Klan was banished as a unit when Exalted Cyclops Walter Turner protested against autocratic realm rule, and in Pittsburgh financial irregularities in the Rich administration resulted in wholesale defections. In 1932 the Klan's sixth Imperial Klonvokation (national convention) was held in Philadelphia's Lu Lu Shrine Temple, but the event was poorly attended and not even locally significant.

Although the secret order made a much greater initial effort in the Empire state, the realm of New York never equaled that of Pennsylvania. Upstate recruitment was directed by Major E. D. Smith from his headquarters in Binghamton, where the local Klan initiated raids on bootleggers and sought to purchase a four-story building for initiations. Kleagles established big chapters in Rochester, Syracuse, Troy, Utica, Albany, Elmira, and Ulster Park, and in 1923 *The New York Times* estimated state membership as 200,-000.

The most sizable inroads were made in Buffalo, where Kleagle J. P. Martin and national lecturer Kenneth Scott began an exhaustive recruiting drive in 1922. The local contingent grew quickly to six thousand members and proceeded to burn crosses within the city, to publish a directory of Buffalo Klan businessmen, and to co-sponsor outdoor rallies near Batavia and Cambria Center. The Catholic community was particularly concerned, and in fact the Bishop of Buffalo publicly placed the onus of Klan growth on "willful misrepresentation" of Catholic doctrine that was preached every Sunday "from certain churches in this city." He may well have been thinking about the Reverend L. E. H. Smith of Ontario United Presbyterian Church. A prominent Klansman and an officer in the Buffalo Council of Churches, Smith was an enthusiastic anti-vice crusader who charged Mayor Frank K. Schwab with shielding gamblers and bootleggers.

Mayor Schwab had no love either for the Reverend Mr. Smith or for the Klan, which had tricked him into speaking to a taxpayers group that was in reality composed of jeering Klansmen. Thoroughly disgusted and anxious to revive the "spirit of harmony" in Buffalo, the mayor ordered Police Lieutenant Austin J. Roche to begin an investigation of the activities of the KKK in his city. Roche was given a free rein, and his expenses were paid from the police secret service fund. By hiring an informer who infiltrated the Klan's inner circle, Roche was able to learn whose names were proposed for Klan membership, who presided at meetings, and what items were discussed. Then, on July 3, 1924, someone purloined the secret files from Klan headquarters in the Calumet Building. Mysteriously, the records fell into the hands of Mayor Schwab, who opened up two alleged Klan membership rolls (one with 1752 names and the other with 4025) to public view at police headquarters. The local press balked at publishing the lists for fear of libel suits; so the roster was published in pamphlet form and sold throughout Buffalo for fifty cents. Businessmen, laborers, mechanics, schoolteachers, and prominent ministers like the Reverend Charles C. Penfold of Sentinel Methodist Church appeared on the lists. One high fraternal official was so embarrassed by the disclosure that he took his own life. Other Klansmen suffered economically when their businesses were boycotted by customers or painted and defaced by roving gangs. Meanwhile, the Buffalo newspapers were publishing pieces of confiscated Klan correspondence which documented the hooded order's role in politics, religion, and law enforcement.

The man most immediately damaged by the theft was District Kleagle George S. Bryant, and he was anxious for revenge. He suspected (correctly) that the culprit was Edward Obertean, a young policeman. Acting quickly, Bryant summoned a well-known Klan investigator, Thomas H. Austin, from North Carolina and together they shadowed their suspect for a week. On the evening of August 31, 1924, Bryant, Austin, and another Klansman forced Obertean's automobile to the curb on a lonely Buffalo street. The policeman defended himself with his revolver, and in the ensuing gun battle, Obertean and Austin were both killed. Bryant, who was wounded, was brought to trial for murder but the charge did not stand.

If the public disclosure of Klan records and the subsequent

double killing did not cause the demise of Klan No. 5, other events soon completed the task. Late in 1924 a local kleagle was arrested for the illegal sale of contraceptives and soon thereafter an audit revealed that twenty-three thousand dollars in initiation fees was missing from the chapter's accounts. The Buffalo Klan movement could not stand the successive crises and by late 1925 was virtually expunged.[8]

Because thirty-seven languages were spoken by New York City's six million residents, only one million of whom were white, native-born Protestants, Imperial Wizard William Joseph Simmons described Gotham as "the most un-American city of the American continent." Highly regarded Columbia University was similarly pegged as the "least American of all schools." But the metropolis and its teeming environs could hardly be overlooked as a source of revenue. Setting up headquarters in a four-room suite at the Hotel Embassy in March 1921, Grand Goblin Lloyd P. Hooper superintended a Klan initiation in Manhattan at least as early as June 10, 1921. Unknown to its managers, the Army-Navy Club was a center of the recruitment campaign. In July a Brooklyn klavern was inaugurated, and in September a Bronx chapter began meeting as the American Civic Association. According to Klan defector C. Anderson Wright there were twenty-one operative klaverns in New York City in December 1922, and at about the same time an upstate Klan official boasted of a Gotham membership of one hundred and fifty thousand.[9] Among the city's more prominent Klan boosters was Clifford Slater Wheeler, a former Army captain who declared: "At the Yale Club in this city, where I am a member, I got quite a few of the boys to join." [10] Many local recruits probably shared the sentiments of a Manhattan physician and Klansman who argued that because politicians commonly catered to the bootleg vote, the vice vote, and sometimes even the violently criminal vote, it was only just for the Klan to force office holders to pay some attention to "the decent, God-fearing, law-abiding vote." Others were perhaps attracted by the extreme anti-Catholic and anti-Semitic philosophy of the pro-Klan New York newspaper, *The American Standard*. A typical diatribe declared, "To receive into your home

Roman Catholics, to give them employment in your office, is to put your home and your office at the mercy of the Roman Catholic system."

"One hundred per cent Americanism" profited from effective, if sporadic, support from the clergy in the nation's first city. Canon William Sheafe Chase of Christ Episcopal Church in Brooklyn cited the Invisible Empire as a band of men "organized to resist the corruption of politics and the lawlessness of our times." The Reverend Newell Dwight Hillis of Brooklyn's Plymouth Congregational Church preached that "the Klan should be defended by every white American who is not under the domination of the Church of Rome," [11] and plaudits came also from the Reverend Roy E. Manne of Grace Methodist-Episcopal Church. At Washington Avenue Baptist Church in Brooklyn, a robed Klansman delivered the sermon at a Sunday service and told an astonished congregation to make certain "that the trade of the country is not controlled by Jews, and the educational institutions of the country are not controlled by Catholicism." [12]

The self-advertised "apostle of the Klan" was Oscar Haywood, associate minister of Manhattan's Calvary Baptist Church, the largest of its denomination in New York. The regular pastor, the Reverend John Roach Stratton, had preached in 1921 that "prejudice against the Jews, Negroes or any other race is dastardly and disgraceful," and he was unaware that his associate was a part-time kleagle for the Invisible Empire. Haywood was therefore able to denounce Catholics and Negroes regularly and to distribute Klan literature from the church for more than a month while Stratton was on vacation.

Despite isolated clerical aid, the Invisible Empire did not prosper in New York City. Even racist Thomas Dixon labeled the movement "stupid and inhuman," adding that "If the white race is superior—as I believe it is—it is our duty as citizens of a democracy to lift up and help the weaker race." Every metropolitan newspaper except C. Lewis Fowler's pro-Klan *American Standard* voiced opposition to the secret order. In December 1922, Judge Francis X. Mancuse of the Court of General Sessions directed the two grand juries then sitting to investigate the Invisible Empire in New York City, and in 1923 the state legislature passed the anti-Klan Walker Bill, which required unincorporated associations to file yearly lists of members, by-laws, and oaths.[13] The most crushing blow was dealt by Mayor John F. Hylan, who labeled the Ku Klux Klan a menace to the city, state, and nation, and who instructed his commissioner of police to "ferret out these despicable disloyal persons who are attempting to organize a society, the aims and purposes of which are of such a character that were they to prevail, the foundations of our country would be destroyed." [14]

Mayor Hylan's mandate was effective. Within two weeks the police turned over the names of eight hundred New York City Klansmen to the district attorney, and detectives broke up meetings of the Brooklyn Klan. Early in 1923 Bomb Squad detectives revealed that thirty policemen were members of the secret order, and at about the same time the Reverend Haywood felt obliged to return to his native North Carolina. Kleagle William McDougal sought to revive Klan fortunes later in the year, but was unsuccessful, and very few Gotham Knights remained for the final humiliation of the local organization. In May of 1927, the Klan was granted permission to take part in a Queens County Memorial Day parade to the Soldier's Monument in Jamaica. Protesting KKK participation, the Knights of Columbus and Boy Scouts resigned from the cavalcade, but fourteen hundred Klansmen gathered on schedule on May 30. They brusquely refused the plea of a police inspector not to march, and broke through a police line to the tune of "Onward, Christian Soldiers." Hostile crowds lined the four-mile parade route, and unrestrained by sympathetic police, taunted and jeered the marchers. Several attempts were made to drive automobiles through the Klan column, and the resultant scuffling and fighting developed quickly into a wild melee. As chaos swept through the streets, robes were torn off, and the Knights were forced to abandon their parade.[15]

New York City thus deserved its "un-American" label, but suburbs of the metropolis were more receptive to the Invisible Empire. Immediately to the north, one thousand Yonkers Klansmen were captained by blackjack enthusiast Frederick Storm, and active chapters were established in such Connecticut suburbs as Stamford, Bridgeport, and Greenwich. To the east, as many as a dozen demonstrations took place in a single night in Long Island's Huntington, Manhasset, Port Washington, Roosevelt, Spring Harbor, Valley Stream, Freeport, Bayshore, Lindenhurst, Babylon, Patchogue, and Cedarhurst communities. In 1923, at the Lynbrook Firemen's Tournament the female Klan was chosen as the most popular organization in Nassau County, and at a week-long celebration in Roosevelt, floats, parades, rallies, and carnivals were the order of the day. In 1923, the Klan won elections in Islip, Babylon, Oyster Bay, and Brookhaven, and in 1924, it took temporary control of the Suffolk County Republican Committee. By that time one resident in seven had reportedly sworn allegiance to the Invisible Empire.[16]

New Jersey suburbs of New York City were equally infected with "one hundred per cent Americanism." King Kleagle George W. Apgar established state headquarters just outside Newark in West Hoboken, where the local Knights met at the First Reformed Church. Aided by Don Bates, Apgar installed a half dozen klaverns across the Hudson River from New York City, including Leif Ericson Klan No. 1 in Paterson and an Elizabeth chapter which included "many prominent businessmen."

The first kleagles in Newark were Orville Cheatham, a physician, and Russell F. Trimble, the owner of the American Novelty Glass Works. They set up shop at 837 Broad Street, and staged their first initiation across the street above Stetter's Café on September 20, 1921. Mayor Alexander Archibald caustically refused an early offer of membership; two thousand other residents of the Garden State's largest city thought better of the proposal and formed George Washington Klan No. 3, which was chartered late in 1922. Forty robed Newark members made a welcome appearance at Grace Methodist-Episcopal Church in 1923, and on another occasion local patriots ignited thirteen crosses in a single evening.

The problems of New Jersey Klansmen were myriad. Internal dissension began as early as 1921, when renegade kleagles from Philadelphia and New York City unsuccessfully sought New Jersey support against Atlanta officials. Moreover, anti-Klan violence was a constant threat. In Perth Amboy, where Klansmen concentrated their attacks upon bootlegging, a hostile mob gathered outside a meeting of two hundred Knights on the evening of August 30, 1923. Police and firemen could not control the anti-Klan excitement, and a hail of bricks and stones crashed down upon the besieged Perth Amboy Odd Fellows Hall. The mob of five thousand grew throughout the night; those Klansmen seeking to escape the building were humbled and automobile windshields smashed. Not until dawn were the police able to escort the Klan members to safety.

A somewhat warmer reception awaited New Jersey Klansmen south of the New York City area. Monmouth County and the North Jersey Shore communities of Asbury Park, Long Branch, Lakewood, and Neptune City were bulwarks of the secret order; larger but less influential klaverns were established in New Brunswick, Atlantic City, and Trenton.[17] The most active downstate chapter was located just across the Delaware River from Philadelphia in Camden. Garbed in United States Army uniforms with Klan insignia, the Camden County Rangers patrolled the public highways to prevent parking by lovers and to protect the klavern's occasional outdoor demonstrations.[18]

Southern by tradition and temperament, Washington, D.C., was a locally significant center of the Ku Klux Klan. Henry B. Terrell and S. F. Poindexter established Columbia Klan No. 1 in February 1921, and in six months initiated three hundred members. According to the *Washington Post,* it reached a 1925 peak membership of 15,133, and even held one initiation in the Capitol Building. In addition, chapters were established in suburban Alexandria, Ballston, Arlington, and Bethesda. In 1923 the secret order established its lobbying headquarters at 1723 Rhode Island Avenue, N.W., and in 1925 the national office was moved from Atlanta to Seventh and I Streets in Washington. Moreover, the District of Columbia was the home of the pro-Klan *Fellowship Forum* and the *National Kourier* and was the scene of the most ostentatious demonstration in Klan history: the great Washington Parade of August 1925.[19]

Widely publicized in advance, the Washington demonstration

was designed to counter reports of national Klan weakness. On the eve of the planned celebration *The New York Times* reported that some forty-three chartered trains were converging on the capital, while automobile caravans arrived from every direction. The event attracted contingents from as far away as Georgia, Indiana, and Kentucky, but the greatest number of arrivals hailed from nearby Pennsylvania, New Jersey, and Virginia.

Over the protests of Catholic, Jewish, and Negro organizations, the parade moved down Pennsylvania Avenue on the afternoon of August 8, 1925. It took about three hours and forty minutes for some forty thousand robed Klansmen to move past the reviewing stand. Grouped according to states, the Knights marched sixteen abreast without masks. Journalist Dixon Merritt described the magnitude of the demonstration:

> I did not see the parade of veterans of the Union armies which swung down Pennsylvania Avenue in the spring of 1865. I did see the parade at the beginning of the World War, and I saw the one at its end. I have seen every big parade since. I think I know that there were more people in the Ku Klux Klan Parade than in any other that I have ever seen in Washington or anywhere else.[20]

The Washington Parade was the greatest public demonstration in the history of the Klan, but it failed to buoy the fortunes of Columbia Klan No. 1, which ceased to function in 1928.

Fifty miles to the north lay bustling Baltimore, a former Know-Nothing citadel where Henry P. Moorehead rented a Klan office early in 1921. A Baltimore speech by Imperial Kleagle Clark on November 16 stimulated the recruitment drive, and in February 1922 the local groups received a charter as Thomas Dixon Klan No. 1. Led by the Reverend James W. Ford, the secret order bought an old Presbyterian church at Madison Avenue and Biddle Street for conversion into a klavern hall. The move was completed in early December, and in celebration, Baltimore Klansmen threw open their doors to the public for a bazaar designed to raise ten thousand dollars for a building fund. Featuring game booths, oyster suppers, and twenty-minute lectures on the principles of "one hundred per cent Americanism," the celebration closed with a song fest by the daughters of Klansmen. In 1923 the Klan presented a charity circus in Hazazer's Hall and publicized its endorsement of Protestantism. Visits were made to the United Brethren Church and the Roland Avenue Methodist Church; at the latter edifice the pastor accepted a check for twenty-five dollars and declared, "I, for one, am glad to get it." [21] So encouraging did Klan prospects appear that Frank Beall resigned as Baltimore's chief highway inspector in order to succeed J. H. Hawkins as Maryland Grand Dragon. Shortly after taking office he announced that there were seventy-two Klans in Maryland with an aggregate membership of thirty-three thousand.

The success of Baltimore's Klan No. 1 did not long continue. In February 1923 an attempt was made to burn the Thomas Dixon klavern, and the following month a Klan assembly at suburban Brooklyn First Baptist Church was almost broken up by an angry mob. Governor A. C. Ritchie campaigned against the Invisible Empire in 1924 and was rewarded with re-election. The final blow was struck by Grand Dragon Frank Beall, who resigned in 1926 and denounced the secret order as "shamefully crooked" and "shockingly immoral."

In the summer of 1921, when the Propagation Department had seventeen recruiters in Texas and seven in New York, there was but one kleagle in all of New England. The Invisible Empire increased the number of solicitors in the region the following year and gained a small but persistent following. To some extent its growth was hampered by the fear of Yankee Protestants that the Klan issue might drive traditionally Republican French-Canadians and Italians into the Irish-Democratic fold.

Never strong in Vermont, New Hampshire, or Rhode Island, the Invisible Empire won moderate success in Connecticut and Massachusetts.[22] In New Haven were the headquarters of King Kleagle (state recruiting director) Earl J. Major, the home of Exalted Cyclops Arthur Mann, and the largest klavern in Connecticut. Chapters also prospered in the New Britain–Hartford area and in the

New York City suburbs of Greenwich, Bridgeport, and Stamford. Massachusetts klankraft was probably strongest in Worcester, but the excitement was all in Boston.

Grand Goblin A. J. Padon, Jr. erred in establishing the head-quarters for the Domain of New England within the domain of Boston Mayor James Michael Curley. After one thousand Boston-area Knights met with Lothrop Stoddard and William J. Mahoney in the North Cambridge Odd Fellows Hall on October 3, 1922, Hub reaction was immediate. The *Boston Telegram* and *Boston Advertiser* editorially attacked the Invisible Empire, the homes of suspected Cambridge Klansmen were showered with bricks, the Boston City Council adopted an anti-Klan resolution, and Jewish and Catholic leaders declared war upon Kluxism. Mayor Curley craftily took full advantage of the situation. Seizing upon the issue of "one hundred per cent Americanism," he barred Boston Klan meetings, even on private property, while ordering his lieutenants to burn a clearly visible cross before political rallies. In an emotion-filled voice, Curley would then point to the symbol and shout to his partisans: "There it burns, the cross of hatred upon which Our Lord, Jesus Christ, was crucified—the cross of human avarice, and not the cross of love and charity. . . ." [23]

Fortunately for the grand goblin, Maine was beyond the oratori-cal and political reach of Mayor Curley. Eugene Farnsworth colo-nized the Pine Tree state from Portland, where the Klan eventually claimed control of fourteen thousand out of twenty-three thousand votes and an enrollment of no fewer than twenty-seven hundred members. The secret order was a temporary force in municipal reform and supported Portland's shift to the council-manager form of government. Moreover, the Invisible Empire gained prestige by attaching its political fortunes to ambitious Ralph Owen Brewster, an old-line Yankee Protestant who never actually joined the Klan. The alliance was based upon common opposition to the Bishop of Portland's plea for local aid to parochial schools. When Brewster entered the 1924 Republican gubernatorial primary against the president of the state senate, the two main issues were the Klan and public support for Catholic education. Brewster won after a re-

count, but the issue of "invisible government" cropped up again in
the general election. National anti-Klan Democrats paraded in and
out of the state to speak for Democratic nominee William Patten-
gall, and the state's top Negro leader turned against the Republicans. But Brewster won easily, and Grand Dragon Farnsworth's earlier statement that he would pick Maine's next governor was given
some credence.

Aside from politics, the outstanding achievement of the Maine
Klan was the erection of a mammoth klavern in Portland in 1923.
Located on an eight-acre site on Forrest Road, the structure included a four-thousand seat auditorium, a 165-by-60-foot banquet
hall, several small meeting rooms, and office space for the entire
realm staff. It allowed the state and local organizations to abandon
their earlier reliance upon rented fraternal halls and to become one
of the best-housed realms in the nation. Apparently overawed by
the local Klan's physical and political successes, the Reverend C. H.
Marvin of Portland's Church of the Messiah, Universalist, affirmed,
"The Knights of the Ku Klux Klan has achieved the distinction of
being the greatest secret order in America."

The accomplishment of the Invisible Empire in Portland was not
characteristic of the urban Northeast, however. In most of the region's large cities, the Klan was unable to convert its substantial
membership into the type of political and economic influence enjoyed by urban Knights in the Midwest, South, and Far West,
where fundamentalist Protestantism remained the dominant ethic.
The Northeast was the most populous, the most urban, and the
most heavily Catholic, immigrant, and Jewish of American sections.
In Buffalo and Pittsburgh, Boston and New York, for example, eligible "one hundred per cent Americans" were proportionately much
less numerous than in Dallas or Indianapolis or Portland or even
Detroit. Moreover, Protestants on the eastern seaboard tended to
be more sophisticated and liberal in outlook than the militant Fundamentalists of other regions who provided most of the Klan's
members.

But the Klan was a persistent force along the Atlantic coast, and
long after the secret order had disintegrated elsewhere it retained

devotees in the Northeast. As Imperial Wizard Evans noted in 1928: "there is not a single Eastern state where we have not a strong and effective membership; Pennsylvania and New York are perhaps the strongest, with New Jersey close behind." [24] Concerned over the threat of Catholic and immigrant domination, they had taken to heart the admonition of their national leader:

> If we love our country, if we revere our ancestors, if we honor the founder of the nation; if we believe in its principles, take pride in its traditions, approve its customs and have faith in the Divine Purpose of its institutions, then we must fight. We must struggle against the alien as we would struggle against any other invader, for they are the most dangerous of all invaders.[25]

IV

THE WEST

The most dangerous weakness in a democracy is the uninformed and unthinking average man.

John Moffatt Mecklin

Just where the West begins is difficult to determine. The Ku Klux Klan regarded the Rocky Mountains as an acceptable dividing line and organized and reorganized the region under such titles as the Western Domain, the Pacific Northwestern Domain, the Domain of the Pacific Coast, and the Domain of the Northwest.

Throughout most of this area the Invisible Empire was weak. In 1922, at the Klan's first national klonvokation, the imperial kligrapp (secretary) reported that 5.1 per cent of the total membership resided in the seven chartered realms of the Far West: Colorado, Wyoming, Utah, Idaho, Washington, Oregon, and California. By 1924 the figure had risen only to 6.1 per cent. Utah, Wyoming, and New Mexico were scarcely touched by the secret order, and the organizations in Nevada, where the Reno klavern boasted of eighteen hundred members, and Montana, where the Billings and Butte chapters were the state's largest, were similarly ineffective. In Idaho, the Boise klavern won the first charter, but the Potato state's two kleagles could generate very little monetary enthusiasm for the Klan. Hooded Americanism fared somewhat better in dry and isolated Arizona, where the only significant chapters were those of Phoenix: Kamelback Klan No. 6 and Klan No. 22. The city was the

home of Grand Dragon McCord Harrison and of more than one
third of the state enrollment, and it was the seat of publication of
Arizona Klankraft. Organized initially by Jack Strutz, the Kamelback chapter claimed the publisher of the *Phoenix Gazette*, Tom
Akers, as its exalted cyclops and local politicians, state officials, and
the managers of the telephone and telegraph companies among its
members. On occasion, capital city Knights tended toward reck-
lessness. A group of members abducted a Phoenix schoolmaster,
whom they charged with immorality, branded his face with car-
bolic acid, and whipped him. Governor George Hunt personally
intervened to secure passage of an anti-Klan law which prohibited
public meetings of masked men and increased the penalties for
hooded violence. In addition, he told the press that he had a partial
list of 892 Arizona Klansmen. Thereafter, those Phoenix members
who did not resign in fright held their Monday night meetings quietly and without fanfare.

But weakness was not the universal characteristic of the Domain
of the West. In Oregon, the Klan was instrumental in passing the
only compulsory public education law in American history; in Colorado, it gained control of the statehouse and almost absorbed the
Republican party; in California, it initiated two thousand persons
in a single evening and participated in a murder case that assumed
national proportions.

In many respects, the Far West was quite unlike the rest of the
country. Large stretches of land were virtually unoccupied; towns
were few and cities fewer. In no western state did Negroes, Catholics, or Jews constitute more than 10 per cent of the populace, and
in most, Mexicans and Orientals represented the most serious minority problem. In the West, as elsewhere, however, the key to
Klan success lay in the peculiar problems and tensions of daily life
in the city. Los Angeles, San Francisco, Seattle, Denver, and Portland were the region's five largest cities; each was visited by kleagles in 1921, and all but San Francisco returned a verdict at least
temporarily favorable to "one hundred per cent Americanism."

13

The Golden State and Beyond

On the evening of April 22, 1922, thirty-seven Klansmen gathered quietly in a wooded glade in Inglewood, California. Their purpose was to raid the suburban Los Angeles home of a Spanish-Mexican family named Elduayen, where an illicit winery was supposedly in operation. Crossing Pine Street under cover of darkness, they surrounded the premises, captured Fidel and Matias Elduayen, and confiscated a flask of liquor. After proceeding to Inglewood and Redondo, where they were unable to find a co-operative jailer, the Klansmen released their prisoners and allowed them to return home.[1]

Back at the winery, the situation was less placid. While some of the group were in the house arresting the Elduayens, a night marshal from Inglewood, who had been told of masked figures surrounding a house, arrived on a commandeered motorcycle. Several hooded raiders blocked the road; the marshal identified himself and demanded that the sentries surrender. A gun battle ensued, and three vigilantes were injured, one of them fatally. The dead Klansman was Marion B. (Med) Mosher, a constable of Inglewood Township; his wounded comrades included his son and a deputy sheriff. The coroner found that Mosher was killed "while acting as a member of an illegal masked and armed mob, personally instigated and directed by members of the Ku Klux Klan." Subsequently, the Los Angeles County Grand Jury returned indictments on five counts of felony against all thirty-seven members of the troupe, including Grand Goblin William S. Coburn, King Kleagle Gus W. Price, and Kleagle Nathan A. Baker.[2]

Well-publicized throughout the nation, the trial began on August 7, 1922. To counter the impressive evidence of the prosecution, the defense argued that the Elduayen home was a haven for bootleggers, that the organization of the raid and its execution were legal in form and substance according to the manner of a *posse comitatus*, and that the Klansmen were patriotic Americans risking martyrdom to teach foreigners respect for the law. Success went to such logic. The presiding judge, who had opposed the investigation from the beginning, told the jury to find the defendants innocent if they had been led by a police officer in search of lawbreakers. All thirty-seven defendants were acquitted.

Despite courtroom vindication, the Inglewood raid threatened to negate the hard-won gains of the Klan along the entire Pacific Coast. In March 1921, Grand Goblin Coburn had opened a three-man office in the Haas Building in Los Angeles, kicking off a drive to add the western United States to the dominion of the Invisible Empire. Responsible for California, Washington, Oregon, Idaho, and Nevada, Coburn's kleagles gave greatest emphasis to the Golden State. In San Francisco, Dr. John B. Eckes served as exalted cyclops of a klavern which met every Thursday night in the Pacific Building. In Oakland, the seventeen-hundred-member chapter held large initiations in a secluded glade in the Contra Costa Hills; in Fresno, Dr. L. F. Luckie led Klan meetings in the municipal auditorium; in Kern County and the Imperial Valley, Homer Pitts, who had once been incriminated in a masked flogging in Atlanta, set up at least a half dozen separate chapters. Kleagles Edgar I. Fuller and B. R. Hodes Took set up a province office in Sacramento, and by mid-1922 the secret order was organized and active in the state capital. The most consistent and verbose Sacramento adherents were the Reverend William E. Harrison of Westminister Presbyterian Church and the Reverend W. A. Redburn of Wesley Methodist Church, both of whom were obsessed with the Catholic peril. Redburn was particularly vitriolic, charging that "nearly all the bawdy houses, bootleg joints, and other dives are owned or controlled by Romanists," and suggesting that convents were places where beautiful women were kept behind bars for questionable purposes.[3]

The Klan was also active in the state's southernmost city, San Diego, where Exalted Cyclops L. E. French and seventy-five associates received a provisional charter on October 1, 1921. Initially they were selective in their membership policy and denied the applications of a bootlegger and other undesirables. But San Diego Klansmen were victimized by a young kleagle who absconded with the accumulated collection from Klan headquarters in the Spreckels Building and drove across the border into Mexico. Disillusioned Klansmen then began to regard state officials in Los Angeles as the source of their difficulty. According to the San Diego chapter treasurer, "All we could get out of Los Angeles was a call for reports, which meant money." At a special meeting on February 21, 1922, the San Diego Klan "adjourned indefinitely" and did not resume its regular meetings at the auditorium for six months.

The true strength of the California Klan lay in the Los Angeles area, where Kleagle Nathan A. Baker took advantage of rumored moral decay, a 100 per cent increase in Negroes and Orientals in a single decade, and the increasing power of the Catholic Church.[4] A native of Colorado, a resident of Maywood, and a deputy sheriff of Los Angeles County, Baker personally contacted scores of consequential citizens in the spring of 1921, and within twelve months the Los Angeles Klan was holding big initiations in Wanda Park near Beverly Hills and in Santa Monica Canyon, and meeting every Wednesday in a hall at Slauson and Moneta Avenues. On several occasions, the Los Angeles Klan gathered under the title of Mounted Rifles at the National Guard Armory of the One Hundred and Sixth Infantry Regiment. In addition to three klaverns in Los Angeles proper, suburban chapters were organized in Wilder, Santa Monica, Huntington Park, Redondo, Hermosa, Long Beach, Glendale,

San Pedro, and Anaheim, and prospects were so encouraging that the *Searchlight* reported on March 4, 1922, that "every city on the coast will have a branch of the Klan in the near future."

The Inglewood raid altered this prophecy. In connection with the investigation by the Los Angeles County grand jury, District Attorney Thomas Lee Woolwine raided Klan headquarters in the Haas Building. Grand Goblin Coburn was taken by surprise. Asking to retrieve his coat from an inner office, he slammed and locked the door, and jammed several membership lists into a hastily addressed envelope. Reopening the door, he raced past the startled district attorney and slipped the envelope into the mail chute. The surprised officers confiscated the remaining files and records and subjected them to close scrutiny. Other Klan secrets came from C. R. Isham, personal secretary to Coburn.

District Attorney Woolwine refused the repeated pleas of King Kleagle Price to return the records and in fact decided to make them public. The revelations were startling. The chief of police and police judge in Bakersfield, seven policemen in Fresno, eighty-one federal employees and twenty-five policemen in San Francisco, and roughly 10 per cent of the public officials and policemen in practically every California city were identified as members of the Invisible Empire. From throughout the state district attorneys hurried to Woolwine's office to peruse the captured membership lists for their counties. In Los Angeles alone, fifteen hundred persons, including United States Attorney Joseph Burke, Chief of Police Louis D. Oaks, and Sheriff William I. Traeger, were named as Klansmen.[5]

Reaction to the daily headlines was swift. One hundred and thirty members of the Ventura Klan resigned as a body and advised others to do the same. In Los Angeles, the Ministerial Union, the Church Federation, the American Legion, and the Spanish-American War Veterans denounced the secret order, and the Eagles and Knights of Pythias denied their halls to Klan meetings. Several large corporations asked to examine the files with the intent of giving employees the choice of resigning from the company or the Klan. The Los Angeles City Council passed a strong anti-mask ordinance, and the city and county governments resolved not to hire Klansmen. In Fresno, seven policemen were dismissed from the force because of Klan affiliation, and in the oil town of Taft, the five Klan members on the board of trustees were removed from office by a newspaper-led recall election. Governor William Stephens ordered state employees and national guardsmen to choose between the state and the Invisible Empire. Elks lodges throughout the state adopted resolutions against the hooded order, and the grand master of California Masons advised his subordinates against becoming Klansmen. A distressed Imperial Palace in Atlanta revoked the commissions of all nineteen kleagles in the state and removed Coburn as grand goblin.

The road to recovery was arduous, and in most parts of California, the Klan never retrieved its earlier momentum. But in Los Angeles the secret order survived the Inglewood fiasco and remained active for at least two more years. In large part this was due to the efforts of the Reverend Robert Shuler, pastor of Trinity Methodist Church and editor of pro-Klan *Shuler's Magazine.* Speaking throughout southern California and as far north as San Francisco, Mr. Shuler professed "to love the Klan for the enemies she has made," and he offered the opinion that "good men everywhere are coming to understand that the Klan is dangerous only to the lawless and un-American elements within any midst." Additional kudos were offered by Pasadena's L. E. Burger, who labeled the Invisible Empire "the most grossly misrepresented organization in America." [6]

Encouraged by such support, the southern California Klan survived the abortive attempt of Forest L. Hudson to form a rival Klan organization and later pressured the national office into reinstating King Kleagle Gus W. Price. In 1922 after its Los Angeles headquarters had been transferred to the Walker Auditorium, the secret order helped Friend W. Richardson win the governor's race over Lee Woolwine, the hated Los Angeles district attorney who had denounced the Klan as "an un-American band of hooded cowards and outlaws." In celebration, in November 1922, the Los Angeles Klan held its first large post-Inglewood initiation, and in the next eighteen months met frequently at huge outdoor rallies at Ocean Park and Ocean Park Heights. It reportedly initiated the largest group in southern California history in January 1924, and demonstrated five thousand strong on "Wobbly Hill" in Los Angeles against the International Workers of the World in March.[7]

One of the most controversial metropolitan area klaverns was that of Anaheim, a rapidly growing Orange County suburban community of twelve thousand in 1925. It was led by the Reverend Leon L. Myers, an outspoken anti-Catholic only recently arrived as pastor of the First Christian Church. Twelve hundred persons heeded his call and took an oath of allegiance to the Invisible Empire. By late fall in 1924 AKIA (A Klansman I Am) and KIGY (Klansman, I Greet You) signs were plastered on Anaheim service stations, garages, and hotdog stands; and widely circulated handbills told of regular anti-papal lectures. Supported by the *Orange County Plain Dealer*, the Klan-dominated congregation at the White Temple sought repeatedly to remove the Reverend James Allen Gerssinger, a "pacifist," from his pulpit. The acme of Anaheim success was reached in 1924, when four Klansmen, including Mayor E. H. Metcalf, were elected to the five-member city council.[8]

Unsettled by such evidence of Klan contamination and fearful that Anaheim would become a joke in southern California, a number of local businessmen formed the USA Club to fight "one hundred per cent Americanism." Pointing to the "Detour Anaheim" signs often encountered in Los Angeles garages, they argued that building operations were being held in abeyance and that industrial plant negotiations were broken off because theirs was a Klan-ridden town. With strong support from the *Anaheim Gazette*, the USA Club forced a recall election against Mayor Metcalf and Councilmen Slaback, Knipe, and Hasson. The Invisible Empire countered by similarly seeking the recall of G. J. Stock, the only non-Klan councilman.

The campaign was predictably acerbic. Convening in the evangelistic tent of the Reverend E. J. Bulgin, the Klan candidates tagged themselves the "law enforcement" or "dry" ticket. The *Ana-*

heim Bulletin promptly retorted that the members of both tickets were dry, and that the real issue was not law enforcement but "SHALL OUR CITY AFFAIRS GO UNDER THE CONTROL OF THE KLAN." [9] The secret order remained confident of success, and planned a victory parade after the election. But the vote on February 3, 1925, was 2043 to 1630 in favor of recall, and all four Klansmen were vanquished. Exultant that "hate, distrust, and suspicion" were rejected, the *Anaheim Gazette* reflected upon the flight of Exalted Cyclops Myers:

> He came to Anaheim and found a verdant pasture on which to feed. He found many here, as he would in any community, discontented and susceptible, who fell easy victims to his oily tongue. He exchanged his sacramental cloth for a Ku Klux robe, and preached Klanism from his pulpit. He alienated a large portion of his congregation. . . . He wrecked his church, and made a desperate attempt to junk the city, but was decisively checkmated by the people Tuesday.[10]

Other area klaverns met similar if less spectacular fates, and most were plagued by internal dissension that often wound up in the courts. By 1926 the secret order had all but vanished from southern California. In 1939, a Los Angeles Klan renascence was undertaken by Grand Dragon C. Earl Snelson, who announced that henceforth the Invisible Empire would be primarily concerned with law enforcement and opposition to "the domination of racketeers." [11] More puissant appeals were apparently necessary because fewer than one hundred persons answered the call. Disenchanted by his incessant failure to arouse local patriotism, Snelson resigned after eighteen months in favor of G. W. Price, who rented a propagation office in the Financial Center Building and arranged for klavern meetings. His brief experiment was cut short by the war, however, and the California Klan passed once again into history.[12]

The Invisible Empire was more influential in Washington than in the Golden State. Seattle was the heart and headquarters of the realm, and the home of its largest chapter, but Walla Walla and Tacoma were also noted for huge klaverns, as was Spokane, where the Reverend C. A. Rexroad served as exalted cyclops at Klan No. 2's Thursday night meetings in the Hyde Building.[13]

A king kleagle in the Invisible Empire and a former major in the United States Army, Luther Ivan Powell was the key figure in Washington klankraft. Frequently utilizing the propaganda film *The Face At Your Window,* he was an imaginative recruiter. He invited seamen from visiting Navy vessels to attend chapter meetings in Seattle, and he even established a one-hundred man klavern aboard the battleship *U.S.S. Tennessee* anchored in Puget Sound. His sixth-floor office in Seattle's Securities Building served as the local center for the Women's Klan, the Royal Riders of the Red Robe, and Seattle Klan No. 4, as state command post for the realm of Washington and Idaho, and as national headquarters of the Junior Order of the Ku Klux Klan. Powell wrote a public pamphlet disavowing violence and initiated publication on June 20, 1923, of *The Watcher of the Tower,*[14] an anti-Catholic weekly which took "The Klan, The Konstitution, and The Kross" as its first-page motto. It offered free subscriptions "to every Protestant minister, who is interested in the Knights of the Ku Klux Klan and who wishes to keep in touch with the work which the order is doing." It also offered an answer to William Randolph Hearst's anti-Klan *Seattle Post-Intelligencer.*

Presided over by Exalted Cyclops John A. Jeffrey and Kligrapp William C. Ott, Seattle Klansmen kept pace with the aspirations of Major Powell.[15] When their number reached two thousand late in 1922, they received a charter as Seattle Klan No. 4. They visited local churches, donated two hundred dollars to the Japanese Relief Fund, and caucused so often at the Palm Cafe on Westlake Avenue that it became known as "The Klansmen's Roost." Regular meetings were usually held in the Moose Hall or Carpenter's Hall, but growing membership prompted building plans for "a combined auditorium, Klub Room, and Klan headquarters." Outdoor initiations were held in a fifty-acre meadow near O'Brien's Station or on the broad plains near Issaquah, where one of the first loudspeaker systems in Washington was set up for a "patriotic address" by the imperial lecturer of the Pacific Northwest Domain. At an alfresco

initiation near O'Brien on July 14, 1923, Kluxism reached its crest in
Seattle. Following an initiation, speech, and barbecue dinner, fifty
thousand persons watched exploding star shells form three K's in
the sky. Included in the throng were foreign-born Royal Riders of
the Red Robe, who met weekly under J. Arthur Herndon, Walter J.
Fowler, and Dr. M. W. Rose at the Swedish Hall. The RRRR,
which was particularly active in Portland, Seattle, and Denver, was
a Klan affiliate for those white Protestants not born in the United
States. Its members wore crimson rather than white and offered "a
real patriotic organization to all Canadians, Englishmen, and other
White, Gentile, Protestants."

The prime indicant of Seattle Klan deterioration came in October
of 1923, when King Kleagle Powell left the city and *The Watcher
on the Tower* ceased publication. In the ensuing fourteen months
the secret order suffered several critical reverses. On November 4,
1924, Initiative Measure 49, a controversial Klan-supported proposal to abolish private and parochial secondary schools failed
51,816 to 26,868 in the city and 176,980 to 118,936 in the state.[16]
Two weeks later an internal revolt broke into the open. Protesting
against "tyranny, despotism and autocracy," eight ranking officers
of Seattle Klan No. 4 announced that "Atlanta is bleeding the Klans
of the country," and submitted resignations to Grand Dragon O. H.
Carpenter. They asserted that the national tax amounted to thirteen thousand dollars in a single year, and revealed that Klan No. 4
had only $299.96 in its treasury. Eleven additional objections were
listed by the insurgents including "the abominable system of
Kleagle propagation," and "the Klan form of government by ap-
pointee officers." Ignoring an attempt by Imperial Wizard Evans to
shift local attention to motherhood and the Catholic Church, hundreds of Seattle Klansmen met in Carpenter's Hall on November
17, 1924, and formed officially the International Klan of America.
Other local Knights simply turned their backs on the controversy
and allowed the Klan to die a quick death in their city. But even at
its peak Seattle Klan No. 4 never rivaled in power and influence the
star klaverns of the West in Portland and Denver.

14

Portland: Headquarters of the Realm

Bragg Calloway stepped from a passenger train in Portland on June 12, 1921. The trip from Houston had been tedious but at least offered the opportunity to contemplate quietly the advantages of his new assignment. Old as west coast cities go, Portland was a conservative and prim scion of the Maine city from which it took its name. Calloway was aware that the Oregon metropolis lacked some of the aggressive spirit of Seattle, the cosmopolitan atmosphere of San Francisco, or the youthful exuberance of Los Angeles, but he knew also that its 258,000 citizens were overwhelmingly white and Protestant, with just enough Catholics, Negroes, Jews, and Orientals to excite patriotic fervor and nativistic intolerance.[1]

But Kleagle Calloway fumbled his opportunity in the favorable Portland environment. After acquiring spacious quarters in the Multnomah Hotel, he then disobeyed instructions from Atlanta by disclosing his recruitment intentions to the daily press. Reaction from the Imperial Palace was swift, and Calloway's tenure in Oregon came to an abrupt halt.

Only two weeks elapsed before Portland had a new champion of the Klan. Major Luther I. Powell, a native of Shreveport, Louisiana, had spent the early months of 1921 canvassing for initiates in such southern Oregon towns as Medford, Klamath Falls, and Rose-burg.[2] He organized the first klavern in Medford, and within a month several local outrages were reported involving a half-dozen Klansmen. Violence notwithstanding, the mayor joined the secret order and the Medford *Clarion* referred to the Invisible Empire as "the very antithesis of lawlessness." But like most enterprising kleagles, Powell soon discovered that intolerance could be peddled with greater lucre in the cities. By July 1, he had become a resident of Portland's Multnomah Hotel and was busily dredging up frater-nal, civic, and social membership lists.

Unlike his predecessor in the Oregon metropolis, Kleagle Powell carefully avoided publicity. Accordingly, when the New York *World* telegraphed Governor Ben Olcott asking for his impression of the Invisible Empire, the chief executive replied on September 22, 1921:

> Because of wholesome conditions in Oregon, with little discon-tent and a satisfied people, the Ku Klux Klan, although endeavor-ing to invade the state, has made little or no progress and I am informed it is now folding its tent like the Arab and as silently stealing away. The Klan has been taken lightly here, and because of the fact that it has made practically no impression on our peo-ple or our institutions, the executive office of this state has deemed action or any particular comment unnecessary.[3]

Even as Governor Olcott dictated his reply, however, the Invis-ible Empire was daily bulking larger in Portland. A "Fiery Sum-mons" had been dispatched to everyone on Powell's comprehensive mailing list, and a small cadre of enthusiastic Knights supported the recruiting drive with personal solicitation. By October there were enough respondents to call the first official meeting. Bedecked in the robes of a king kleagle and standing by the door of the Woodmen of the World Hall, Major Powell congratulated the initi-ates while an organist played softly "Are You Going To Leave the Old Homestead, Jim, Today?" Within four months the chapter was chartered as Luther I. Powell Klan No. 1.

The first assemblage of Portland Klansmen also provided the oc-casion for the introduction to hooded service of Fred L. Gifford,

who was destined to become the paramount Klan figure in the
Domain of the Pacific Coast. Of iron-grey hair and average build,
Gifford was a native Minnesotan who had spent thirty of his forty
years in Portland, mostly as a telegraph operator for the Southern
Pacific Railroad and as a business agent for the Electrical Workers Union. The father of four was working as a field superintendent
for the Northwestern Electric Company for two hundred and fifty
dollars a month when Powell tapped him as first exalted cyclops of
Klan No. 1. Gifford's carefully chosen subordinates included W. D.
"Ole" Quinn and C. W. Hurd, both employees of the Pacific Telephone and Telegraph Company, and Kligrapp Frank Parker, a former Catholic turned militant Protestant.[4]

Operating unobtrusively for several months, the Invisible Empire
quite suddenly became a much-discussed Portland institution on
December 22, 1921. The catalyst was a public declamation on "The
Truth About the Ku Klux Klan" before six thousand persons at the
municipal auditorium. Supplementing his oratory with the propaganda film, *The Face at Your Window*, the Reverend Reuben H.
Sawyer of the East Side Christian Church told the hushed audience
that the Klan had come to Portland, "not simply for a brief visit,
but to be enrolled among the permanent organizations of your city."
He predicted that the day would come "when the world will recognize and acknowledge that it was a most distinguished honor to
have occupied even the humblest position under such a leader as
ours, and in such an organization as that represented by these
thousands of Portland's best citizens." [5]

In the spring of 1922, Klan lectures in the five-thousand-seat auditorium became so popular that overflow crowds posed a serious
civic problem. On May 9 more than fifteen hundred persons had to
be turned away when Sawyer delivered the first of two preach-
ments on "Almighty God's Most Potent Force." Robed Klansmen
were at the doors and in the aisles, and on the stage a team of
hooded Knights presented a series of drills and tableaux.

The auditorium was also oversold for a Klan gathering on the
evening of May 10, 1922. Unable to gain admittance to the building, more than a thousand persons surged up and down Third

Street, and eighty-three policemen and fourteen deputy sheriffs were required to restore order. An outraged Catholic delegation officially protested further Klan use of public facilities, but Mayor George Baker, who was himself rumored to be a Klansman, refused to take any action:

> You have said there are 8000 or 10,000 members here in Portland. Do you think you can suppress that kind of an organization with a handful of policemen? To attempt such suppression would only stir up riots worse than anything this town has ever known before.[6]

While Sawyer's vainglorious speeches convinced many that the Invisible Empire was a decent, law-abiding fraternal order, the secret organization launched a full-scale campaign to improve its image. Fifty thousand dollars was pledged to the Women's Christian Temperance Union's Children's Farm Home, baskets of food were distributed individually to the needy, and a Klan Kommunity Kit was organized. (The Community Chest contributed to Catholic and Jewish charities.) The secret order also sponsored a Christmas Eve party in the municipal auditorium, where Kris Kringle exhibited a "vast cargo of gifts for all." Neither was Protestantism neglected; no fewer than eighteen churches were visited on a single Sunday in May 1922. At one church, the congregation cheered when three robed Klansmen left a fifty dollar "token of appreciation" with evangelist John Wood Anderson. In order that Portlanders not confuse local Knights with Klansmen who were reportedly engaging in acts of violence elsewhere in the country, Powell, Sawyer, and R. H. Davis arranged for the publication of an "open letter" to Oregon Klansmen. They emphasized "our solemn obligation to support the constitution and all constitutional laws. Above all things also, we believe in law and order, and this outstanding fact must be impressed upon the minds of the public."

The eminent success of the public relations campaign was signaled by crosses which glared nightly from Mt. Tabor and Mt. Scott and by automobile kavelkades which periodically clogged Portland streets. At his Blue Mouse Theater, "100% John Hammrick" booked *The Birth of a Nation* for a return engagement, and "100% Berry" compiled a "100% Directory" which purported to list those firms that either promoted or sympathized with the Invisible Empire.[7] By the summer of 1922, Portland membership exceeded ten thousand and accounted for well over half the Oregon total, although new chapters were planted in Corvallis, Pendleton, Salem, Eugene, Myrtle Creek, Astoria, Lebanon, Marshfield, and Roseburg.[8] State headquarters were established in Portland at 453 Pittock Block, and plans were announced for a downtown ten-story office building. Free Klan lectures were sponsored at the Couch School and Tenwillinger School in February 1923, and handbills invited all good citizens who wished to know the truth about the Klan and "one hundred per cent Americanism" to attend. At such meetings and at special klonvokations, Klan speakers hammered at the numerous problems facing "real Americanism." Three were singled out for special attention: (1) opposition to control of public affairs by aliens of any kind, (2) opposition to alien land ownership, and (3) establishment of genuine compulsory education.[9]

As the affluence and influence of Klan No. 1 rose, Fred L. Gifford moved up to be Oregon grand dragon. His replacement as exalted cyclops was the Reverend James R. Johnson, a spry widower of sixty who worked as a carpenter during the week and preached on the Sabbath to congregations that could not support a full-time pastor. An intense believer, Johnson counseled each Klansman "to shape and mould his life and character like the life and character of Christ" and to remember "that no good deed will ever be overlooked." But he also won fame for the frequency and belligerence of his attacks upon the Roman Church, typical of which was a boast at suburban Oak Grove Community Church: "I warn the Catholic Church now, keep your dirty hands off the public schools."

That the elected head of the Portland Klan should be primarily noted for his anti-Catholicism was no accident. Negroes, comprising less than one per cent of the population and increasing by only five hundred between 1910 and 1920, scarcely constituted a threat. Portland's twelve thousand Jews were also of little concern, and Gifford even sought to muzzle anti-Semitic speeches by Klansmen.

The foreign-born, particularly Orientals, suffered more noticeably; prejudice against the Japanese led in 1923 to an American Legion–sponsored, anti-alien land ownership bill. As Grand Dragon Gifford remarked in Atlanta:

> The Klan in the western states has a great mission to perform. The rapid growth of the Japanese population and the great influx of foreign laborers, mostly Greeks, is threatening our American institutions, and Klans in Washington, Oregon, and Idaho are actively at work to combat these foreign and un-American influences.[10]

The Catholic Church remained the primary antagonist, however. As Professor Mecklin has noted, anti-Catholicism was part of the intellectual baggage of migrants from the great central Mississippi Valley and was responsible for the strength of the American Protective Association in Portland in the 1890's. Moreover, the small Oregon Catholic Church had prospered, and by 1926 the number of Portland parishioners exceeded twenty-seven thousand.[11] During the era of "normalcy," Sister Lucretia, an "escaped nun," and V. K. ("Bearcat") Allison, an "escaped priest," were popular visitors in the city; and the Portland exalted cyclops once remarked that "the only way to cure a Catholic is to kill him." Especially vitriolic was Klan lecturer Paul Packard, who declared at the tabernacle at Alberta and Mallory in 1923:

> Will Al Smith be elected to the presidency? As one American I stand before you to contend that we have enough real red-blooded Protestant American citizens to swear with our hand raised to heaven that we will float our horses in blood to their bridles before we will see a Roman Catholic sitting in our presidential chair.[12]

Fortunately, neither Al Smith nor the Pope sought election in Oregon, but candidates almost equally pernicious were involved in the May 1922 primary. The central contest, the Republican gubernatorial primary, pitted Governor Ben Olcott against Senator Patterson and Charles Hall, a telephone executive in Marshfield and a former president of the Oregon Chamber of Commerce. Klan support went to Hall, who stressed a program calling for compulsory attendance of all children in public schools. Prior to the Klan endorsement, Hall had been expected to run third behind Governor Olcott and Senator Patterson.

Welcoming the rebuff of the Invisible Empire, Governor Olcott issued an official proclamation five days prior to the election:

> Dangerous forces are insidiously gaining a foothold in Oregon. In the guise of a secret society, parading under the name of the Ku Klux Klan, these forces are endeavoring to usurp the reign of government, are stirring up fanaticism, race hatred, religious prejudice, and all of those evil influences which tend toward factional strife and civil terror. Assaults have been committed in various counties of the state by unknown, masked outlaws, the odium of which has reflected on the Ku Klux Klan.[13]

Exalted Cyclops J. R. Johnson immediately issued a public rejoinder and accused the governor of introducing racial and religious prejudice into the campaign. The Klan leader stated certain "generally recognized facts":

> 1. The United States was founded by Protestants of the white race, mainly Anglo-Saxons.
> 2. Every race predominantly Protestant has been and is a progressive free people. Where such predominance does not prevail there is a conspicuous absence of progress and freedom.
> 3. The Klan presupposes its right to establish and carry on an organization exclusively American, whose members are pledged and dedicated to a defense of the principles and ideals of American liberty and justice.

While Governor Olcott was the prime object of Klan concern on May 19, Republican Congressman C. N. McArthur and three Portland public service commissioners were also listed for oblivion. Moreover, the secret order sought to elect a thirteen-man Multnomah County legislative delegation friendly to the Klan.[14] In the final weeks of the primary campaign the Invisible Empire became the dominant issue, and expressions of prejudice became so vitriolic that the *Oregon Daily Journal* ceased publishing letters to the editor on racial or religious matters. The newspaper later argued that it was "idle to contend that the Ku Klux Klan and its political activities were not the dominant note in the primary campaign from the beginning." The counting of the ballots on May 19 resulted only in a disquieting stalemate in state politics. Governor Olcott won a razor-thin, five-hundred-vote victory—in fact, Hall was first announced as the winner. Congressman McArthur also survived the Klan challenge with a narrow 15,449 to 14,311 plurality over the most threatening of his five opponents.[15] The secret order tasted of victory in other political contests, however. In Portland, Charles Hall led Governor Olcott 19,185 to 18,361, despite the fact that all three Republican newspapers supported the incumbent. Klansmen Dolph Walker and John H. Rankin won positions on the public service commission, and twelve of thirteen Klan-supported candidates for the legislature were nominated, although this involved the defeat of all but three incumbents. Grand Dragon Gifford explained that: "The only things that the Ku Klux Klan looked at in picking the right man to vote for was [*sic*] their loyalty to the free public schools, loyalty to the government of the United States, and the question of anti-alien land law bills. We requested and exacted no pledges, nor did we attempt in any way to pledge a single candidate. We simply ascertained his views on the principles above set forth." Conspicuous among the right-thinking victors was veteran legislator K. K. Kubli, a Harvard-educated businessman whose initials earned him a free membership in Klan No. 1. He received 23,018 votes and ran second in the field of thirty-six.

In its successful campaign to elect "none but real Americans" to public office, the Invisible Empire had important allies in the Federation of Patriotic Societies and the Oregon Good Government League. Formed in 1917 to break the power of the corporations, the Federation functioned as the political arm of seventeen fraternal orders, including the Loyal Orange, the Odd Fellows, Masons, and Knights of Pythias. Although the Klan was never formally admitted to membership, there were enough Klansmen in the member lodges to elect Grand Dragon Gifford as director of the

Federation in 1922. As such, he managed to synchronize the political endorsements of the Klan with those of the patriotic societies. Gifford also served as an officer in the Good Government League, a quasi-debating society composed of many of the same elements as the Federation. Noted for its political endorsements (called yellow tickets from the paper they were printed on), the League degenerated into a front organization designed to lend an air of respectability to Klan pronouncements.

Because neither Klan nor anti-Klan forces had been satisfied with the primary election, the struggle for political control remained in abeyance until November. With registered Republicans outnumbering Democrats by 238,000 to 90,000 in 1922, Oregon would ordinarily have been considered safe for the G.O.P. But 1922 was not a conventional year, and the Klan's post-primary boast that "Hall's defeat means a Democratic governor next fall" was no idle threat. Moreover, perennial Democratic hopeful Walter Pierce was not one to let an opportunity slip away. Openly bidding for Kluxer support, the LaGrande Klansman endorsed the compulsory education bill, emphasized the necessity of keeping "America as a land for Americans," supported the anti-alien land ownership proposal, and pointed out the "dangers of allowing the Mongolian races to gain a foothold on the soil of our state." As if to warrant a triumph, Pierce noted that he was a ninth-generation American Protestant and that "my wife and all her relatives are Protestants." Less naked, but similar strategy was followed in Portland by McArthur's congressional opponent, Elton Watkins, who advocated restrictive immigration laws and "the exclusion of Orientals and aliens not fit for citizenship." [16]

Overshadowing every encounter between office-seekers, however, was a controversial initiative proposal on compulsory public education that was also to be submitted to the voters in the general election.[17] Sponsored through the petition stage by Ancient and Accepted Scottish Rite Masons and contrived primarily to abolish Catholic schools, the measure required all children between eight and sixteen years of age to attend public schools.[18] As the Knights of Pythias, the Federation of Patriotic Societies, the Oregon Good

Government League, the Loyal Orange, and the Ku Klux Klan locked arms in support of "Free Public Schools for Red-Blooded Children," voters were told that the common school was the foundation upon which American freedoms rested. Incorporated with such entreaties was a certain recognition that education should serve an egalitarian function: "The American public school puts in the minds of children, democracy, love of equality, belief in your fellow man, genuine equality, that comes from mingling with all classes, and knowing them as equals and friends in useful mind-improving competition." [19]

Although the Klan did not originally propose the compulsory education bill and did not initiate its submission to the electorate, the secret order did give the measure its full and public endorsement. Basic strategy was to shift voter attention from the threatened abolition of parochial education to the assertion that Catholics sought to destroy the public schools. Portland Klansmen circulated pictures of nuns teaching in tax-supported institutions,[20] and Klan orators William McDougal and R. H. Sawyer lectured throughout the city on behalf of the education bill. With somewhat perverted logic, Sawyer declared on May 27, 1922:

> The Ku Klux Klan swears allegiance to the flag and not to the church. The constitution and the Bible are inseparable. The Bible is the highest authority.
>
> One of our purposes is to try to get the Bible back into the schools, such as it was in the old days. The little red schoolhouse on the hill is the cornerstone and foundation for our government. Within the next few years we hope to see only native born Americans rule the government instead of foreigners.

According to advocates of the school bill, only two classes of people opposed compulsory public education: (1) those who believed the rights of the church should take precedence over the rights of the state, and (2) blue-bloods who cherished class distinction and social caste. Under the direction of Archbishop Alexander Christie, the Catholic Civil Rights Association organized special committees to oppose Initiative 49 (the compulsory public education bill) in each of Oregon's 130 parishes, and it eventually collected and spent more than $50,000 in the campaign. But the Catholic Civil Rights Association was only one of many diverse Klan adversaries. Episcopalians, Lutherans, Seventh Day Adventists, and Presbyterians generally supported parochial and private education, and large newspaper advertisements were purchased by such *ad hoc* committees as the Jewish League for the Preservation of American Ideals, the Protestant Committee for Freedom in Education, and the Non-Sectarian and Protestant School Committee. The presidents of Chicago, Yale, Stanford, Columbia, Princeton, Texas, and George Washington universities openly condemned the bill, professors from Reed College and the University of Washington voiced strong disapproval, and two hundred Oregon lawyers publicly stated that the school measure would be declared unconstitutional if approved. The controversy raged so savagely that two newspapers predicted that animosity would permanently endure if the bill became law. But nothing deterred the champions of compulsory education, who declared two days before the election that the test of the politician was his attitude toward the public school. "If he hesitates, if he departs one inch from the old idea that the public school is the SCHOOL OF AMERICA, and the ONLY school, if he hesitates in his loyalty to THAT school, he is a traitor to the spirit of the United States, and your vote should tell him so."

Although Governor Olcott was backed by the *Portland News,* *The Morning Oregonian,* and the *Portland Telegram,* he recognized that anti-Catholicism and the Ku Klux Klan periled traditional party loyalties.[21] His campaign strategy called for minimizing the expected cross-over to the Democrats by playing down the religious issue and remaining noncommittal on the school measure. "The monster of invisible government" was fair game, however. The governor invited all good citizens to support his drive "against masked riders or cloaked and disguised figures who unlawfully skulk about on secret missions for unknown ends," and he demanded the resignation of all Klansmen serving as state officers or members of state boards. The reaction of the president of the Oregon Board of Chiropractic Examiners was quick. Admitting his Klan membership, Dr. R. E. Ellsworth resigned his official position and somewhat vindictively labeled the governor "a filthy mess of political garbage."

The extreme vilification of the 1922 campaign came to an end on November 7, a day of jubilation for the Invisible Empire. Winning by 132,000 votes to 98,000, Walter Pierce became Oregon's first Democratic chief executive in half a century and its first ever from east of the Cascade Mountains. Equally significant was the election success of the compulsory public school bill, which overcame the opposition of 30,000 Catholics and 65,000 Protestants and won adoption 107,498 to 97,204. According to the Invisible Empire, Oregon was only the first of many states to abolish parochial education.[22]

Klan triumph was especially noticeable in Portland, where controversial Initiative 49 piled up two-thirds of its victory margin and where Pierce outdistanced Olcott 43,612 to 35,224.[23] With strong support throughout the city, an almost solid Klan delegation was sent to the state legislature from Multnomah County. Every circuit judge endorsed by the secret order retained his position; the only incumbent to fail was a Catholic, W. N. Gatens. Elton Watkins unseated Republican Representative C. N. McArthur and became Portland's first Democratic congressman since 1879.[24] Only in the race for two city commissioners, where the Klan and the Federation of Patriotic Societies endorsed separate two-man tickets, did the Invisible Empire stumble. Reflecting the fact that the combined patriotic societies with over 20,000 members could outvote the Klan, Federation nominees ran first and third while Klan candidates George B. Cellars and Alva Lee (Big Steve) Stephenson finished fourth and sixth with 18,292 and 16,018 votes respectively.

The Invisible Empire achieved the zenith of its Oregon success early in 1923. In the state legislature K. K. Kubli was elected Speaker of the House and his "Kubli Klan" forces were ably led by Klansmen William F. Woodward, a member of the Portland Board of Education, and Cyril G. Brownell. Although many of their proposals were defeated in the Senate, where the secret order was relatively weak, two Klan measures were successful: a garb bill prohibiting the wearing of religious habits by public school teachers and a property bill preventing aliens ineligible for citizenship (which of course meant Japanese and Chinese) from owning land in the state. When a vacancy occurred for the post of collector of customs of the Port of Portland, a Klansman was named to the position. The most blatant example of Klan weight came on March 3, 1923, at the close of the state legislature session. At a banquet held at the Portland Chamber of Commerce in honor of the birthday of Fred Gifford, Grand Dragon of the Realm of Oregon, Governor Walter Pierce and Mayor George L. Baker were among the speakers and guests.[25]

Klan No. 1 attained a membership of fifteen thousand by the fall of 1923.[26] Many prominent businessmen, including public utility officials, hotel keepers, and banking employees professed allegiance to the Invisible Empire, and the *Portland Telegram* reported that the police department was "full to the brink with Klansmen." The *World's Work* observed that it was "not the bad people of the state, but the good people—the very good people," that accounted for the secret order's success, but a former Klan official reported there was also "a large minority that is normally destitute, religiously delinquent, mentally minus, and semi-illiterate." [27]

Klan strength in Portland did not rest solely on its regular membership. Wives and mothers were encouraged to join the Ladies of the Invisible Empire (Loties), while foreign-born males, otherwise qualified as one hundred per cent Americans, were eligible for the Royal Riders of the Red Robe. Organized in the early summer of 1922, the Loties made their headquarters at 326 Pittock Block, and met regularly at the Red Men's Hall or municipal auditorium. They were particularly solicitous about the purity of race, which they symbolized with white robes set off by red, white, and blue sashes. The Royal Riders, similarly well-clad in red sheets, were led at Klan functions by Dr. Martin Rose, a physician in the Morgan Building. Awake to every potential source of income, the secret order provided for younger patriots by organizing in Portland a Junior Citizen's Club on March 29, 1923.[28]

In addition to such auxiliary organizations there were special groups within Klan No. 1 itself. Composed entirely of Klansmen, the Portland Police Vigilantes was an armed, one-hundred-man force. Nominated or approved by Grand Dragon Gifford, each man was commissioned as a police deputy. Equally ominous was the Black Patrol, a nine-man strong-arm squad sworn to "eternal secrecy." During the I.W.W. strike of 1923, the Black Patrol gathered together suspected "Wobblies" and escorted them out of the city.[29]

Not all the activities of Klan No. 1 were so sinister. Portland Knights time and again motored to nearby Forest Grove or Hillsboro to have a hand in initiations or simply to listen to their well-drilled band, the Scotch Kilties. Members from the big city comprised "most of the Klansmen in the line of march" at a statewide gathering in Salem, where an airplane flew low over the capitol building carrying a huge fiery cross and a "Join K.K.K." sign. In Portland, the local group had its headquarters at 404 S.W. Second Avenue, and usually held its meetings either on leased grounds or at the Armory, the municipal auditorium, or the Salvation Army Hall. Occasionally venturing to induce the school board into awarding contracts to non-Catholic firms, Klansmen were usually content to participate in such traditional Portland celebrations as the Rose Carnival.

The gamut of Klan activities led to the establishment late in 1922 of the *Western American*. Published briefly in Astoria before relocation in Portland and edited by transplanted Tennessean Lem A. Dever, the Klan magazine appeared weekly on city newsstands. It referred to the metropolitan press as "Portland's pope-bossed, Jew-kept, scandal mongering dailies" and adopted a policy vigorously anti-Catholic in both tone and content. Promising to "keep after Rome, as Rome is keeping after the Ku Klux Klan," the *Western American* stated its belief that there was nothing "that could advance the world in progress any more than the destruction of the Roman Catholic hierarchy and all of its man made teachings."[30]

Such maxims met relatively little overt resistance in the city of Portland. Exceptions were Frank S. Baillie, grand master of Oregon Masons, and Dr. Ernest Halliday of the Congregational Church, who told the Portland Rotary Club that the Klan's hood was a "symbol of banditry." Archbishop Christie, the Catholic Truth Society of Oregon, and the *Catholic Sentinel* were also consistent foes of "one hundred per cent Americanism," but their influence was essentially limited to the small Catholic community. The most effective anti-Klan voice was that of the *Portland Telegram,* which joined the *Corvallis Gazette Times* and the *Capitol Journal* in refusing to bow to the Invisible Empire. Portland's three other metropolitan newspapers were journalistic cowards that broke their silence only after the Klan was declining. Their approach was typified by the *Oregon Daily Journal,* which declared in 1922: "The mistake of Catholics, Jews, and others is that they take the Ku Klux Klan too seriously." But the fight of the *Telegram* was costly. In one month its white, Protestant owners lost five thousand subscribers and its advertisers were threatened with boycott.[31] The newspaper finally folded in 1933, when it was merged with the *News.* According to *The Morning Oregonian,* "the Klan wrecked the old *Telegram.*"

Had the Portland Klan been able to avoid internal dissension, it might well have weathered such meager opposition from without. Ironically, deep fissures developed as a direct result of the secret order's 1922 political success. Mayor George Baker and Speaker of the House Kubli each sought the Klan endorsement for senator in 1924. Gifford leaned originally toward Baker while *Western American* editor Lem A. Dever championed the cause of Kubli. Several months later the Grand Dragon abandoned Baker and threw his support to George Kelly of Portland. Just prior to the election, the vacillating Gifford realized that no one could defeat Senator McNary, and he once again shifted allegiance, this time to the incumbent. As a result, the Klan gained nothing and alienated George Baker, K. K. Kubli, and George Kelly.

While the Invisible Empire was wrestling with the problems of senatorial nomination, two new controversies foamed. The first was a complete divorce between the Klan and the Federation of Patriotic Societies, a circumstance brought about because Gifford attempted to split the Loyal Orange by organizing a group of clandestine Orange lodges, and because the Klan supported persons friendly to the utility corporations for membership on the Public Service Commission. The latter action was particularly treasonous to the Federation, which had long opposed eight-cent street-car fares, high telephone rates, and "excessive" profits for big business. W. E. Elford, secretary of the patriotic societies, charged that the Grand Dragon was a tool of the public utility corporations, and he announced that "there will be no armistice between us and the Klan until it is purged of Gifford and Giffordism." This marked the end of a potent alliance.

No less damaging to the fortunes of Klan No. 1 was the antagonism between the Grand Dragon and King Kleagle Luther I. Powell, the founder of the Portland organization. The breach had several causes, including the Simmons-Evans dispute on the national level, with Powell supporting Colonel Simmons, and Gifford backing the eventual winner. (The Portland Klan itself also supported Evans.) There was also a sharp personality clash, because both men nurtured ambitions of political domination in the Northwest. Spending most of his time in Seattle, Powell had lost ground to Gifford by October 1923. Returning to Portland, Powell sought to rebuild his position by staging an elaborate "Klan Frolic" in the Portland Auditorium complete with prizes, speakers, parades, Christmas trees, and Klan marriages. More important he signed a contract to increase Klan No. 1 membership to fifty thousand. The task was obviously impossible of attainment, and Gifford allowed his rival just enough time to look ridiculous before dismissing him without payment. Disillusioned, Powell announced his intention of establishing an anti-Gifford monthly entitled *Klansman's Progress* and issued a public statement damning "the autocratic and political aspirations of the grand dragon and his official henchmen, W. D. Quinn and Charles Hurd, who as ward politicians have served their purpose well, so well, in fact, that the Gifford machine has had a steam roller effect upon the free thinking minds of real Americans and Klansmen."

The natural outcome of such in-fighting was charges and counter-charges of corruption. The public learned that the much-ballyhooed, fifty-thousand-dollar Klan donation to the W.C.T.U. Children's Farm Home had never materialized and that oil well stocks sold by Gifford through the Royal Riders of the Red Robe were worthless.[32] Even more serious was the apparent failure of the Skyline Corporation, formed in 1922 to raise funds for a million-dollar Klan headquarters in downtown Portland. Enthusiastic Klansmen invested thirty thousand dollars, of which Gifford retained 3 per cent as his commission. The remainder was not accounted for and the building was never constructed.

Early in 1924, Klan No. 1 did move to a new home, but it was four blocks from the proposed construction site in a cramped portion of the Odd Fellows Hall. Non-payment of dues became a serious problem, and Treasurer P. L. Wadley mailed an anxious letter to the Portland faithful:

> The dues are $6.00 per year, payable in advance.
> You will want your 1924 dues card to avoid being temporarily suspended for non-payment of dues, as the 2nd DEGREE IS NOW ABOUT READY TO BE CONFERRED. This degree requires six months (at least) in good standing.
> . . . Your help on the Immigration Bill, the Compulsory School Bill and the bill for the taxation of church property is needed now, more than ever.
> While dollars and cents will not make you more of a Klansman or the lack of it any less of one, the efforts of each one of us is needed and must be put to the front to overcome the enemies of THESE UNITED STATES.[33]

The ardent appeal did not revive the old spirit, however, and the once puissant Portland Klan began to crumble. Public indication of weakness came in May when three Klan-supported county commissioners, including well-known Klansmen John H. Rankin and Dolph Walker, were confronted with a recall election. Rankin was a particularly loyal Knight who always stood at the klavern door and greeted the members. The three were accused of graft in connection with construction of the Ross Island and Sellwood bridges and charged with responsibility for increased public utility rates. Klan support was again extended to the commissioners, and special yellow tickets instructed Portland Knights to vote straight down the line against recall. Because the *Catholic Sentinel* broke with tradition and involved itself heavily in the election, Klan strategy called for emphasizing that recall was favored by the "great Catholic machine" and that "only those who measure up to the standard of REAL AMERI-CANISM should be elected." A special issue of the *Western American* proclaimed: "Recall Movement Papal Drive." [34] But the result was disaster, for all three commissioners were turned out of office.

The Klan's impotence in May 1924, was indicative of its fading glory.[35] By November it was no longer an important political force and could avoid defeat only by remaining uncommitted or by endorsing incumbents who were certain winners. In the general election, the featured race was for mayor of Portland. The conflict brought together George Baker, who sought an unprecedented third term; W. N. Gatens, a Catholic and a former circuit judge who had fallen victim to the Klan in 1922; John H. Rankin, the recalled county commissioner and a Klansman; and three other candidates. Gatens looked upon Baker as his chief opponent and sought to malign the Mayor with the charge of yielding to "secret societies and clandestine influences." His advertisements described Baker's "naturalization" into the Klan and charged that hooded bigotry and the city government had "linked unseen hands in this campaign. They stand for Baker. Do you stand for them?"

But Baker had severed his ties with the Ku Klux Klan a year earlier, and in 1924 the yellow, green and red paper tickets issued by the Klan and the Good Government League instructed members to vote for Rankin for mayor.[36] The Invisible Empire could take little pride, therefore, when Baker overwhelmed Gatens by 41,810 votes to 21,579, because John H. Rankin, the only true Klansman in the race, could garner only sixteen hundred votes.[37] Nor was the state result any more encouraging because Klan governor Walter Pierce failed in a bid for re-election. Oregon's experiment in invisible government was at an end.

It was left to Lem A. Dever, the outspoken editor of the *Western American*, to deliver the coup de grâce. Resigning in disgust in October 1924, Dever issued for public sale a red, paper-covered pamphlet entitled *Confessions of an Imperial Klansman*. He apologized for "promoting this giant fraud instead of opposing it," and somewhat unrealistically argued that "I myself was not prejudiced regarding religion." He also hopefully inaugurated the anti-Klan periodical *Harpoon,* which in its only issue bared the inner workings of the Pacific Northwest Domain.[38]

Because Dever had been well-respected by most Oregon Klansmen, his revelations had an immediate and devastating effect. Imperial Wizard Evans attended a Klan klonklave at the Portland auditorium in an unavailing attempt to stem the tide. Gifford himself even lost heart, resigning as grand dragon several months after. Finally, in May 1925, came the revealing announcement that the *Western American* had suspended publication and "merged" with the *National Kourier.*[39] The news from Washington was equally discouraging. In 1925 the Oregon compulsory public education law was struck down by the United States Supreme Court as an infringement on property rights. The Federal District Court in Oregon had previously held the law unconstitutional, and the state had appealed the decision.[40]

By the end of 1925 nothing was seen in the newspapers, and little was heard, of the Portland Klan. A few Knights refused to give up the ghost, however, and in August 1925 M. S. Belser arrived from Atlanta hoping to lead a resurgence. He announced that Klan No. 1 no longer had any interest in politics and would concentrate instead on public schools and law enforcement. But Belser was unsuccessful, and the secret order disappeared from Oregon early in 1926.

Fred L. Gifford meanwhile lapsed into insignificancy for twelve years. Then in November 1937 he called a meeting in the Grosvenor Building and heralded the rebirth of the Oregon movement. Claiming sixteen thousand members, the dreaming old man told the small group that the Klan would henceforth be concerned with Fascists and Communists rather than Catholics and Negroes. Apparently Hitler and Stalin provoked only apathy, for the "one hundred per cent" spirit was not rekindled and Gifford returned immediately to obscurity.

15

Denver: The Triumph of John Galen Locke

Along the eastern front of the Rocky Mountains at the juncture of the South Platte River and Cherry Creek lies the largest city between the Missouri River and the Pacific Ocean. Self-sufficient, isolated, and complacent, Denver had no significant rival in either size or importance for five hundred miles in any direction. Already a metropolis in 1920 with 256,000 inhabitants, it comprised nearly one-third of Colorado's total population. The Queen city of the West was overwhelmingly white, Protestant, and native born; its non-white population increased by only 649 between 1910 and 1920. But 35,000 Catholics were the object of growing concern.[1] Like Portland, Denver was noted for its conservatism and its tradition of intolerance. In the 1890's, it was the home of ten thousand members and twenty-five chapters (councils) of the American Protective Association and the seat of such anti-Catholic and nativistic magazines as the *Rocky Mountain American* and the *Mercury*.[2] A generation later, adherents of the Klan were in many instances the sons and daughters of those who led the A.P.A. in Denver.

Early in 1921, Imperial Wizard William Joseph Simmons visited the Colorado capital on a western recruiting trip. Friends arranged a Sunday afternoon meeting with several Denverites at the fashion-

able Brown Palace Hotel. Reviewing the history and aspirations of
the Invisible Empire, Simmons persuaded his guests to lead the
Colorado crusade for "one hundred per cent Americanism." A hasty
initiation followed, and a local klavern was organized under the
innocuous title of the Denver Doers Club.[3]

Although zestfully led by physician John Galen Locke and Grand
Goblin A. J. Padon, Jr., the Denver Doers Club made slow progress
in its first months and attracted few recruits. Not until June 17,
1921, did it cast aside its misleading title and, in an open letter to
the *Denver Times,* publicly announce its affiliation with the Invisible Empire: "The local Klan, consisting of the very best citizens of
Denver, has been under course of construction for some time. . . .
We proclaim to the lawless element of the City and County of
Denver and of the State of Colorado that we are not only active
now, but we were here yesterday, we are here today, and we shall
be here forever." [4] Three weeks after the announcement the secret
order made its first appearance in the city. A caravan of automobiles swooped down on Curtis Street in downtown Denver and
stopped before a theater. Bearing red torchlights, masked Klansmen posted a crude sign demanding the re-engagement of a film
dealing with a patriotic theme.

Threats were apparently a popular diversion of the Denver Klan
in the early months of its organization. The president of the local
chapter of the NAACP was warned to restrict his activities, and in
January 1922 a letter on Klan stationery was delivered to Ward
Gish, custodian of an apartment house. Reproached for "intimate
relations with white women" and "use of abusive language to white
women," the Negro janitor was told to leave town before February
1; otherwise, "the climate of Denver will be injurious." As a parting
admonition the letter warned: "Nigger, do not look lightly upon
this: Your hide is worth less to us than it is to you." [5]

Understandably diffident, Ward Gish turned the warning over to
the police and hastily departed from the city. District Attorney
Phillip C. Van Cise took personal responsibility for the case and
persuaded the janitor to return. Commissioned by the grand jury to
probe the threats and their relationship to the local Klan, Van Cise

asserted that "Gish or anyone else who receives threatening letters will be given protection, and it is my intention to try and put the Klan out of business in this city."

A former war hero, Van Cise pressed his anti-Klan campaign with vigor, infiltrating the local chapter with five secret agents. His persistence dissuaded the Denver Klan from again engaging in crude threats, but the tempo of secret order activities actually increased. Emphasis was placed upon charity, Christianity, and public benevolence. Highland Christian Church of the Reverend William Oeschger on the north side and Grant Avenue Methodist Church of the Reverend James Thomas in south Denver were focal points of Klan strength, as was First Avenue Presbyterian Church, where the pastor once delivered a sermon on "the Klan as a defense against Catholic hierarchy encroachments." Oeschger in particular was an apostle of the Klan. In 1924, he served as exalted cyclops of Klan No. 1 and later in the same year accepted five hundred dollars from robed Knights during worship services in his church. When evangelist Aimee Semple McPherson appeared in Denver in July 1922, she was surprised in her suite at the Brown Palace Hotel by three hooded men. They presented her with "$64.20 as a love gift" for her two young children, and promised that Klansmen everywhere "will watch over you, admire you, and protect you." Local members also donated one thousand dollars to Atlanta's Klan-sponsored University of America and one hundred dollars to the Denver Y.M.C.A.[6]

A particularly offensive form of "benevolence" was the Klan tendency to seek an association with persons in death who had had nothing to do with the Invisible Empire in life. In late February 1922, five Klansmen appeared at the Fairmont Cemetery funeral of a well-known physician and left a floral arrangement honoring him as a "real American." In November of the same year, during the funeral of Policeman Richie Rose, a non-Klansman who had died in the line of duty, six Klansmen dramatically appeared just as the body was being lowered into the grave. The leader of the hooded entourage presented a cross of flowers and vowed that Klan No. 1 would never allow Rose's widow and children to live in want.

To those who failed to qualify as "one hundred per cent Americans," the Invisible Empire offered only robust hostility. In 1920, the city's seven thousand Negroes were effectively segregated in a deteriorating East Denver ghetto near downtown and just north of Capitol Hill. But white supremacy was a cardinal principal of klankraft, and local patriots increased in number when Negro students attended a white high school social affair in February 1923. At the regular klonklave of Klan No. 1 on February 8, a unanimous resolution was approved for public communication to Lucius F. Hallett and the Denver Board of Education:

> Referring to Article 9, Section 8, of the Colorado constitution, providing that no distinction or classification of pupils shall be made on account of race or color, we assume to call your attention to the operation of this provision as affecting the school work and the social relations of pupils.
>
> Their school work is compulsory, and in its arrangement, any such distinction or classification is inhibited. Their social life together is not compulsory, but wholly voluntary, and, in that relation, we are advised by competent legal authority, the inhibition does not apply.
>
> We, therefore, respectfully insist that, insofar as the school authorities assume to direct or chaperone the social life of public school pupils, provision be made for separate functions for the white pupils and separate functions for the negro pupils.
>
> Any intrusion by members of either race, into the social affairs of the other will not be tolerated.[7]

Slightly more numerous than Denver Negroes in 1920 were eleven thousand Jewish residents, many of whom resided in the West Colfax section of the city. The Klan was concerned with their "international" character and frequently routed Friday evening automobile caravans past synagogues and through West Denver neighborhoods. Shouting insults from behind their white hoods, local Klansmen apparently derived pleasure from the interruption of the pre-Sabbath preparations of devout Jews.

More important than white supremacy or anti-Semitism was prejudice against the Catholics and foreign born, who were the most numerous, widely distributed, and threatening of Denver's minority groups in 1920. The fifteen thousand predominantly Catholic recent immigrants were concentrated in heavily East European Globeville on the northern edge of the city, although some Italians were moving into the Highlands. Combined with at least twenty-thousand, native-born Catholics scattered throughout Denver, the aliens were regarded as a severe threat to "one hundred per cent Americanism." Significantly, the Klan's *Protestant Herald* was usually made up almost entirely of anti-papal diatribes and of attacks upon Father Matthew Smith and the *Denver Catholic Register.* The monsignor also related that he was physically threatened and that at least a half dozen automobile drivers had swerved out of their way to run him down as he crossed streets. Klan No. 1 adopted an official cigar, Cyana—or, "Catholics, you are not Americans"—and it surreptitiously printed and distributed hundreds of allegedly pro-Catholic pamphlets "containing a list of Catholic tradesmen and urging that Catholics should not patronize heretics but should trade with Roman Catholics only." Catholic businessmen suffered greatly as a result; one reported a loss of 35 per cent in business volume. Meanwhile the most crowded restaurant in Denver was that of Gano Senter, grand titan of the Northern Province of Colorado, where a large sign announced: "We Serve Fish Every Day—Except Friday." [8]

Utilizing such anti-Negro, anti-Semitic, and anti-Catholic appeals to best advantage, Kleagle Hi Grimm mailed invitations to members of the Loyal Orange and Masonic lodges. The response was overwhelming, and Denver exalted cyclopes were hard pressed to find meeting places to accommodate an expanding enrollment. Yeager Mortuary, Woodmen Hall, the Mining Exchange Building, Fort Campbell Auditorium, and Knights of Pythias Hall served as temporary klaverns prior to 1923, while Table Mountain, nine miles west of Denver and Castle Mountain, near Golden, were the most frequent sites of klonklaves after that time. Initiations were usually held in Estes Park or at the Klan's Cotton Mills Stadium in south Denver, and the consistent attraction was the mammoth, two-hundred-member Imperial Klan No. 1 band. As was the case in most other cities, chapters of the Women of the Ku Klux Klan, the

Junior Klan, and the Royal Riders of the Red Robe were organized in Denver.

From its inception, the Denver klavern was paramount in the Realm of Colorado. Organized and chartered well in advance of the klaverns in Pueblo, Boulder, Canon City, Grand Junction, and Colorado Springs, Klan No. 1 enlisted approximately half of the state's 45,000 Knights and provided the realm with most of its top officials.[9] Significantly, Denver was the home and headquarters of Dr. John Galen Locke, grand dragon of Colorado and one of the most colorful and powerful Klansmen in the nation.

Dr. Locke was born in New York State and was a graduate of the College of Physicians and Surgeons in Manhattan. He moved to Denver in 1893 at the age of twenty and practiced medicine in the Colorado capital for twenty-eight years. Denied membership in the Denver Medical Society for failing to keep abreast of developments in the medical field, Dr. Locke abandoned his profession and small private hospital in 1921 and placed his unusual talents in the service of the Invisible Empire. A short, stout fellow who took great pride in his Van Dyke beard and carefully trimmed moustache, he was a charter member of the Denver Doers Club and rose rapidly to the position of grand dragon. A brick building next to the present site of the Denver Athletic Club housed his private office and the sliding wall-section leading to the basement headquarters of the Realm of Colorado. Furnishings were lavish and included Dr. Locke's high-backed leather chair and a copy of the United States seal in solid gold. The environment was similar at his South Denver home, where trophies of the hunt and curious weapons adorned the walls.[10] Always bejeweled with numerous rings, the egotistical and pompous Grand Dragon was a superb organizer and inspired almost fanatical loyalty among his followers. In 1924 the *Denver Express* tagged him the most powerful man in Colorado and declared that his powers were those of an absolute dictator: "He may at his pleasure remove any officer in the state of Colorado. He may also suspend any man from the order without a hearing . . . public officers are completely subservient. They either obey or are kicked out of the organization."

Grand Dragon Locke waited until the municipal election of May 1923 before seriously committing the Klan in local politics. The mayoral campaign pitted Republican incumbent Dewey C. Bailey against Democrat Benjamin F. Stapleton. The challenger accepted the endorsement of the Invisible Empire, but was unsure of Klan strength, and prudently presented himself to the public as an opponent of the KKK. Stapleton declared shortly before the election that "True Americanism needs no mask nor disguise," adding that "any attempt to stir up racial or religious prejudice or religious intolerance is contrary to our constitution and is therefore un-American." For his part, Mayor Bailey was handicapped by newspaper opposition, his underworld associations, and a reputation for giving property valuation advantages to wealthy contributors. Thus Stapleton was presented as a reform candidate and won a 37,370 to 31,007 vote victory.

At first Stapleton was a capable mayor who cracked down on inefficiency and reorganized the police department. But the honeymoon ended in June 1923, when the secret order asked permission to use the city auditorium for a lecture. Despite protests from many citizens—especially Catholics, Negroes, and Jews—the Mayor granted the Klan request, citing constitutional guarantees of free speech. Shortly thereafter, the public learned that the Mayor's newly appointed manager of public safety, Rice W. Means, was a Klansman and had accepted the position with the understanding that he would be named city attorney within ninety days.[11]

While serving as manager of public safety, Means permitted police officers to use abusive methods in punishing citizens and visitors for petty offenses. After becoming city attorney, Klansman Means once stepped down from his official post to defend a Denver laundry proprietor accused of forcing a woman to work more than eight hours per day. The public was not impressed by the unusual spectacle of a public official going to battle for a man accused of violating the criminal code.

Criticism of the Stapleton regime received additional stimulus in November. On the night of the tenth, burning crosses were placed at various locations in the city. The city council demanded an investigation, but the new manager of public safety, Klansman Reuben W. Hershey, reported that the police department could find no trace of any crosses. Mayor Stapleton added that his personal inquiries into the incident were similarly unsuccessful.

The close working arrangement between the Mayor and Dr. Locke began to weaken early in 1924, when Stapleton decided to resist the Grand Dragon's play for political power. But the pressure against the Democratic executive from the opposite direction was already formidable; anti-Klan forces were circulating recall petitions throughout the city to force Stapleton's removal from office. Suddenly without allies, the Mayor eagerly reverted to the KKK fold. Grand Dragon Locke accepted this change of heart, but warned Stapleton never again to betray the trust of the Invisible Empire: "if you do it again, may God help you." As the price of Stapleton's reinstatement, Locke secured the appointment of Klansman William Candlish as chief of police.[12]

In the spring and summer of 1924, the Invisible Empire very likely attained its maximum power and influence in Denver. Its members included state representatives, state senators, the mayor, city attorney, manager of public safety, police chief, police inspector, two deputy sheriffs, the Colorado secretary of state, at least four judges, two federal narcotics agents, and scores of policemen.[13] Its officers represented a cross section of Denver society. Grand Dragon Locke, Grand Klokard Marshall H. Dean, and Klan No. 1 Exalted Cyclops A. L. Douglass were all local physicians. Prominent restaurateur Gano Senter served as grand titan, and Northside preacher William Oeschger was a local klaliff (vice-president). The two klokanns (executive committeemen) were District Judge Clarence J. Morley (later governor of Colorado) and advertising man Walter Durbee; the kludd (chaplain) was a "Captain Stewart."

Rank and file Denver Klansmen were less prominent socially and politically than their officers and were drawn primarily from lower- or middle-class citizens. The secret order was particularly strong in three sections of the city: (1) a spacious area east of the South Platte River as far as Emerson Street, (2) Berkeley and the North

Denver Highlands, and (3) South Denver. The first area was over-whelmingly lower and lower-middle class and was deteriorating rapidly in 1920. South Denver was somewhat more respectable, as was the Berkeley-North Denver Highlands area. Italians were buying into the latter neighborhood, where the residences were generally well-kept, low brick bungalows.[14] In addition to the three primary areas of concentration, much smaller numbers of Klansmen lived just north of the East Denver Negro ghetto and in a half-mile-square section of Capitol Hill. The secret order also had widely scattered representation in Park Hill and in relatively affluent neighborhoods east of Washington and Chessman Parks. Noticeably weak in East European Globeville, Jewish West Colfax, and in Barnum, Valverde, Montclair, and Elyria, Klan No. 1 was described by Father Matthew Smith, editor of the *Denver Catholic Register*, as consisting of down-at-the-heels businessmen, who joined in return for its promise to coerce members to trade with them, and of attorneys, physicians, and clergymen of mediocre professional character, who used the Klan as a crutch.

Although important businessmen of Denver were apparently not counted among the membership, there is every reason to believe that their interests were protected by Klan government. For more than a generation a fight had been in progress over the ownership and rates of the Denver Tramway Company. While Stapleton was mayor and a Klansman was serving as city attorney, the case went to the private transit corporations and at a valuation that was double the previous figure.[15]

The naming of William Candlish as Chief of Police was the final example of Klan domination of the city administration. Within one week of the March 1924 appointment, a petition for the recall of Mayor Stapleton was filed with the city clerk. The petition contained more than twenty-six thousand signatures and necessitated a special mayoral election on August 12, 1924. The choice of the anti-Klan forces was former mayor Dewey C. Bailey, who made every effort to establish the Invisible Empire as the single overriding issue of the race. Campaigning among Catholics, Jews, and Negroes, he labeled the Klan unconstitutional, un-American, and "absolutely opposed to the principles of religious freedom upon which this country was founded."

Bailey received unexpected support from the Denver County Democratic Assembly, which approved 670 to 174 a resolution denouncing the Ku Klux Klan and "any administration that permits itself to become the working tool of the Klan." Observing that "Never before has the executive officer of the city . . . been so repudiated by the party which put him into power," the *Denver Post* repeatedly issued the challenge: "Shall the Ku Klux Klan, an anonymous, secret, masked society, rule Denver, or Shall the people rule Denver?" Famed Juvenile Court Judge Ben Lindsey capped the Bailey campaign with a ringing denunciation of his fellow Democrat and an appeal to the people "to rescue their homes and their fair city from this white hooded menace—the blackest it has ever faced. At this juncture this can be done only by voting against Klansman Benjamin F. Stapleton." [16]

As campaign manager for the Mayor, Grand Dragon Locke countered such anti-Klan entreaties with tight organization and thorough precinct work. From temporary Klan headquarters in the Brown Palace Hotel, members distributed thousands of "I'll Vote Again for Ben" bumper stickers and divided themselves according to election districts. This time there was no doubt about where Stapleton stood on the issue of invisible government. At a Klan rally on Castle Mountain on the evening of July 14, 1924, the Mayor pledged: "I have little to say, except that I will work with the Klan and for the Klan in the coming election, heart and soul. And if I am re-elected, I will give the Klan the kind of administration it wants."

Election day was quiet and orderly, but almost eighty thousand persons went to the polls in the heaviest balloting in Denver history. Stapleton was retained in office by a resounding 55,635 to 24,277. The Mayor was strong in most of the city and carried all sixteen election districts. Only in heavily Jewish West Colfax did Bailey strength hold firm. The most impressive Stapleton margins were piled up in Klan-dominated districts, R, S, and T in South Denver, where the Mayor outdistanced his rival by the convincing

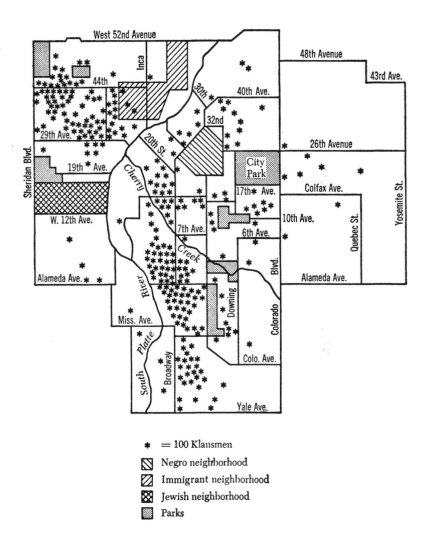

∗ = 100 Klansmen
◪ Negro neighborhood
◩ Immigrant neighborhood
▨ Jewish neighborhood
▦ Parks

Figure 3. Distribution of Klan Strength in Denver, 1924

margin of 12,020 to 2,391.[17] Bailey had expected to run behind in the area but not by such an avalanche.

Klan No. 1 was elated by the Stapleton victory. On the night of the election Denver members gathered at the Knights of Pythias Hall and proceeded by automobile to Castle Mountain. As the precinct returns indicating success mounted, the Klansmen ignited two crosses—one white and one red—in celebration. Grand Dragon Locke, who was the first to congratulate the Mayor, met with reporters the following day at his office. Labeling army-style discipline the key to his success, he blustered: "The Klan had charge of the campaign and election of Mayor Stapleton, and is entitled to credit for his overwhelming victory at the polls." [18] His sentiments were echoed by the anti-Klan *Denver Post*, which mused that the victory was "one of the greatest, if not the greatest, in the city's political history," proving "beyond any doubt that the Ku Klux Klan is the largest, most cohesive and most efficiently organized political force in the State of Colorado today." [19]

Having won control in the city of Denver, the secret order turned its attention to the 1924 state and county elections. Opting to work within the Republican party, Grand Dragon Locke reached an understanding with wealthy Senator Lawrence Phipps in July 1924. The deal specified that Phipps, who was not a Klansman, should provide the main portion of the campaign funds and that the Klan should take the rest of the ticket, including the short-term Senate seat left vacant by Samuel D. Nicholson. The top of the slate, with the exception of Phipps, would be solidly Klan—Clarence J. Morley, a controversial judge distrusted by many of his colleagues, for governor; Rice W. Means, a former Democrat and the son of an American Protective Association leader, for senator; and incumbent Carl S. Milliken for secretary of state. All were warned by Locke that "the Klan will support no man in the coming election unless he signs his name on the dotted line to all the pledges and promises the Klan demands." Klan strategy also called for the rout of Judge Benjamin Lindsey by Klansman Royal Reed Graham and for the election of scores of lesser state and county aspirants.

The first hurdle for the Phipps-Klan slate was the Denver Republican County Assembly, which met at the city auditorium in early August to elect delegates to the state and congressional assemblies and to designate candidates for the various county offices to be filled at the November election. The Invisible Empire controlled a clear majority of the delegates, and Police Chief Candlish made certain that the galleries were packed with Knights. Grand Dragon Locke directed Klan maneuvering from Mayor Stapleton's box in the rear of the auditorium while Rice Means acted as floor leader. Organization and preparation were superb, and Klan-sponsored nominations and resolutions were railroaded through against ineffective opposition. District Attorney Van Cise met with boos and catcalls when he rose to oppose the tactics of those in control, and most Republican candidates and delegates not sympathetic to the Invisible Empire left the auditorium in disgust.

Klan power was not nearly so evident at the Republican state convention which met two days later. The huge Denver Klan delegation voted solidly behind floor leader Means; as a result Morley, Milliken, and Means were approved for state office. But the vote on other issues often went against the Invisible Empire, affirming that Klan strength lay primarily in Denver and adjacent counties.[20]

Anti-Klan forces in the capital city were not resigned to their fate, however. Within a fortnight of the county convention a group of one hundred Republican business and professional men, led by Van Cise, issued a formal statement charging Grand Dragon Locke with dominating the county assembly and the Klan itself with having exploited the convention "for the secret and private ends of certain of its self-seeking leaders." The Van Cise Committee announced the formation of the Visible Government League and promised to present to the voters a complete county legislative and judicial ticket. On September 2, 1924, Van Cise scheduled a public meeting of the league in the city auditorium to denounce "invisible" control of the Republican party. Grand Dragon Locke ordered the Klan to saturate the meeting; his charges responded so devotedly that at least 70 per cent of the audience was loyal to the Invisible Empire. They booed, stamped their feet, and sang "Onward Christian Soldiers" from 8:45 P.M. until the early hours of the morning, seeking to drown out the words of the district attorney. According to Judge Sam Johnson, more than half the crowd was armed with revolvers. But Van Cise delivered his address in spite of the uproar, and the meeting miraculously closed without violence.

The Colorado general election of 1924 was fought almost entirely along Klan and anti-Klan lines. A liberal governor, William E. Sweet, and a liberal administration ran for re-election on the Democratic ticket with the tacit support of the La Follette men in the state. Opposing them was the reactionary Phipps-Klan Republican slate, most of whose members gave professions of loyalty to the Invisible Empire on Table Mountain. In return, Grand Dragon Locke bedecked Klansmen throughout the state with buttons reading, "Means, Morley, Milliken," stationed at least three Knights in every Denver precinct on election day, and admonished his flock to remember that "We are not Republicans or Democrats but Klansmen." True to tradition, the *Denver Post* opposed most Klan candidates, but made no recommendation for governor, declaring that all five alternatives were "awful."

The result on November 5, 1924, was an apparent endorsement of "one hundred per cent Americanism" in Colorado. Phipps and Means became senators, and former Klokann Clarence Morley was elected to the governorship. Klan-backed Republican candidates also took over the offices of lieutenant governor, auditor of state, attorney general, secretary of state, regent of the University of Colorado, and state supreme court justice.[21] According to *The Christian Century*, the Colorado result offered the nation's "most striking instance of Klan control in the election."

The success of the Invisible Empire was particularly noticeable in Denver, where four of seven District Court benches were filled by Klansmen. Two of the three Klan statewide candidates ran better in the city than in the remainder of Colorado. Morley received 56 per cent of the vote in Denver and 53 per cent of the total elsewhere. Milliken was approved by 65 per cent of the local electorate, and by only 61.7 per cent of voters outside the city. However, Rice W. Means received only 51.7 per cent of the Denver total, while accumulating 52.9 per cent in the rest of the state. The most significant capital city contest involved the re-election attempt of Judge Benjamin B. Lindsey, a veteran of twenty-five years on the bench and the recognized father of the juvenile court system. "The greatest man the state ever produced" had long campaigned for the restriction of child labor, the protection of juvenile rights, and the rehabilitation of youthful offenders.[22] Lindsey's opponent in 1924 was Royal Reed Graham, an admitted Klansman who was characterized by the *Denver Post* as unfit for "any job, however small." The campaign was fought on a low level, and the November election result was exceedingly close. Each side accused the other of fraud, and several recounts were made. For over two years no winner was declared. Finally, the Colorado Supreme Court threw out the returns of a disputed West Colfax precint, thereby awarding the election to Graham, who had committed suicide while waiting for a decision. Meanwhile Lindsey packed his books, burned his records, and despite his long service to Colorado, moved to California. The Klan long savored this result, and in 1927 the Grand Dragon boasted: "But for the splendid work of Denver Klan No. 1, in all probability Judge Lindsey would still be sitting arrogantly on his little juvenile throne." [23]

Less than one week after the Klan's stunning 1924 election success, Imperial Wizard Hiram Wesley Evans, Kansas Grand Dragon Charles H. McBrayer, and Georgia Grand Dragon Nathan Bedford Forrest visited the Colorado capital to join the celebrations. Arriving in a private Burlington railway car, they were met at the station by Governor-elect Morley, Grand Dragon Locke, and Judge A. T. Orahood and escorted by a detachment of Denver policemen to a flower-laden suite in the Brown Palace Hotel. Local Klan leaders feted the visiting dignitaries at breakfast and then spent the entire morning in conference with the Imperial Wizard.

In the late afternoon and evening, Evans attended a dinner given in his honor by Dr. Locke at the Denver Athletic club, addressed a meeting of female Kluxers, and motored to nearby Englewood for a speech before the local chapter. The highlight of the evening came later at a huge initiation at the Cotton Mills Stadium in South Denver. While the two-hundred member Klan No. 1 band serenaded an estimated thirty thousand onlookers, five thousand persons were "naturalized" into the Invisible Empire. After the ceremony the Imperial Wizard told the new Klansmen that they had joined "the most wonderful movement the world has ever seen."

When the Colorado legislature convened early in 1925, Klan power was everywhere evident. *The Nation* reported that the Grand Dragon's office was reckoned as important as the Governor's for those who sought official favors, and an aide of Morley's had as his primary responsibility the carrying of written messages between the capitol building and Locke's office. Klansmen were named to dozens of patronage jobs, and an attempt was made to make all important positions appointive. Dr. Locke was appointed a colonel in the state medical corps, the director of recruiting and publicity for the Colorado National Guard, and a member of the State Board of Medical Examiners. The Governor himself made little attempt to conceal his interest in the secret order. In 1925 he led two hundred marching Klansmen down Sixteenth Avenue through the shopping district, and on March 7 of the same year met with high Klan officials in Washington's Congressional Club.

Hooded Americanism clearly was an important and popular force in Denver early in 1925. A highly successful Ku Klux Klan Boxing and Wrestling Tournament was held at the Cotton Mills Stadium, and a Klan picnic at Lakeside Park attracted almost fifty thousand participants. But the demise of the Colorado Klan empire was not long in coming. Confidence in the Grand Dragon was shaken when the federal government launched an investigation of Locke's alleged mismanagement of Klan funds and his failure to pay any income tax since 1913. A federal judge ordered the Grand Dragon to produce his financial records; when he reported them misplaced he drew a fine of fifteen hundred dollars and ten days in jail. Then a dispute erupted over the validity of his National Guard appointment. Although Governor Morley offered his aid in the difficulties, Locke resigned his official state positions under fire four months after legislative adjournment. Important also was the amicable unification of Klan opponents at a mass meeting in the Denver auditorium on February 11, 1925.

More serious threats to the Invisible Empire in Colorado came on July 1, when an embarrassed national office asked for the resignation of the Grand Dragon. Before the cheers of twenty thousand Klansmen at the Cotton Mills Stadium, Locke announced his refusal to comply. Two weeks later Imperial Wizard Evans asked the rebellious group to turn over all Klan funds and property to the parent organization. The result was an internal dispute within the Denver klavern itself. Most members publicly withdrew from the Invisible Empire, adopted the title of Minute Men of America, and seized local Klan real estate. Another faction remained loyal to Evans and banished the recalcitrants from the Klan.

The growing weakness of the Realm of Colorado was soon reflected in politics, and Governor Morley and Senator Means both fell upon evil days. The Governor's open support of state legislation to outlaw communion wines in churches, and his attempt to abolish state nursing services marked the beginning of his eclipse. In the 1926 off-year elections William E. Sweet gained revenge as both Morley and Means were turned out of office. Denver Mayor Benjamin Stapleton avoided a similar fate only by publicly repudiating the Ku Klux Klan.[24]

After 1926 the Invisible Empire ceased to be a factor in Colorado. John Galen Locke's tax suit dragged on until early in 1935, when the former grand dragon was completely exonerated. He died of coronary thrombosis on April 1 of the same year and was buried in Fairmont Cemetery. Members of the discredited Klan did not appear openly but stole into the graveyard at night to burn a cross before the crypt.

In the 1940's one Denver preacher, a protégé of Gerald L. K. Smith, began publishing the *Western Voice*, an anti-Negro, anti-Catholic, anti-Jewish, anti-United Nations, anti-labor smear sheet. The breadth of his intolerance was reminiscent of Denver's Protestant crusade in the 1920's, but he was never able to recapture the charisma, power, and influence of Grand Dragon John Galen Locke.[25]

V

THE KLAN AND THE CITY

We invested $21,000 in this place and we're not going to be
chased out. We had to move out before, from the southeast side,
when all those Negroes moved in and we practically gave that
house away. We're not running again.

Tom Stramik
Chicago, 1966

The Bureau of the Census revealed in 1920 that the United States
had made the long-awaited transition from a rural to an urban nation. In 1910, 54.2 per cent of its people lived on farms or in cross-
roads villages of fewer than 2,500 inhabitants; by 1920, only 48.6
per cent could be so classified. For the first time in American history less than half the population conformed to the Jeffersonian
ideal.

Recognizing 1920 as a watershed in our national development,
historians have tended to interpret the ensuing decade as an era of
conflict between two well-defined groups in American life, the one
rural, white, dry, Anglo-Saxon, and Protestant, and the other urban,
wet, recent immigrant, and Catholic.[1] A contest between conservative and liberal, and past and future, it featured many of the great
luminaries of the period: William Jennings Bryan, Clarence Darrow, Billy Sunday, H. L. Mencken, and Al Smith. Viewed in this
perspective, Prohibition, Sacco-Vanzetti, the 1924 Democratic Convention, the Scopes Trial, immigration restriction, and the presidential campaign of Governor Smith were but skirmishes in a
conflict of vastly greater import.

This neat rural-urban dichotomy tends to veil rather than illumi-

233

nate the truth when applied to the Ku Klux Klan, however. Considering the city as a single entity obscures the fact that speakeasy and farmhouse were hardly more diverse than elements within the city itself. The urban migration of rural, old-stock Americans is a phenomenon almost as old as the nation itself and ranks in significance with the more celebrated and recent movement of immigrants and Negroes to the city. Thus every metropolis contained a myriad of racial, ethnic, and religious cultures, not all of them congenial. Moreover, the prevailing notion that tolerance and acceptance are more easily spawned in the heterogeneous environment of a large city than in a smaller community is at best too simple, and perhaps mistaken.

16

The Urban Klansman

An important by-product of the urban confrontation of cultures was the success of the Ku Klux Klan in metropolitan areas. Certainly the Invisible Empire did not have great appeal in every city, but neither did it attract widespread support among the farmers and townspeople of many states. Generally, whenever the secret order was strong on a statewide basis, it was more attractive to white Protestants in populous communities than in Robert Lynd's Middletown or along Sinclair Lewis's Main Street.

Because the official records have never been found and in all probability no longer exist, the precise size and distribution of membership of the Invisible Empire cannot be determined.[1] But any comparison of rural, small-town, and urban Klan strength must necessarily begin with an evaluation of total membership, which has been variously estimated at between one and nine million.[2] The commonly accepted figure of about four million was first suggested in 1924 by Stanley Frost, author of several articles and a book on the secret order and a reported friend of *Fiery Cross* editor Milton Elrod. Frost was exceedingly vague, however, and greatly over-estimated the size of such realms as Maryland, Oregon, Texas, California, Mississippi, and Tennessee. His evaluation was readily accepted because both the Klan and the anti-Klan camps stood to gain by exaggerating the size of the threat.[3] A more realistic examination would reveal that in actuality the Invisible Empire enrolled approximately 2,030,000 persons between 1915 and 1944, and never at any time numbered as many as 1,500,000 active members (see Table 8). Of the two million total, at least one million, or 50 per cent, resided in metropolitan areas of more than 50,000 persons. No fewer than 650,000, or 32 per cent, resided in metropolitan areas which in 1920 contained more than 100,000 persons (see Table 9). The traditional ascription of Klan strength to residents in small towns clearly ignores a most important facet of Klan support. On a percentage basis, Indianapolis, Dayton, Portland, Youngstown, Denver, and Dallas were the hooded capitals of the nation, but Chicago's twenty klaverns and 50,000 Knights accounted for the largest single total.

Almost as important as mere numerical representation was the disproportionate influence which urban klaverns exercised within both state and national organizations. Seattle Klan No. 4, Little Rock Klan No. 1, Marion County (Indianapolis) Klan No. 3, or Robert E. Lee (Birmingham) Klan No. 1 never enrolled over one-third of the Klan's statewide total membership, but each was clearly dominant within its realm. Similar, if not greater, supremacy was enjoyed by Denver, Portland, Los Angeles, Chicago, Detroit, Philadelphia, Pittsburgh, and Dallas Klansmen. Ohio had no dominant chapter; those of Akron, Dayton, Columbus, Youngstown, and Cincinnati were all immense.

An important factor in this heavy urban influence was the source of Klan leadership. Most officials at the Imperial Palace had lived their productive lives in a large city, and townspeople or farmers did not win prominence in most state organizations. That Illinois Grand Dragon Charles Palmer hailed from Chicago was typical rather than exceptional. Texas's H. C. McCall, Brown Harwood, Zeke Marvin, and Marvin Childers came from Houston, Fort Worth, Dallas, and San Antonio. Oklahoma's N. Clay Jewett was from Oklahoma City; Maryland's Frank Beall from Baltimore; Alabama's James Esdale from Birmingham; Wisconsin's William Wieseman

Table 8

DISTRIBUTION OF KLAN MEMBERSHIP BY STATES*

Realm	Total	Realm	Total
Indiana	240,000	Washington	25,000
Ohio	195,000	Virginia	20,000
Texas	190,000	Connecticut	20,000
Pennsylvania	150,000	West Virginia	18,000
Illinois	95,000	Mississippi	15,000
Oklahoma	95,000	Wisconsin	15,000
New York	80,000	Maine	15,000
Michigan	70,000	Massachusetts	12,000
Georgia	65,000	Dist. Columbia	7,000
Florida	60,000	South Carolina	5,000
New Jersey	60,000	Minnesota	5,000
Alabama	55,000	Delaware	5,000
Oregon	50,000	Utah	5,000
California	50,000	Rhode Island	5,000
Louisiana	50,000	Idaho	5,000
Missouri	45,000	South Dakota	5,000
Colorado	45,000	Arizona	4,000
Kansas	40,000	North Dakota	3,000
Tennessee	35,000	Montana	3,000
Kentucky	30,000	New Hampshire	2,000
Iowa	28,000	Vermont	2,000
Nebraska	25,000	Nevada	2,000
Maryland	25,000	Wyoming	1,000
Arkansas	25,000	New Mexico	1,000
North Carolina	25,000		
		Total	2,028,000

* The above totals include all male and female persons initiated into the Klan between 1915 and 1944. The figures are personal estimates, which are based to some degree on the claims of William Joseph Simmons, Edward Young Clarke, Hiram Wesley Evans, and Robert L. Duffus, the estimates of the New York *World, Washington Post, The New York Times,* and *The Imperial Night-Hawk,* the evaluations of Charles Alexander, Emerson Loucks, and David Chalmers, and the report of the imperial kligrapp at the 1924 Klonvocation.

from Milwaukee; Oregon's Fred Gifford from Portland; Ohio's Charles Harrod and Clyde Osborne were from Columbus and Youngstown, Colorado's John Galen Locke was from Denver; Indiana's David Stephenson and Walter Bossert were from Evansville and Indianapolis; Connecticut's Harry Lutterman and New Jersey's Arthur Bell from suburban New York City; Tennessee's J. R. Ozier and M. S. Ross from Nashville; and Georgia's Nathan Bedford Forrest was from Atlanta. These grand dragons may have occasionally denounced the iniquities of urban politics or offered lip service to the virtues of farm and country, but they chose the city for themselves and thereby set the pattern for the Invisible Empire.

Predictably, the source and character of the Klan press was also urban. With the exception of such short-lived and insignificant periodicals as the *Tyler* (Texas) *American* and the Tullahoma, Tennessee, *Klan Krusader,* almost every Klan-supported newspaper or magazine, including such major journals as *The Fiery Cross, The Kourier, Dawn, Searchlight, The Watcher on the Tower, The Western American, The Kluxer, The Pitchfork, The American Standard,* and *Col. Mayfield's Weekly,* was headquartered and published in a large city and received the bulk of its advertising revenue from urban businessmen.

Among the questions hardest to answer about the urban Klan are those which concern the character of its membership and the nature of its appeal. Who was the urban Klansman? Why did he turn to the Invisible Empire? The questions defy simply answers but must be analyzed if the movement is to be understood. It will not suffice to call Klan members cowards and scoundrels or to dismiss the secret order as a simple manifestation of ignorance and bigotry. Most members were not innately depraved or anxious to subvert American institutions. Rather they regarded their initiation as a patriotic gesture and believed the tenets of "one hundred per cent Americanism" to be both moral and Christian. As sociologist Frank Tannenbaum has observed: "Sincerity is a common virtue, and must not be denied in an analysis of group behavior."

There is general agreement among students of the Invisible Em-

Table 9

City	Total	City	Total
Akron	18,000	Minneapolis-St. Paul	2,500
Albany-Schenectady-Troy	11,000	Mobile	3,000
Allentown-Bethlehem	2,000	Nashville	3,500
Atlanta	20,000	New Bedford	—
Baltimore	5,000	New Haven	2,000
Birmingham	14,000	New Orleans	3,000
Boston-Somerville-		New York-Yonkers-New	
Cambridge	3,500	Rochelle	16,000
Bridgeport	1,500	Newark-Elizabeth, N. J.	5,000
Buffalo	7,000	Norfolk-Portsmouth, Va.	4,000
Charleston, W. Va.	2,000	Oklahoma City	5,000
Chattanooga	2,500	Omaha-Council Bluffs	3,500
Chicago	50,000	Patterson-Clifton, N. J.	4,500
Cincinnati-Covington	15,500	Philadelphia-Camden	35,000
Cleveland	2,500	Pittsburgh-Carnegie	17,000
Columbus	16,000	Portland	22,000
Dallas	16,000	Providence, R.I.-Mass.	3,000
Davenport-Rock Island-		Reading, Penn.	1,500
Moline	4,000	Richmond	2,500
Dayton	15,000	Rochester	1,500
Denver	23,000	St. Joseph	2,500
Des Moines	3,000	St. Louis-E. St. Louis	5,000
Detroit	35,000	Salt Lake City	1,000
Erie	3,000	San Antonio	6,000
Fall River	—	San Diego	2,000
Flint	2,000	San Francisco-Oakland	3,500
Fort Wayne	3,000	Scranton	2,500
Fort Worth	6,500	Seattle	8,000
Gary-Hammond	10,000	Spokane	2,500
Grand Rapids	2,000	Springfield, Ill.	2,500
Hartford	2,000	Springfield-Holyoke, Mass.	2,000
Houston	8,000	Springfield, Ohio	3,000
Indianapolis	38,000	Syracuse	1,500
Jacksonville	3,500	Tacoma	2,000
Jersey City-Bayonne	4,000	Tampa-St. Petersburg	2,500
Kansas City, Mo.-Kan.	5,000	Toledo	1,500
Knoxville	3,000	Trenton	2,000
Little Rock-N. Little Rock	7,500	Tulsa	6,000
Los Angeles-Long Beach	18,000	Utica-Rome, N. Y.	1,500
Louisville	3,000	Washington	7,000
Lowell	—	Wichita	6,000
Memphis	10,000	Wilmington, Del.-N. J.	3,500
Miami	4,000	Worcester	2,500
Milwaukee	6,000	Youngstown-Warren	17,000
		Total	653,000

* All members, male and female, who resided in the standard metropolitan area, are included. The figures are personal estimates.

pire that the typical Klansman was decent, hard-working, and patriotic, if narrow-minded. But very little specific research has been done on the socio-economic status of the average member. Most observers have placed the responsibility for nativist resurgence on the "common man" rather than upon either social extreme. Former Kleagle Edgar Fry described his associates as "successful business and professional men, nearly all of them devout church members, married men with families, and just the sort of men to make up a prosperous community." His sentiments were echoed by seventy-three Pennsylvania exalted cyclopes, who declared upon oath in 1927 that the Klan membership of their state was "gleaned from the average walk of life and such as composes our Protestant churches, our lodges, commercial clubs, and other civic organizations." John Moffatt Mecklin, surely the most quoted of all authorities, regarded "the good solid middle class, the backbone of the nation" as providing the bulk of the membership; sociologist Guy B. Johnson theorized in 1922 that "prosperous business and professional men" were dominant; and in 1924, Arthur Corning White interpreted the movement as the "middle class, caught between capital and labor." [4] More recently, Irving Leibowitz of Indianapolis described the Invisible Empire as "made up largely of people of substantial and decent standing," and Professor Charles Alexander found the secret order to be "remarkably cross-sectional" in the Southwest, including "a good portion of the substantial people." Less flattering portraits have meanwhile been drawn by Frederick Lewis Allen and Richard Hofstadter. Allen viewed the secret order as drawing mostly upon the "less educated and less disciplined elements of the Protestant community," while Hofstadter labeled the average Knight "relatively unprosperous and uncultivated." [5]

This study has sought to re-open the inquiry into the socio-economic character of the Ku Klux Klan. The evidence indicates that in the city the secret order was a lower-middle-class movement.[6] Few men of wealth, education, or professional position affiliated with the Invisible Empire; the exceptions, such as Dr. John Galen Locke in Denver and Vice President Edwin Debarr of the University of Oklahoma, usually served in high Klan office. White-collar workers in general provided a substantial minority of Klan membership and included primarily struggling independent businessmen, advertising dentists, lawyers, and chiropractors, ambitious and unprincipled politicians and salesmen, and poorly paid clerks. The greatest source of Klan support came from rank and file nonunion, blue-collar employees of large businesses and factories. Miserably paid, they rarely boasted of as much as a high school education and more commonly possessed only a grammar or "free school" background. Their religious loyalty was to conservative, nonritualistic Protestant denominations such as the Baptist, Methodist, or Christian churches.

Although evidence regarding the geographical background of the membership is meager, there was a statistically significant correlation between Klan success and population growth.[7] For example, the secret order was active and strong in such cities as Detroit, Memphis, Dayton, Youngstown, Dallas, and Houston, all of which claimed high growth rates between 1910 and 1930. Conversely, it was weak in comparatively stable Boston, St. Louis, New Orleans, Providence, and Louisville. But Klansmen were not necessarily urban newcomers. On the contrary, in the only city for which statistics are available (Knoxville), one-third of the members were lifelong residents and the remainder had lived in the community for an average of more than nine years. These figures suggest that urban newcomers were the cause rather than the source of Klan strength.

The appeal of "one hundred per cent Americanism" to urban, lower-middle-class Fundamentalists was undoubtedly complex. It was not, however, related to a suppressed penchant for violence. The notion must be dispelled that Klansmen were essentially sadists reveling in murder and torture. Scores of floggings, tar and featherings, and other forms of physical abuse were reported in the South between 1920 and 1925, and no fewer than six murders were directly attributable to the secret order. But lawlessness had a long tradition in the region, and not all violations of justice could be charged to the Klan account. This basic fact was recognized by both the American Civil Liberties Union and *The New Republic*, which declared in 1927: "Some hoodlums signed up in order to participate in night-riding, but it is safe to say that 90 per cent of the total membership never indulged in such practices." Outside the South only a very small number of members partcipated in any form of violence. In fact, in many parts of the country (such as Perth Amboy, New Jersey; Niles, Ohio; and Carnegie, Pennsylvania), Klansmen were more often the victims than the instigators of foul play.[8]

Table 10

COMPARATIVE KLAN OCCUPATIONAL CHART*

Community	Total Membership	Blue-Collar		White-Collar	
		Number of Persons	Percentage of Membership	Number of Persons	Percentage of Membership
Knoxville	399	283	70.9	116	29.1
Chicago	110	43	39.1	67	60.9
Aurora	73	26	35.6	47	64.4
Winchester	180	134	74.4	46	25.6

* The above percentages include only those members about whom precise occupational information is available. In Chicago and Aurora the information is biased in favor of white-collar workers because anti-Klan elements were quick to identify the names of independent businessmen on the Klan lists. The occupational distribution of Klansmen in other cities could not be determined. The figures are based on Tables 3, 5, 6, and 7.

Fear of change, not vindictiveness or cruelty, was the basic motivation of the urban Klansman. He was disillusioned by the Great War and its aftermath, by the Senate rejection of the League of Nations, and by the economic recession which came in the summer and fall of 1920. He was aware of the Red Scare and of reports of "petting parties," "wild dancing," and other indications of a revolution in morals. Sensing that the traditional values, religion, and way of life of an older America were in danger, he donated ten dollars to a hypocritical secret society in a vague attempt to halt the forces of time. Ordinarily, the decade of the twenties is thought of as an era of "normalcy." Actually, it was a period of rapid, almost bewildering, change; the Model T, the telephone, the radio, the airplane, and the motion picture were transforming American life. But the changes of greatest concern to the urban Knight were ethnic and racial, not technological.

Two far-reaching, distinct migration patterns provided the basis for the phenomenal career of the Ku Klux Klan. The first was a shift in the sources of European immigration, particularly noticeable after 1890, from the English, Irish, Scandinavians, and Germans of earlier years to the peasantry of southern and eastern Europe— Hungarians, Italians, Slovaks, Czechs, and Poles. The predominantly Catholic and Jewish newcomers frightened nativists by clinging tenaciously to Old World customs and celebrations, by establishing hundreds of foreign-language newspapers, and by voting for the supposedly corrupt and inefficient urban political machines. Spurred by Lothrop Stoddard's *The Rising Tide of Color* and Madison Grant's *Passing of the Great Race,* older Americans made excited appeals for immigration restriction. Their basic fear was that if the immigration flow were not shut off or drastically reduced, then white, Anglo-Saxon Protestants would become a minority in the land of their fathers, and the nation would be ethically transformed.

The second major migration pattern of concern was that of American Negroes from farm to city and from South to North. First noticeable about 1910, the trend was accelerated by World War I, which restricted the supply of foreign labor, increased the demands of industry, and encouraged many industries to experiment with Negro labor. An additional factor was the boll weevil, which ravaged hundreds of thousands of acres of fertile cotton fields and forced white farmers temporarily to abandon their custom of advancing money to field hands. The traditional Negro dependence upon southern agriculture was weakened; between 1910 and 1920 the Negro rural population fell by 239,000 while the urban total increased by 874,000. Almost four hundred thousand Negroes moved to southern cities in the decade, and an even larger number trekked to the urban North. During the twenties the black stream became a flood and an additional six hundred thousand Negroes crossed the Mason-Dixon line.[9] The impact was startling, particularly in the Midwest. In the twenty years between 1910 and

1930 the non-white population of Chicago increased from 44,000 to 160,000, that of Detroit from 6,000 to 125,000, and that of Indianapolis from 22,000 to 44,000.

Ultimately, both migration patterns posed a threat to white Protestants throughout the United States, but the immediate impact was primarily upon urban residential stability. By both choice and necessity the immigrants and Negroes crowded into ghettos, often located near the center of the city. White Protestants, on the other hand, were more likely to reside nearer the edge of a community. Thus divided geographically as well as religiously, socially, economically, and politically, the inner core and the residential fringe were consistent opponents and created an intra-urban environment favorable for the growth of the Ku Klux Klan.

Neighborhood transition has been a neglected but omnipresent dimension of American urban history for at least the last one hundred years, but its rapidity and extent increased markedly in the first quarter of the twentieth century as immigrants and Negroes crowded into burgeoning cities.[10] Some physical expansion of the bulging racial and ethnic ghettos was inevitable; but equally threatening to the tranquillity of the older (i.e. white Protestant) residents was the desire of ambitious second-generation immigrants and successful Negroes to escape completely from the old neighborhoods and to buy or rent in the "zone of emergence," [11] the broad belt separating the core of the city from its outer residential fringe. The "zone of emergence" was usually made up of working-class neighborhoods of modest homes and apartments, and it was here, among white laborers, that the Invisible Empire thrived. Unable to afford a fine home far removed from minority problems, the potential Klansman could not live along Chicago's Lake Shore Drive or Indianapolis's Fall Creek Parkway, or in Memphis's Hein Park or Atlanta's Druid Hills. Rather, he was forced by economic necessity to live in older transitional areas close to his place of employment. He was bewildered by the rapid pace of life and frustrated by his inability to slow the changes which seemed so constant and so oppressive. He perhaps remembered an earlier neighborhood transition and was frightened at the prospect of a Negro or a Pole coming into his block and causing him to sell his house at a low price. Unable to escape and hesitant to act alone, the threatened citizen welcomed the security and respectability of a large group. Seeking to stabilize his world and maintain a neighborhood status quo, he turned to the promise of the Klan. Not a reaction against the rise of the city to dominance in American life, the Invisible Empire was rather a reaction against the aspirations of certain elements within the city.

The problems of the potential Klansman were complicated by his economic condition. Whether a struggling café proprietor in Indianapolis, a lumber mill worker in Knoxville, a milkman in Chicago, or a cotton oil company employee in Memphis, he had obviously been left at the post in an economic race he perhaps only inadequately understood. His wages were below average, his tasks often menial, his responsibilities slight, and his opportunity for advancement remote. Yet this was an age heavily influenced by the Horatio Alger notion that hard work would be rewarded and that all Americans had ample opportunity in the competition for prestige and economic advantage. Having fought his way above the lowest rungs of the financial ladder, the potential Klansman remained something less than a success. Life seemed to offer him little dignity or personal significance. Moreover, he was faced with increasing competition from Catholics and from a new kind of Negro, who seemed anxious to take his job and live in his neighborhood. What was he to do? [12]

Then a kleagle arrived in the city. Capitalizing on the psychological principle that the easiest idea to sell someone is that he is better than someone else, he told his eager listeners that the country belongs to the sons of the men who built it. Catholics, Jews, Negroes, and foreigners could only undermine the national heritage. The recruiter offered enough mystery to be attractive, enough crusading spirit to be appealing, and enough idealism to be impressive. Pointing to the KKK as the greatest Protestant organization on earth, the kleagle tendered the urban worker the opportunity to become a Knight of the Invisible Empire for only ten dollars. Here indeed was new hope. As a member of a vast and secret body of "one hundred per cent Americans," the initiate was able to derive a modicum of self-esteem from comparing himself with members of unfavored groups. As Professor Gordon Allport has observed, snobbery is a way of clutching at one's own social and economic status and is particularly common among those who have little of either. Moreover, the Klansman found solace in the belief that his participation and his patriotism were essential to the continued survival of constitutional freedoms. His klectokens, "naturalization," and white robes served as a salve for his wounded pride and enabled him to fight rather than face the future.

Every metropolitan chapter of the Invisible Empire was in some respects unique. The environment of heavily Catholic Detroit differed markedly from the atmosphere of smaller Denver, which was more homogeneous racially and ethnically; the situation in Atlanta was unlike that in Portland. Even within the same city conditions were never the same; Chicago's Austin Klan No. 6 was not faced with the same problems as Englewood Klan No. 2 or Logan Square Klan No. 9. The zeal and ability of recruiters, the degree of major newspaper opposition, the year of peak strength, and the quality of local leadership were important variables. Certainly the political situation differed greatly from city to city. Indianapolis, Chicago, Detroit and Memphis Knights were forced to contend with unfriendly municipal administrations, whereas a neutral chief executive presided in Knoxville, and pro-Klan politicians occupied the mayoral posts in Denver, Portland, Atlanta, and later, Indianapolis.

But whatever the local situation, urban klaverns faced peculiar problems which served to differentiate them from their small-town or rural counterparts. Survival required a significant adjustment in methods and manner from more traditional methods of Klanishness. Urban Knights could rarely defy city police and parade unmolested through busy downtown streets, nor could they drag moral transgressors from their homes or drive errant Negroes from the community. Burning crosses were utilized somewhat more frequently and with greater effect in the small towns. But because urban

Klansmen were less ostentatious and spectacular than their rural counterparts is no indication that they were less active or powerful.

"Harvest Jubilee and Rube parties," river excursions, "Kolossal Klan Karnivals," barbecues, picnics, and weekly meetings in rented fraternal halls were among the myriad activities of the Klansmen in the cities. Particularly exciting were the large outdoor initiations which normally required a short drive to nearby "naturalization grounds." While urban Klansmen never participated in organized community drives and rarely conducted large-scale charity campaigns of their own, they did lend much assistance to the individually needy. Most of the giving was spontaneous and haphazard and usually included the distribution of food and gifts at Christmas and financial support for impoverished widows. Particularly ambitious in this regard was Dallas Klan No. 66, which established and operated for several years a seventy-five-thousand-dollar institution for homeless children.

Church visitations were an important part of the urban Klan routine, and many Klansmen long remembered the silent reaction of a startled congregation as robed Knights appeared unexpectedly during their services. The alliance with Protestantism was partly the result of conviction and partly the result of clerical assistance. Caleb Ridley in Atlanta, James R. Johnson in Portland, Oscar Haywood in New York City, A. C. Parker in Dallas, and William Oeschger in Denver were among scores of clergymen who served in high Klan positions. But such men were not typical of their co-religionists, and were frequently, like Ridley, drummed out of their own churches. In 1923 Rabbi Samuel Mayerberg warned in Chicago: "Protestantism is on trial. Protestantism must destroy Ku Kluxism or Ku Kluxism will destroy Protestantism." The church survived the crisis capably; virtually every denomination publicly and officially denounced the Klan, and, with the exception of Chicago, opposition to the Invisible Empire was almost everywhere spearheaded by Protestants.

The most distinguishing characteristic of urban Klansmen was a preoccupation with politics. Usually unable to demonstrate publicly or to achieve their goals through intimidation, they turned early to the ballot box as the best method of preserving "one hundred per cent Americanism" in the cities. State-wide contests sometimes gained prominence, as in the campaign of Walter Pierce and compulsory public education in Oregon, Clarence J. Morley and Rice W. Means in Colorado, Earle B. Mayfield in Texas, Ralph Owen Brewster in Maine, and Ed Jackson in Indiana. But primary emphasis was usually placed upon local elections. Strategy varied from city to city with success coming most often when the secret order functioned as a balance of power within the two-party system rather than as an independent political force. Thus did Klan support elect Republican Mayor John Duvall in Indianapolis and Democratic Mayors Benjamin Stapleton and Walter Sims in Denver and Atlanta. Seeking success outside the two major parties, Klan candidates W. Joe Wood in Memphis and Charles Bowles in Detroit met defeat. Similarly, the Invisible Empire's choices for lesser political offices were unsuccessful when they failed to ally with other independent political pressure groups. Regardless of methods, however, the secret order never earned anything more than short-term political success and was usually forced from power as soon as anti-Klan elements awakened the community to the menace and united behind a single candidate. It is significant and indicative of the fact that the Klan was not a movement of economic protest that its political endorsements were made primarily on the basis of race, religion, and attitude toward the KKK rather than upon economic philosophy.[13]

Although the Invisible Empire had only a minor impact upon presidential politics, its national influence was well demonstrated at the 1924 Democratic Convention. In broiling heat, the delegates at Madison Square Garden split almost evenly on a vote to denounce the Ku Klux Klan by name. The motion failed by one vote. The bitterness engendered carried over into the selection of a presidential nominee and smashed the uneasy coalition between the two great wings of the party. Only after 103 ballots, the longest deadlock in convention history, was John W. Davis of West Virginia nominated for President. By that time the Democratic party was so badly divided that only a major depression and the Roosevelt coalition would restore it to health.

The contending forces in American life that tore apart the 1924 Democratic National Convention were also at work in the nation's cities. Roman Catholic and Fundamentalist, Gentile and Jew, Prohibitionist and wet, Negro and white, old immigrant and new came together in urban America as nowhere else and faced each other in direct political, economic, and social competition. The result was not always harmony, understanding, and tolerance. The Ku Klux Klan provided a focus for the fears of alienated native Americans whose world was being disrupted. In the city the Invisible Empire found its greatest challenge, and in the city it met its ultimate defeat.

Epilogue

In the summer of 1924, the Invisible Empire could boast that it was the most powerful fraternal and nativistic organization in American history. Neither as violent, fanatical, or racially oriented as its namesake of the post–World War II era, nor as socially acceptable or economically conservative as the John Birch Society, the Ku Klux Klan was much more broadly based than either and, with two million members, almost qualified as an authentic folk movement. The secret order's immense lower-middle-class constituency provided the movement with a gross revenue of perhaps forty million dollars between 1920 and 1925, discrediting the theory that financial support of such magnitude could come only from wealthy industrialists seeking mass support for individual objectives.

But the Klan fell from the heights of national power to obscurity between 1923 and 1929. Relatively inactive during the 1930's, it ceased to exist during World War II. The exact rate of deterioration may never be known, but decline was so rapid that it could not long escape public notice. In August 1925, Dixon Merritt unequivocally stated in *The Outlook* that the national organization had been losing members, and in December the secret order itself gave a hint of growing weakness: "The early church was bitterly persecuted,

251

but it prospered. The Masons were bitterly persecuted, but they weathered the storm. The Klan is having its testing period. Will it survive? Let God and time answer."

By the early months of 1926 it was obvious that the strength of the Ku Klux Klan had greatly diminished. In February, *The New York Times* completed a nationwide survey of the secret order and pronounced it definitely on the wane: "Everywhere it shows signs of dissolution; nowhere are there indications of gain." Early in the summer, at the completion of a similar study, William Starr Myers of Princeton University concluded, "There would seem to be no question that the Ku Klux Klan as an organization has passed its zenith and already is on the wane." As decline continued without abatement, affiliation with the Invisible Empire became a distinct political liability and candidates began to seek votes on the ground that they no longer belonged to the society. In the 1926 congressional and state selections the Klan lost much of the ground it had gained two years earlier, particularly in Colorado, Indiana, Oregon, and Ohio. Early in 1928 the Imperial Wizard himself finally admitted the obvious: "There is some truth in reports of our weakness; we have lost strength at certain points."

The attempt of Alfred E. Smith to become President in 1928 was a temporary godsend for the faltering Invisible Empire. The son of Irish immigrants, the affable New York Governor was the very antithesis of the Klan ideal; he was alien, wet, and representative of urban bossism. Most importantly, he was a Catholic. Imperial Wizard Evans defined the danger, and *The Kourier* predicted that Smith would be "the worst beaten man who ever ran for the presidency as a nominee of a major party." The Klan's battle against "priest-rule" included bonfires, speeches, and pamphleteering in more than twenty states. When Herbert Hoover won a landslide victory, the Invisible Empire boasted that it had nailed "Smith's political hide to the Klan's barn door."

Apparent Klan success at the polls, however, obscured long-term indications of decay and exaggerated the secret order's relatively small influence on the Republican victory. Of a peak membership of one and one half million in 1924, less than 10 per cent had taken part in the Klan's crusade against Smith. The depression further shortened the chapter rolls and a new exodus began. Frantically the Klan began to search for a new issue which would unite America's native white Protestants.

In the early 1930's the secret order increasingly regarded Communism as the nation's greatest enemy. The bolshevik menace was, of course, never clearly defined; but it obviously included trade unionism as well as Negro "uppitiness." The Klan helped defeat the efforts of the C.I.O. to organize southern textile workers, and it warned Negroes to reject the "Red" tenet of an egalitarian society. Its frequent boasts that "Communism Will Not Be Tolerated," and its occasionally violent activities in support of the racial and moral status quo generated considerable publicity, but few recruits.

As the decade came to an end, control of the Invisible Empire passed finally from the hands of Hiram Wesley Evans. In January 1939 he accepted an invitation to attend the dedication of the Catholic Cathedral of Christ the King on the grounds of the Klan's old, white-pillared Imperial Palace. The local press lauded his action, but it galled rank-and-file Klansmen who, in their enthusiasm to hate Communists, had not forgotten that Catholics were something less than "one hundred per cent American." They communicated their displeasure to the national office, and on June 10, 1939, in a ceremony at the Henry Grady Hotel, the Dallas dentist stepped down after almost seventeen years as imperial wizard.

Evans's successor was a bespectacled and balding, forty-two-year-old former veterinarian from Terre Haute, Indiana. James Arnold Colescott was a capable administrator and a veteran of sixteen years of Klan service. He re-affirmed the order's white-supremacist and anti-Catholic traditions, announced a new recruiting drive, and sent kleagles into thirty-nine states. Old members did not return to the colors as anticipated, however, and younger men were too concerned about a possible war with the Axis to bother with imagined internal threats to "one hundred per cent Americanism." In most cities, the Klan membership drive was a total failure.

The end came in 1944. The federal government presented Colescott with a bill for $685,000 for back taxes on the Invisible Empire's profits in the 1920's. The secret order had neither the enthusiasm nor the klectokens to meet the crisis. On April 28, 1944, its national officials gathered in secret and voted to disband the Invisible Empire. Several weeks later James Colescott closed his imperial office and retired to Florida.

The debilitating factors that caused the Klan's precipitous decline in the 1920's and its official demise two decades later were as varied as the factors that had earlier contributed to its growth. Aside from immigration restriction (for which the Invisible Empire took credit), the kleagles had promised much more than the Klan could deliver. It could neither restore the Bible to primacy in the public schools, nor restrict the activities of the Catholic Church, nor return the Negro to rural docility, nor stop neighborhood transition. Opposition from liberal Protestants, metropolitan newspapers, and members of minority groups severely damaged the klaverns of Detroit, Dallas, Chicago, Denver, and many other communities.[1] Moreover, most urban chapters were torn apart internally by charges of corruption arising from the Simmons-Evans dispute on the national level or from the colliding ambitions of local Klan officials. In 1925 alone Niagara, New York, Klansmen broke away to form the Independent Protestant Knights of America; Denver Klansmen renamed themselves the Minute Men of America; Illinois and Indiana Klansmen created the Independent Klan of America; and Pennsylvania members formed the American Debating Society. A particularly damaging secession was that of six hundred members of the powerful New Haven, Connecticut, klavern. Declaring that no American worthy of the name could any longer affiliate with the national body, they resigned in a group to maintain their "self-respect." In a public statement they labeled the secret order "a travesty on patriotism and a blasphemous caricature professing Protestantism."

The ultimate weakness of the Invisible Empire, however, was its lack of a positive program and a corresponding reliance upon emotion rather than reason. The distinctive white garb, super-secret ritual, and guarded open-air meetings were calculated to appeal to man's weakness for the mysterious. But emotion proved to be a two-edged sword. Having aroused eager patriots to the imminent dangers facing Americanism, the Klan could not pacify them by repeating an eight-page ritual four times a month and passively awaiting election day. Inevitably, the unusual became commonplace, and emotional fervor waned. Without a meaningful *raison d'étre* the Invisible Empire was exposed as a ludicrous sham, for neither its infantile mumbo jumbo nor its exaggerated claims could bear objective scrutiny, even among those it counted as Knights. The genuine American sense of decency finally asserted itself and consigned the once mighty Klan to obscurity.

As a result of the continuing refusal of the American people to accept literally as well as theoretically the words of the Declaration of Independence and Statue of Liberty, the problems brought into sharp focus by the Ku Klux Klan have not been solved; the roots of intolerance remain. The techniques perfected by Edward Young Clarke and his kleagles remain available for any who would implement them: first, the affirmation of a program of the most resoundingly patriotic aims, and secondly, the singling out of a controversial and unpopular portion of the community for attack. Although the Ku Klux Klan is no longer an effective and viable force in American life, the Klan mentality remains.

Notes

PART I

1. *Variety* estimated in 1963 that the movie had grossed more than *Gone with the Wind*. Walter Lippmann, *Public Opinion* (New York, 1922), p. 92. See also Tom Murray White, *"The Birth of a Nation: An Examination of Its Sources, Content, and Historical Assertions About Reconstruction"* (unpub. Master's thesis, University of Chicago, 1952).

2. Simmons may have been intoxicated during his many viewings. Ralph McGill, *The South and the Southerner* (Boston, 1959), p. 133. See also Charles O. Jackson, "The Ku Klux Klan, 1914-1924: A Study in Leadership" (unpub. Master's thesis, Emory University, 1962), p. 6.

3. The Klan must have had an unusual interpretation of this well-known chapter, the tenth verse of which reads: "Be kindly affectioned one to another with brotherly love; in honour preferring one another."

4. The official Klan version of the founding was that as a youth Simmons had a vision of galloping horsemen in the sky and had then sworn to establish the memorial organization. It is more likely that the idea did not occur to Simmons until 1915. Either he read about *The Birth of a Nation* or knew of Tom Watson's statement in connection with the Leo Frank case that, "another Ku Klux Klan may be organized to restore Home Rule," in *The Jeffersonian*, August 12, 1915. Quoted in Stetson Kennedy, *Southern Exposure* (Garden City, N.Y., 1946), p. 165.

CHAPTER 1

1. Former Kleagle Edgar Irving Fuller wrote that Frost was the real founder of the Klan and that Simmons stole the idea. Fuller, *The Maelstrom: The Visible of the Invisible Empire* (Denver, 1925), p. 22. See also, U.S. Congress, House Committee on Rules, *Hearings on the Ku Klux Klan*, 67th Cong., 1st Sess., 1921, p. 69. Hereafter cited as *Klan Hearings*.

2. Simmons, William Joseph, *Imperial Proclamation of the Imperial Wizard, Emperor of the Invisible Empire, Knights of the Ku Klux Klan* (Atlanta, 1917). Rare Book Room, Library of Congress.

3. Winfield Jones, *Knights of the Ku Klux Klan* (New York, 1941), p. 76.

4. According to Fuller, Simmons was dismissed from the Methodist Conference because "he was mentally inefficient and morally delinquent." Fuller, p. 26. It is entirely possible that Simmons was thinking of the lucrative fraternal insurance field when he organized the Klan. Of the 92 persons who joined the secret order in the first few months, 42 signed up for a total of $53,000 worth of Klan life insurance. This feature did not survive the early years of the Klan, but was revived briefly in the mid-twenties by the Empire Mutual Life Insurance Company of Kansas City. William Joseph Simmons and William G. Shepherd, "How I Put Over the Klan," *Collier's*, LXXXII (July 14, 1928), 31-3.

5. Ward Greene, "Notes for a History of the Klan," *American Mercury*, V (June 1925), 241. A crank telegram, dated April 2, 1917, contended that over ten thousand men were already sworn into the Ku Klux Klan "to destroy those who make blood profit from war." Justice Department File 9-5-304, National Archives.

6. Simmons's earnings before 1920 averaged only $2000 per year. Testimony of Simmons, *Klan Hearings*, 69-70.

7. William Joseph Simmons, *America's Menace or the Enemy Within* (Atlanta, 1926), p. 66.

8. Edward Young Clarke testified in 1924 that when he took over as imperial kleagle in June 1920, "there were only ten or fifteen Klans, and approximately a membership of three thousand." U.S. Senate, Committee on Privileges and Elections, *Senator from Texas: Hearings*, 68th Cong., 1st and 2nd Sess., 1924, p. 422. Hereafter cited as *Senator from Texas*.

CHAPTER 2

1. The contract is reprinted in full in Winfield Jones, *Knights of the Ku Klux Klan* (New York, 1941), pp. 228-30. See also "For and Against the Ku Klux Klan," *The Literary Digest*, LXX (September

24, 1921), 38; and *The Whole Truth about the Effort To Destroy the Ku Klux Klan* (Atlanta: Knights of the Ku Klux Klan, 1923), pp. 2-6.

2. Of every $10 collected as a "klectoken," or initiation fee, $8 were taken in commissions and only $2 were available for general use. Indications are that in their first year of operation Tyler and Clarke split only $57,000. Testimony of Simmons, *Klan Hearings*, p. 158.

3. Ward Greene maintains that the Klan got its start when an ambitious photographer gave twenty Negroes a quarter each to pose in sheets as Klansmen and then sold his pictures to the mass media. *The New York Times* placed them in its rotogravure section. Greene, "Notes for a History of the Klan," p. 242. See also testimony of Simmons, *Klan Hearings*, p. 87.

4. The relationship of Masons to the Klan has been the subject of considerable disagreement. Masonic leaders denounced the secret order in the strongest terms, but the Klan was quite successful in recruiting among the adherents of Masonry, and more than half the members of some klaverns were Masons. See particularly *Searchlight*, July 1, 1922, and November 11, 1922; *Tolerance*, December 24, 1922; and *The New York Times*, June 17, 1922.

5. Payment by commission was a major cause of ultimate Klan failure because it led to the initiation of many individuals who joined for personal revenge or financial gain.

6. The Klan attributed the New York *World* attack to a desire to increase circulation and the fact that Joseph Pulizer was Jewish. Guy B. Johnson, "The New Ku Klux Movement" (unpub. Master's thesis, University of Chicago, 1922), p. 95.

7. Accurate financial records for later periods are unavailable because the only statements ever given to the Klan membership presented a mere recital of assets and liabilities. For example, see *The Imperial Night-Hawk*, August 29, 1923, p. 1, and January 23, 1924, p. 1, Table 2.

8. When the exposé first began, the Klan threatened to bring suit for $10 million, but the secret order soon began to realize the beneficent effects of the press exposure. According to Fuller, "The *World* and its combination of papers did more to spread the Klan throughout the nation than all the propaganda that Clarke and Mrs. Tyler could have devised in years." Edgar Irving Fuller, *The Maelstrom: The Visible of the Invisible Empire* (Denver, 1925), p. 19; and New York *World*, September 8, 1921, p. 2.

9. Mrs. Clarke identified her husband in Mrs. Tyler's bed at 183 South Pryor Street in Atlanta. Fortunately, the *World* photographed the record of the arrest, because the relevant page later disappeared from the records of the Atlanta police department. New York *World*, September 19, 1921.

10. Paul Meres Winter went on to declare that the office of imperial wizard entailed greater responsibilities than that of the President

of the United States. See Winter, *What Price Tolerance?* (Newlett, N.Y., 1928), pp. 18-20.

11. Simmons and Shepherd, "How I Put Over the Klan," *Collier's*, LXXXII (July 28, 1928), 47.

12. Official records of this litigation and other Klan-related legal suits of the period in Fulton County Superior Court have been destroyed in accord with Georgia law. Only those cases which were appealed to the Georgia Supreme Court or Court of Appeals were preserved.

13. *Minutes of the Imperial Kloncilium, Knights of the Ku Klux Klan. Meeting of May 1 and 2, 1923* (Atlanta, 1923), *passim*.

PART II

1. Laura Rose, *The Ku Klux Klan or Invisible Empire* (New Orleans, 1914), p. 75.

2. See Table 8 for the number of members by state.

3. Gunnar Myrdal, *An American Dilemma: The Negro Problem and Modern Democracy* (New York, 1944), I, 560.

4. A Catholic, Percy was the son of Mississippi's well-respected anti-Klan senator, Leroy Percy. See W. A. Percy, *Lanterns on the Levee: Recollections of a Planter's Son* (New York, 1941), pp. 232 and 237.

CHAPTER 3

1. So labeled by an editorial in Illinois's anti-Catholic newspaper, *The Rail Splitter*. Reprinted in *Searchlight*, June 10, 1922. Catholics accounted for about 2 per cent and Jews about 5 per cent of the Atlanta population. U.S. Bureau of the Census, *Census of Religious Bodies: 1926*, I, 365-6. Hereafter cited as *Religious Bodies: 1926*. See also Robert H. Mugge, "Negro Migrants in Atlanta" (unpub. Ph.D. diss., University of Chicago, 1957), *passim*.

2. Robert Ramspeck was later a congressman from Georgia. An earlier charter was granted on December 4, 1915, but the Klan was not incorporated until July 1, 1916.

3. Wade was formally banished in 1922 from the Invisible Empire, when he publicly denounced both Simmons and Clarke and instituted legal action against Klan officials in Fulton County Superior Court. He later helped organize the anti-Klan National Defenders.

4. According to Winfield Jones, "No citizen of Atlanta has a higher standing in the public estimation than Judge Etheridge." Jones, *Knights of the Ku Klux Klan* (New York, 1941), p. 107. See also *Searchlight*, June 16, 1922; New York *World*, September 19, 1921; and testimony of Paul S. Etheridge, *Klan Hearings*, p. 59.

5. Rivers was a charter member of Grand Klan No. 285, an Atlanta chapter chartered in 1928. The original charter is in the possession of an Atlanta resident who prefers to remain anonymous. An un-

even treatment of the early years is Marion Monteval, *The Klan Inside Out* (Claremore, Okla., 1924), 165-9.

6. Charles P. Sweeney, "The Great Bigotry Merger," *The Nation*, CXV (July 5, 1922), 10; and testimony of C. Anderson Wright, *Klan Hearings*, p. 17.

7. Georgia Governor Hardwick made the dedicatory speech at the home of Simmons, who also received two automobiles and $25,000 as "gifts" from his followers.

8. The JOUAM was also an anti-Catholic fraternity, and membership in that body was considered an excellent recommendation for membership in the Klan. One page of the eight-page *Searchlight* was ordinarily devoted to the activities of the JOUAM.

9. Miss Julia Riordan, who had taught in Atlanta for 20 years, was reportedly discharged in 1921 because she was a Catholic. Testimony of Rowland Thomas, *Klan Hearings*, pp. 8-15 and 59.

10. *Searchlight*, August 8, 1921; reprinted in the New York *World*, September 16, 1921. See also *Atlanta Journal*, September 9 and 23, 1922.

11. E. F. Stanton, *Christ and Other Klansmen; or Lives of Love: The Cream of the Bible Spread upon Klanism* (Kansas City, 1924), pp. 10-11.

12. *The Atlanta Georgian* occasionally sniped at the Klan and opposed it politically. In 1921, *Enquirer-Sun* editor Julian Harris, the son of Joel Chandler Harris, wrote that his was "the only daily in Georgia to oppose the Klan and was the first in the South to attack it." The Klan's explanation was that "Tom Loyless was married into the Roman Church and Julian Harris was born into it." See particularly *Columbus Enquirer-Sun*, November 8, 1923. See also Theodore Saloutos, *The Greeks in the United States* (Cambridge, 1964), pp. 246-8.

13. In 1921, Atlanta was the base of 25 kleagles operating under Grand Goblin M. B. Owen in the Haynes Building. New York *World*, September 9, 1921; *Searchlight*, May 6 and 13, 1922; *Atlanta Constitution*, November 28 and 29, 1922; *Tolerance*, December 24, 1922; and *The Fiery Cross*, December 8, 1922.

14. Article XIII, Section 5, *Constitution and Laws of the Knights of the Ku Klux Klan, Inc.* (Atlanta, 1921). Rare Book Room, Library of Congress.

15. Simmons estimated in 1921 that only 30 per cent of Klansmen owned robes and that the wholesale price of the regalia was $4.50. The robe factory began operation on August 16, 1923, and charged Klan officials as much as $40 each for their special robes. Testimony of Simmons, *Klan Hearings*, p. 133; Report of T. J. McKinnon, Manager of Plants, to 1924 Klonvokation, reprinted in Edgar Irving Fuller, *The Maelstrom: The Visible of the Invisible Empire* (Denver, 1925), p. 133; and *Dawn*, July 28 and August 25, 1923.

16. See particularly Frank Bohn, "The Ku Klux Klan Interpreted," *The American Journal of Sociology*, XXX (January 1925), 395-6.
17. In 1921, the New York *World* estimated Atlanta Klan membership at 40,000. Most local members belonged to Klan No. 1, but East Point Klan No. 61, chartered on November 12, 1920, and several other klaverns also operated in the Atlanta area.
18. Governor Hardwick refused to condemn the secret order in 1921, and Senator Tom Watson said he was known as "the King of the Ku Klux Klan in Georgia." It is not likely that either of the men was a Klansman.
19. Testimony of Simmons, *Klan Hearings*, p. 72. The Klan opposed a Chamber of Commerce proposal to adopt the city-manager plan in 1922, and the measure was defeated 7041 to 6010.
20. Evidence of Sims's Klan affiliation is available in a collection of testimony, never tried, gathered by the Indiana Attorney General between 1926 and 1928. See testimony of William J. Mahoney, *State of Indiana* v. *Knights of the Ku Klux Klan*, p. 133 A.
21. Governor Walker addressed the 1924 Klonvokation in Kansas City, and was reported to have said in 1922, "If anybody gets an indictment against a Klansman—or a Klan itself—I AM GOING TO WRITE OUT A PARDON IMMEDIATELY." *Columbus Enquirer-Sun*, November 23, 1924; and *Atlanta Journal*, September 7 to 25, 1922.
22. The case was listed as *William Joseph Simmons* v. *H. W. Evans, et al.*, No. 556,553, In Equity, of the Superior Court of Fulton County.
23. According to James L. Key, the primary issues in the campaign were "the Georgia Railway and Power Company and the *Atlanta Constitution*." Sims's victory was 7967 to 6566. J. O. Wood again led the field for the state legislature, but by a smaller margin than in 1922.
24. The floggers were soon released by Governor Eugene Talmadge.

CHAPTER 4

1. A Negro laborer accused of the rape and murder of Antoinette Rappal, a sixteen-year-old white girl, was forcibly taken from police officers and, before 15,000 men, women, and children, burned alive. Almost insensible to the atrocity in their city, Memphis newspapers remained primarily concerned with the reported crimes of the German Army some 4000 miles away. *The Commercial-Appeal*, May 15 to 25, 1917; National Association for the Advancement of Colored People, *Thirty Years of Lynching in the United States, 1889-1918* (New York, 1919), pp. 25-6; and William D. Miller, *Memphis During the Progressive Era* (Memphis, 1957), *passim*.
2. The Memphis Negro percentage declined, however, from 48.8 per cent in 1900 to 37.7 per cent in 1920. The foreign-born total, small to begin with, also declined between 1910 and 1920.

3. An uninspiring writer, Mooney was a native of Kentucky. An admiring study of his career is Sister Mary Leonita Geraghty, "The Life and Editorials of C. P. J. Mooney" (unpub. Master's thesis, Creighton University, 1932).

4. This judgment is based upon newspaper estimates, interviews with former Memphis Klansmen, and an analysis of election returns. My neighborhood analysis owes much to the superb study of Rayburn W. Johnson, "Land Utilization in Memphis" (unpub. Ph.D. diss., Department of Geography, University of Chicago, 1936), *passim*.

5. Stratton was not a serious candidate and dropped out of the race prior to the election when he failed to get Crump's endorsement. See Virginia Phillips, "Rowlett Paine, Mayor of Memphis, 1920-1924," *West Tennessee Historical Society Papers*, XIII (1959), 110-114.

6. They also charged that the city stables and the fire department were "honeycombed with Klan." *The Commercial-Appeal*, October 29, 1923; and *Memphis News Scimitar*, October 17, 1923.

7. In practically every instance of disorder police said Klansmen were involved. *The Commercial-Appeal*, November 5 to 15, 1923. See also William D. Miller, *Mr. Crump of Memphis* (Baton Rouge, 1964), pp. 137-8; and Ralph G. Martin, *The Bosses* (New York, 1962), p. 135.

8. The Klan ticket received the following vote:

Cliff Davis	11,736	Putnam Dye	8351
H. A. Roynon	9042	Chas. Divine	8283
W. Joe Wood	8639	J. Fitzhugh	8086
Met Selden	8360		

9. According to the contending factions, the 24,732 votes for mayor were divided as follows:

	Official Result	Klan Claim
W. Joe Wood	8639	11,725
Rowlett Paine	12,978	8936
Lewis T. Fitzhugh	3105	4041

10. *The Commercial-Appeal*, November 13, 1923. V. O. Key reports the belief that "some discretion in counting the ballots" was common in Shelby County. *Southern Politics in State and Nation* (New York, 1949), pp. 62-3.

11. Ingram's Klan activities had everything to do with his removal, and he had repeatedly refused to sever his connection with the secret order. Squire Connell of Eads explained his vote for the Klansman: "I do not belong to the order of which Coroner Ingram is a member, but I take up his case because he is an old Confederate soldier and doesn't deserve such treatment." *The Commercial-Appeal*, January 3 to 22, 1924.

12. Klan and anti-Klan feeling did not reach the intensity that it did

in 1923, and both sides expressed satisfaction with the conduct of the election officials. The Klan candidates, who did better in the county than in the city, were also strong in Arlington, Buntyn, Collierville, Hollywood, Frayser, New South Memphis, and Southern and Highland Avenue. Joseph J. Williams, Klan candidate for trustee, lost the city by a vote of 13,175 to 5995; and Will Taylor lost the same precincts by 12,838 to 6833. They also lost the county, but by smaller margins. *The Commercial-Appeal,* August 8, 1924.

13. The disturbance was the outgrowth of an attempt by James Esdale, a Birmingham attorney and Klan official, to gain access to Memphis Klan records.

CHAPTER 5

1. The original membership applications and the dues records of Knox County Klan No. 14 between 1923 and 1928 are owned by the Department of Special Collections of the Emory University Library. Hereafter cited as Klan No. 14 Papers.

2. Fry became a kleagle on April 7, 1921, after being introduced to the Klan by another kleagle, probably J. F. Lowry. Tennessee recruitment was directed from Chattanooga by King Kleagle J. M. McArthur. The New York *World,* September 7 to 18, 1921; A. W. Murray to James Deadman, Knoxville, September 29, 1926, Klan No. 14 Papers; and Henry P. Fry, *The Modern Ku Klux Klan* (Boston, 1922), pp. 12-22.

3. For example, six masked Klansmen marched into the Lonsdale Baptist Church and left $25 with the pastor. *Searchlight,* April 21, 1923. See also *Searchlight,* January 16 to June 3, 1922; and *Knoxville Journal,* September 24, 1923.

4. Estimate of *Knoxville Journal,* September 16, 1923.

5. Part of the demonstration was held at Chilhowee Park. The fair committee originally set the date aside as "Ford and traveling man's day." *Knoxville Journal,* September 19 to October 5, 1923; *The Fiery Cross* (Michigan Edition), September 21, 1923, and November 9, 1923; and *Dawn,* September 29, 1923.

6. Howard Stawford to C. B. Lee, Knoxville, June 13, 1926. Klan No. 14 Papers. See also *Knoxville Journal,* September 26, 1923.

7. C. B. Lee to Exalted Cyclops, Kligrapp, Terrors, and Klansmen of Buncombe Kounty Klan No. 151, Knoxville, October 18, 1926. Addressed to the Asheville, North Carolina Klan, this letter said that 15,000 Klansmen were expected on Armistice Day and that 500 persons would be initiated. See also Henry A. Grady to A. W. Murray, Raleigh, October 11, 1926. Klan No. 14 Papers.

8. Kligrapp's Quarterly Report for Knox County Klan No. 14, April 17, 1928. Klan No. 14 Papers.

9. Of the 184 members who listed an exact educational achievement, the average was 7.7 years of formal education.

CHAPTER 6

1. The general account of the Klan in the Southwest may be consulted in several well-written and thorough studies by Charles C. Alexander, who has added Texas, Arkansas, Louisiana, and Oklahoma to Colorado and Pennsylvania as the only states about which adequate studies of the Invisible Empire may be said to exist. See Charles C. Alexander, *The Ku Klux Klan in the Southwest* (Lexington, Ky., 1965); *Crusade for Conformity: The Ku Klux Klan in Texas* (Houston, 1962); and "Invisible Empire in the Southwest: The Ku Klux Klan in Texas, Louisiana, Oklahoma, and Arkansas" (unpub. Ph.D. diss., University of Texas, 1962).

2. *Senator from Texas*, p. 682.

3. Dallas *Morning News*, July 12, 1922; New York *World*, September 9 to 17, 1921; Henry P. Fry, *The Modern Ku Klux Klan* (Boston, 1922), pp. 185-8; and Lois E. Torrence, "The Ku Klux Klan in Dallas" (unpub. Master's thesis, Southern Methodist University, 1941), pp. 67-9.

4. Two Dallas newspapers, the *Morning News* and the *Dispatch*, fought the Klan. The *Times-Herald* took no definite stand. See Dallas *Morning News*, April 4, 1922; Sam Acheson, *35,000 Days in Texas: A History of the Dallas News and Its Forbears* (New York, 1938), pp. 275-9; and Alexander, *Crusade for Conformity*, p. 12.

5. Testimony of J. F. Collier, auditor of the Dallas Klan for the 1922-1923 fiscal year, *Senator from Texas*, p. 400.

6. Testimony of Clarence Wilson, *Indiana* v. *Klan*, Reel 201, pp. 136-144. *Wisconsin Kourier*, December 19, 1924; testimony of Erwin J. Clark, *Senator from Texas*, pp. 60-61.

7. Vanderbilt has no record of Evans's admission. Charles O. Jackson, "The Ku Klux Klan, 1914-1924: A Study in Leadership" (unpub. Master's thesis, Emory University, 1962), p. 83.

8. *Senator from Texas*, pp. 465-7.

9. Testimony of D. C. McCord, klaliff of Dallas Klan No. 66, *Senator from Texas*, pp. 372-3.

10. Neither senatorial candidate was overly concerned with civil liberties. Each charged the other with seeking Negro support in the "white" primary. Anti-Klansman Ferguson remarked, "I wouldn't have the office of constable, even, if I had to get it by nigger votes." Dallas *Morning News*, August 13, 1922.

11. It is interesting to note that the courthouse and many stores closed at noon, perhaps because October 24 was also designated "League of Texas Municipalities Day."

12. It is perhaps significant that Dallas, with only 4 per cent of the

state's population, was credited with over 13 per cent of the Texas Klan total.

CHAPTER 7

1. The Norfolk police chief and the Newport News officials subsequently denied the reports.
2. *Searchlight,* May 27 to October 21, 1922; *The New York Times,* October 31, 1922; and David M. Chalmers, "The Ku Klux Klan in the Sunshine State: The 1920's," *Florida Historical Quarterly,* XLIII (January 1964), 209-15.
3. According to Kleagle Henry P. Fry, Chattanooga manufacturers were opposed to the Klan because they felt it might drive Negro workers North. Fry, *The Modern Ku Klux Klan* (Boston, 1922), p. 92. See also *The Outlook,* CXXXIV (April 25, 1923), 742.
4. M. S. Ross to C. B. Lee, Atlanta, November 9, 1927; and J. R. Ozier to A. W. Murray, Nashville, December 4, 1926. Klan No. 14 Papers.
5. Miss Robie Gill, the supreme commander of the female Kluxers, later married Comer. See Charles C. Alexander, "White Robed Reformers: The Ku Klux Klan Comes to Arkansas, 1921-1922," *Arkansas Historical Quarterly,* XXII (Spring 1963), 21-3.
6. Of a more benevolent nature was the reported Klan contribution of $1000 to the widow of a Houston electrician. *Klan Hearings,* p. 79; *Dawn,* September 29, 1923; *The Commercial-Appeal,* August 22, 1922; and *Atlanta Journal,* August 22, 1922.
7. The first grand dragon in the realm was Edwin DeBarr, a University of Michigan Ph.D. and a vice-president of the University of Oklahoma.
8. *Searchlight,* July 1 to August 5, 1922; *The New York Times,* April 2, 1924; *The Nation,* CXVII (September 5, 1923), 239; and Marshall Houts, *From Gun to Gavel: The Courtroom Recollections of James Mathers of Oklahoma* (New York, 1954), p. 235.
9. *Minutes of the Imperial Kloncilium,* pp. 6, 8, and 23; Howard A. Tucker, *History of Governor Walton's War on the Ku Klux Klan* (Oklahoma City, 1923).
10. The New Orleans Klan was quite active in 1921, when Mayor Andrew J. McShane and Commissioner Stanley Raye condemned the order as un-American. However, no klavern was reported in the city in 1924 when Louisiana law required the filing of membership lists with the secretary of state. Thomas E. Dabney, *One Hundred Great Years: The Story of the Times-Picayune from Its Founding to 1940* (Baton Rouge, 1944), p. 417.

PART III

1. The Lynds pegged the strength of the Muncie, Indiana, Klan at 10 per cent of the total population, or 3500, in 1923. Robert and Helen Lynd, *Middletown: A Study in Contemporary American Culture* (New York, 1929), pp. 481-4.
2. Bohn, "The Ku Klux Klan Interpreted," *The American Journal of Sociology*, XXX (January 1925), 385-407. There is a widespread impression that the Klan did not utilize the anti-Negro theme in the Midwest or the anti-Catholic theme in the South. Almost as good a case could be made for precisely the opposite position. The traditional view is taken by Norman F. Weaver, "The Ku Klux Klan in Wisconsin, Michigan, Indiana, and Ohio" (unpub. Ph.D. diss., University of Wisconsin, 1954), p. 271.

CHAPTER 8

1. Despite a 148 per cent increase in the Chicago Negro population between 1910 and 1920, they comprised only 4.1 per cent of the total in 1920. For background information, see Lloyd Lewis and Henry Justin Smith, *Chicago: The History of Its Reputation* (New York, 1929), pp. 444-6; and Bessie Louise Pierce, *As Others See Chicago* (Chicago, 1933).
2. Anti-Catholicism was rampant in Chicago in the 1890's, when no fewer than five American Protective Association periodicals were published in the city. Donald Kinzer, *An Episode in Anti-Catholicism: The American Protective Association* (Seattle, 1964), p. 256.
3. On the morning of August 16, 1921, the Klan placed a full-page advertisement in the *Chicago Tribune*.
4. Chicago City Council, *Journal of Proceedings* (September 19, 1921) p. 1074. See also Duncan Chambers Milner, "The Original Ku Klux Klan and Its Successor, "A Paper Read at a Stated Meeting of the Military Order of the Loyal Legion of the United States, Commandery of Illinois, October 6, 1921 (Chicago, 1921), *passim*.
5. Interview with former Chicago Klansman who prefers to remain anonymous, Chicago, August 7, 1965. In September 1921, O. B. Williamson testified: "I was told that their large following in the North was in Chicago." *Klan Hearings*, p. 39. Significantly, Guy B. Johnson, a now prominent sociologist, noted in his Master's thesis early in 1922: "outside the South, the states or cities which lead in Ku Klux strength are: the Pacific Coast states; Ohio, especially Cincinnati; Pennsylvania; New York; and the City of Chicago." Johnson, "The New Ku Klux Movement" (unpub. Master's thesis, University of Chicago, 1922), p. 6.
6. The extent of neighborhood tension is perhaps indicated by the fact that Chicago recorded twenty-four fire bombings of Negro

homes between July 1, 1917, and July 27, 1919. Chicago Commission on Race Relations, *The Negro in Chicago: A Study of Race Relations and a Race Riot* (Chicago, 1922), pp. 123-9. A more recent study has shown that the Chicago Negro community developed a strong race consciousness, or racial awareness, between 1916 and 1919. Carol A. Wills, "Chicago's Negro Community During the First World War Era" (unpub. Master's field paper, University of Chicago, 1965), p. 6.

7. Most of the Chicago klaverns had low charter numbers, meaning that they were chartered early. In addition to Klans 2 and 4 already mentioned, Chicago claimed William Joseph Simmons Klan No. 1, Chicago Klan No. 5, Austin Klan No. 6, Logan Square Klan No. 9, and Garfield Klan No. 11. The Hermosa klavern, however, was numbered 111.

8. In the 1924 Indiana gubernatorial primary, Lake County went for Klansman Ed Jackson. East Chicago *Calumet News*, September 20 and November 15, 1923; *Chicago Daily News*, April 5, 1923; *The Fiery Cross*, April 6, 1923, to January 11, 1924; and *Gary Post-Tribune*, June 23, 1923.

9. The Joliet gathering included Klansmen from Indiana and other parts of Illinois. The Klan took films of the ceremony, but Chicago Police Chief Charles Fitzmorris refused a permit for their public presentation in the city.

10. The best account of the demonstration appears in the *Chicago Tribune*, August 20, 1922. *The Chicago Defender* claimed that it had fifty spies present at the initiation. See *Defender*, August 26, 1922.

11. The event went so smoothly that it is difficult to escape the impression that the Rev. Mr. Myers was forewarned of the visit. Interesting also is the fact that the *Tribune* had a photographer on hand to snap pictures. *Chicago Tribune*, August 21, 1922.

12. Another reported philanthropy of the Chicago Klan was the University of America in Atlanta. According to one source Chicago klaverns subscribed $100,000 for the institution, including $10,000 by Austin Klan No. 6 and $5000 by Englewood Klan No. 2. It is most unlikely that such sums ever reached Atlanta.

13. In contrast, there were many instances of violence against Klansmen in Chicago, particularly of the homemade bomb variety. See, for example, *Chicago Daily News*, April 2, 1923; *Chicago Tribune*, April 8, 1923; *Dawn*, December 15, 1923; and *Abendpost*, June 15, 1922.

14. *Chicago Tribune*, February 10, 1923.

15. *Chicago Tribune*, September 16 and 22, 1921. An earlier editorial took no position, but remarked that "the objects of the society [Klan] as stated in its constitution are commendable." *Chicago Tribune*, August 27, 1921.

16. *Chicago Tribune*, December 6, 1922. Catholics and Negroes ac-

cused the *Tribune* of being slightly favorable to the Klan. See *Chicago Broad Ax*, July 5, 1924; *Tolerance*, December 31, 1922; and *Chicago Defender*, November 4, 1922.

17. The official Catholic newspaper of the archdiocese, *The New World*, was no beacon of tolerance, however. While denouncing Oregon's compulsory education law as bigotry, it was supporting anti-blasphemy laws in Italy. *The New World*, January 19, 1923. See also *Abendpost*, January 10 and March 20, 1923; *Dawn*, November 4, 1922; and *Chicago Defender*, August 26, 1922.

18. Judge David removed himself from a court case involving the Klan nine months later because he felt "too strongly against it." *Chicago Daily News*, November 12, 1922, to January 9, 1923.

19. *Grady K. Rutledge, et al. v. Robert Shepherd, et al.*, B-93874, Cook County Circuit Court, 1923.

20. O'Donnell was a native of Carroll County, Indiana, and had been a member in 1921 of Governor Dunne's ineffective National Unity Council. *Dawn*, May 12, 1923; *Searchlight*, August 19 and September 23, 1922; *Chicago Defender*, October 14, 1922; and Irving Leibowitz, *My Indiana* (Englewood Cliffs, N.J., 1964), p. 215.

21. Deposition of Harry Junker in *Harry Junker v. American Unity Publishing Company*, 423-23-S-388057, Cook County Superior Court, 1923. In somewhat different fashion, names of Klansmen were made available to the public in Indianapolis, Buffalo, Denver, and Los Angeles.

22. The Washington Park neighborhood was to experience a marked racial change in the next two decades, and by 1940 it was part of the Negro ghetto. See Frederick Burgess Lindstrom, "The Negro Invasion of the Washington Park Subdivision" (unpub. Master's thesis, University of Chicago, 1941).

23. Deposition of William R. Toppan in *William R. Toppan v. American Unity Publishing Company*, 323-23-S-387494, Cook County Superior Court, 1923.

24. Interview with a former member of Chicago's Englewood Klan No. 2, who prefers to remain anonymous, Chicago, August 7, 1965. See also *Junker v. A.U.L.*; and *Tolerance*, March 11, 1923.

25. The Klan, of course, was not above using the boycott itself against un-American groups. The whole doctrine of Klannishness was based upon the concept of preferential treatment for fellow Knights. *Dawn*, June 23, 1923; and *The American Standard*, June 1, 1924.

26. Chicago probably accounted for about one-half the Illinois Klan membership, which Robert L. Duffus estimated at 131,000 in May 1923, and which Stanley Frost pegged at between 50,000 and 200,000 early in 1924. Duffus, "The Ku Klux Klan in the Middle West," *The World's Work*, XLVI (August 1923), 363; *Chicago Tribune*, December 8, 1922; *The New York Times*, December 12, 1922; and Stanley Frost, *The Challenge of the Klan* (Indianapolis, 1924), p. 19.

27. *Tolerance,* December 24, 1922, and February 4, 1923; and *Dawn,* May 19, 1923.

28. It was originally hoped that Al Smith would deliver the feature address, but the New York governor was unable to come to Chicago for the occasion.

29. Dixie Shea was trapped and captured by Thomas Watson Klan No. 16 of Chicago in the summer of 1923. He was officially turned over to police in Paris, Illinois, where he was wanted for the theft of other Klan membership rolls. *Dawn,* June 16, 1923.

30. Other possible sources of information for the American Unity League were James E. Brockman and Audrey J. Heather, against whom the Klan sought injunctions to prevent them from revealing secrets. *Chicago Tribune,* January 18, 1923; and *Dawn,* March 24, 1923.

31. The order for transferring the Klansmen was later rescinded by "powerful city hall officials," reportedly Alderman John P. Garner of Austin, a close friend of Mayor Thompson. *Chicago Tribune,* January 1, 1923, to January 25, 1923; and *Abendpost,* December 7, 1922, to January 1, 1923.

32. The owner of the Hotel Sisson was listed by the A.U.L. as a member of the Klan. *Tolerance,* February 4, 1923, p. 5.

33. The cases against Green and Novotny were formally dismissed on December 28, 1923, in accordance with court orders. *Chicago Civil Service Commission Records* (Chicago, 1924), p. 534.

34. State of Illinois, *Journal of the House of Representatives of the 53rd General Assembly,* January 16, 1923, p. 54; and State of Illinois, *Journal of the Senate of the 53rd General Assembly,* June 18, 1923, p. 1350. For a general discussion of the constitutionality of anti-mask laws, see David Fellman, *The Constitutional Right of Association* (Chicago, 1963), particularly Chap. V.

35. Millard undoubtedly won the votes of many Masons who were not Klansmen, but by the same token some members of the Invisible Empire doubtlessly remained at home or voted for another candidate. Millard ran well in Hermosa, Grand Crossing, Chatham, Austin, Englewood, Woodlawn, South Shore, Logan Square, Belmont, Morgan Park, Avondale, and Irving Park.

36. The central issue in the campaign was not immigrant versus native; *Abendpost,* the largest German language newspaper west of the Hudson River, supported Leuder just as did the Klan. Robert L. Duffus estimated that the Klan polled or influenced about 20 per cent of the total vote in the April election. See Duffus, "The Ku Klux Klan in the Middle West," p. 371; George C. Sikes, "Thompson Rule in Chicago Ended," *The Outlook,* CXIII (March 14, 1923), 481; and Carroll Hill Woody, *The Chicago Primary of 1926: A Study of Election Methods* (Chicago, 1926), p. 18.

37. Each of these wards, especially 8, 37, and 40, had given large votes to Arthur Millard in the February Republican primary.

38. All five simon-pure Thompsonites were defeated. *Chicago Daily News*, April 1 and 4, 1923; *Chicago Tribune*, April 4, 1923; and *Abendpost*, February 28, 1923.

39. The jewelry story of George A. Penrose at 61st and Calumet was bombed in October 1923. *Dawn*, October 20, 1923; and *Chicago Daily News*, April 6, 1923.

40. *Tolerance* was published regularly until early in 1923, although it was reduced from sixteen pages to eight in the fall of 1923, and printed as few as two dozen names of Klansmen per week.

41. At one large outdoor Chicago Klan demonstration the coffee company gave the secret order a percentage of the revenue from all sales of "Liberty Bell" brand coffee. *Dawn*, November 3, 1923.

42. *Dr. Guy E. Krolick v. Tolerance Publishing Company*, 23-S-386402, Cook County Superior Court, 1923. The case was dismissed because Dr. Krolick failed to file a declaration. See also *Chicago Tribune*, February 3 and 6, 1923.

43. Brooks won the case because he was never initiated. But he was awarded only one dollar. *Brooks v. American Unity Publishing Company*, 323-23-S-387485, Cook County Superior Court, 1923. See also *Tax Fee Book 273*, p. 371. The President of William R. Johnston Manufacturing Company also brought suit against *Tolerance* after he was accused on June 10, 1923, of soliciting members for the Invisible Empire. *William R. Johnston v. Tolerance Publishing Company*, 124-24-S-398127, Cook County Superior Court, 1923.

44. Although Wrigley was not a Klansman, the secret order reportedly built up membership in Chicago by using his name. *Tolerance*, December 24, 1922, to February 4, 1923; and *William R. Wrigley v. Tolerance Publishing Company*, 223-23-S-386399, Cook County Superior Court, 1923.

45. The original statement that Wrigley was a Ku Kluxer was made over the protests of majority stockholders and directors of the publishing company, who reportedly repudiated the alleged application. *Grady K. Rutledge v. Julius Thasky*, 722-22-S-379280, Cook County Superior Court, 1922.

46. *The Fiery Cross*, February 9 and 16, 1923; and *Searchlight*, February 10, 1923. See also Edgar Allen Booth, *The Mad Mullah of America* (Columbus, Ohio, 1927), p. 69.

47. Jones was given a $2500 bonus by the Klan in 1923. His contract is reprinted and details of the case are related in *Senator from Texas*, Part 3, pp. 695-701. See also, *The New York Times*, June 29, 1924; *Dawn*, May 5, 1923; and Marion Monteval, *The Klan Inside Out* (Claremore, Okla., 1924), p. 118.

48. Robert L. Duffus, "Ancestry and End of the Ku Klux Klan," *The World's Work*, XLVI (September 1923), 527-8. See Table 3 for Chicago Klan occupational chart.

49. At first *The Birth of a Nation* was banned in Chicago, and motion

picture operators at the Auditorium Theater were arrested. *Chicago Daily News*, February 12, 1924; *Dawn*, February 9, 1924; *Searchlight*, February 16, 1924; and *The Imperial Night-Hawk*, January 2, 1924.

50. Only two persons were elected to the Superior Court who were not present or former judges, and the Klan claimed to have supported them both. *Dawn*, November 3 and 10, 1923. The Klan also supported a bond issue for the zoo, which was defeated. *Chicago Tribune*, November 7, 1923.

51. *Dawn*, November 10, 1923.

52. Chicago Klans 2, 4, 6, 10, 16, 17, 26, 70, 95, and 108 were those affected. *Dawn*, November 24 and December 1, 1923.

53. In 1939, at a Joint Meeting of Patriotic Organizations in Chicago, a Mr. Grainger announced that the Klan was again becoming active in the city, with nine chapters in Chicago and six others in the suburbs. *Anti-Defamation League Memorandum*, April 13, 1939.

54. Anti-Catholicism was probably the single most important factor in Chicago Klan growth. One person testified that "there was, according to common knowledge and belief, a large and flourishing order of members of the Ku Klux Klan in said city of Chicago engaged in a strenuous campaign against the Roman Catholic Church and Roman Catholics. . . ." *Junker v. American Unity Publishing Company*, 423-23-S-388057 Cook County Superior Court, 1923. This impression was confirmed by an interview with a former Klansman in Chicago on August 7, 1965.

55. Englewood, for instance, served as a buffer between an overcrowded black ghetto and a fearful southwest Chicago. See Zorita Mikva, "The Neighborhood Improvement Association: A Counter-Force to the Expansion of Chicago's Negro Population" (unpub. Master's thesis, University of Chicago, 1951), pp. 80-82.

CHAPTER 9

1. The president of the A.P.A. from 1893 to 1896 was William James Henry Traynor, a resident of Detroit since 1867, and the secretary was Charles T. Beatty. Traynor reappeared in the ranks of anti-Catholics during the Klan era with a booklet containing a "concise digest of Roman Catholic principles." Donald Kinzer, *An Episode in Anti-Catholicism: The American Protective Association* (Seattle, 1964), pp. 59-60, 92, 242, and 253. See also Emerson Hunsberger Loucks, *The Ku Klux Klan in Pennsylvania* (Harrisburg, 1936), p. 11.

2. A 1923 survey ascertained that 77 per cent of the Negro newcomers gave social rather than economic reasons for their coming. Robert C. Adams, "Social Reasons Bring Negroes to Detroit," *The Detroiter*, XIV (August 30, 1923), 7-9.

3. According to Gunnar Myrdal, "Detroit is almost unique among Northern cities for its large Southern-born population and for its Ku Klux Klan." Myrdal, *An American Dilemma: The Negro Problem and American Democracy* (New York, 1941), I, 568.

4. The figure of 75,000 was estimated by a Klan official in 1924, and also by Professor Norman F. Weaver. See *Detroit News*, August 21, 1924; and Weaver, "The Ku Klux Klan in Wisconsin, Michigan, Indiana, and Ohio" (unpub. Ph.D. diss., University of Wisconsin, 1954), p. 271. One estimate placed Michigan membership at 875,130, a totally absurd figure. See *Washington Post*, November 2, 1930. Detroit contained 27.1 per cent of the state's population in 1920.

5. The Klan estimated that 11,000 were present, and the *Free Press* estimated 8000. *Detroit Free Press*, June 14, 1923; *Detroit News*, June 14, 1923; *Detroit Times*, April 5, 1923; and *The Fiery Cross*, July 6, 1923.

6. The Chicago anti-Klan publication, *Tolerance*, was also sold on Detroit streets. *The Fiery Cross* (Michigan Edition), November 16, 1923; and *Detroit News*, September 14 and October 12, 1923.

7. William J. Laurence, candidate for the council, who was endorsed by the Klan in the October 9 primary, secured a temporary injunction against further endorsement by the secret order because it caused him "irreparable damage." *Detroit News*, November 2 and 7, 1923; and *The Fiery Cross* (Michigan Edition), November 2, 1923.

8. When financial irregularities were uncovered in the chapter's accounts, a Klan creditor brought suit in Circuit Court. Deposition of Manly L. Caldwell in *Clayton C. Gilliland* v. *Symwa Club, Ku Klux Klan, A Michigan Corporation* in Wayne County Circuit Court, case 117851. No transcript of the case is available, but various depositions are on file, and the Detroit newspapers gave good coverage to the court proceedings. Percy C. Howe said he was a member of Symwa, and he believed that fact made him a Klansman. *Detroit News*, January 23, 1930.

9. *Detroit News*, August 21, 1924; *Detroit Evening Times*, December 5, 1939; and Winfield Jones, *Knights of the Ku Klux Klan* (New York, 1941), p. 152. One source estimated Wayne County membership at 50,000 and Michigan membership at 265,000. See *Henry C. Warner* v. *Arthur S. Nichols, et al.*, filed in Wayne County Circuit Court, case number 132314, in March 1928 and tried in July 1928.

10. In the Republican primary the Klan made its best showing in Lansing, Flint, Saginaw, Jackson, Kalamazoo, and Detroit.

11. The official revised totals, minus disputed ballots, were as follows:

Smith	116,775
Bowles	102,602
Martin	84,462

Bowles could have won only if he had received credit for all of his spoiled ballots. *Detroit News,* November 20 and 22, 1924.

12. According to a long-time civil rights worker in Detroit, the Klan candidate should have won the 1924 mayoralty election. Interview with Josephine Gomon, Detroit, December 11, 1964. The discarded ballots were divided as follows:

Misspelled Bowles's name	4455
No X marked	4645
Surname only	2473
Wrong first name	655
Wrote name twice	339
	12567
Spoiled ballots	2653
	15220

Detroit News, November 2, 1924.

13. Most of the land bought by the Klan was in the southwest quarter of Section 13, Town Two South, Range 9 East. *Gilliland* v. *Symwa* and *Detroit News,* January 22 to 25, 1930.

14. The furniture was returned to the building when the six constables received a check signed by Arthur S. Nichols. *Detroit News,* January 7, 1925; see also *Detroit News,* November 8, 1926.

15. *Detroit Free Press,* July 12, 1925.

16. T. J. Woofter, Jr., ed., *Negro Problems in Cities* (Garden City, N.Y., 1928), pp. 75-7. Weaver, pp. 285-6.

17. *Detroit News,* September 10 to 15, 1925. See also Robert Shogan and Tom Craig, *The Detroit Race Riot: A Study in Violence* (Philadelphia, 1964), p. 20; and Irving Stone, *Clarence Darrow for the Defense* (Garden City, N.Y., 1941), p. 474.

18. *Detroit News,* September 13, 1925.

19. But according to one Negro, "Ninety-nine per cent of the colored vote will be anti-Klan." *Detroit Free Press,* October 31, 1925; and *Detroit News,* November 2, 1925.

20. John J. Leary, Jr., staff correspondent of the New York *World,* wrote a series of articles on the part played by the Klan in the 1925 election campaign. *Detroit Free Press,* October 31, 1925, and November 2, 1925.

21. Henry Ford had recanted by 1925, and the more violent pronouncements of his *Dearborn Independent* were stilled. But two years earlier the Independent Order B'rith Abraham's annual convention in Atlantic City accused Ford of being a financial backer of the Klan if not an actual member. Although the rumor was denied by Ford and the Klan, it was frequently voiced. See *Dawn,* June 2 and 30, 1923; *Detroit Free Press,* November 1, 1925; *Searchlight,* May 19, 1923; William M. Likins, *The Trail of the Serpent* (n.p., 1928), pp. 76-7; and *Detroit Times,* October 30 and 31, 1925.

22. Even today the extreme northwest portion of Detroit is populated by Anglo-Saxon, northern-born Protestants. David Greenstone, *A Report on the Politics of Detroit* (Cambridge, Mass., 1961), pp. 1-9.

23. *Detroit News*, March 17, 1926, and February 15, 1929. Danceland was the scene of several Klan meetings. *Detroit News*, January 24, 1930.

24. After 1925, R. J. Witteman, Fred W. Gower, W. F. Jackson, and Charles Spare served as exalted cyclopes. Testimony of Charles Spare and deposition of R. J. Witteman in *Gilliland* v. *Symwa Club et al. Detroit News*, February 26, 1924, February 22, 1928, and January 23, 1930.

25. *Detroit News*, May 31, 1935. See also Morris Janowitz, "Black Legions on the March," in Daniel Aaron, ed., *America in Crisis: Fourteen Crucial Episodes in American History* (New York, 1951), pp. 306-7.

26. Detroit was the location for an insignificant meeting of Michigan, Ohio, and Indiana Klansmen on November 27-28, 1937. *Detroit News*, November 19, 1937. The Klan's interest in the Motor City in the late 1930's probably stemmed from the fact that Imperial Wizard James Colescott had lived there in 1924. In 1940 Detroit was one of the leading cities for Klansmen according to the national headquarters. See also *Detroit Evening Times*, December 5, 1939.

27. Grand Dragon to All Klansmen (Mimeographed), Detroit, October 11, 1941; and Grand Dragon to Klansmen, Detroit, October 9, 1941. Both letters are in the files of the Chicago office of the Anti-Defamation League.

CHAPTER 10

1. The most recent history of the city is undistinguished and takes very little note of the Klan. Jeannette Covert Nolan, *Hoosier City: The Story of Indianapolis* (New York, 1943).

2. In a careful recent study Professor Emma Lou Thornbrough has determined that Klan responsibility for the enactment of segregation measures in Indianapolis and the state in the 1920's was minor. More important in the implementation of anti-Negro policies were neighborhood civic organizations and the White Supremacy League, which were distinct from the Klan. Thornbrough, "Segregation in Indiana During the Klan Era of the 1920's," *The Mississippi Valley Historical Review*, XLVII (March 1961), 594-619.

3. Wilma Dykeman and James Stokely, *Seeds of Southern Change: The Life of Will Alexander* (Chicago, 1962), p. 108.

4. *The State of Indiana* v. *The Knights of the Ku Klux Klan, et al.,* Marion County Circuit Court, 41769 (1925-1929), now available in the Indiana State Library, Indianapolis. Hereafter cited as *In-*

diana v. *Klan*. See particularly testimony of Hugh Pat Emmons and D. C. Stephenson. See also Alva W. Taylor, "What the Klan Did in Indiana," *The New Republic*, LIII (November 16, 1927), 330.

5. *Searchlight*, March 4, 1922; Dixon Merritt, "Klan and Anti-Klan in Indiana," *The Outlook*, CXX (December 8, 1926), 465-7.

6. It was a hot night but two thousand persons heard the diatribe. Gunsolus also spoke from the pulpit of the Garfield Christian Church on at least one occasion. See *Searchlight*, August 5, 1922; *The Fiery Cross*, December 8, 1922; and Irving Leibowitz, *My Indiana* (Englewood Cliffs, N.J., 1964), p. 189.

7. The Klan regretted that all Hoosier Knights did not subscribe to the newspaper and admitted that it depended very largely upon street sales. Official Mandate, Realm of Indiana, October 6, 1923, p. 3.

8. Testimony of William M. Rogers, *Senatorial Campaign Expenditures*, Part 3, pp. 2325-6. Circulation estimates for *The Fiery Cross* range from 50,000 to 400,000. Taylor, pp. 330-32. *The Fiery Cross*, January 19 to December 21, 1923, *passim*.

9. The list also included Klan membership numbers for each individual. *The Fiery Cross*, April 2 and May 19, 1923; *Dawn*, May 19 and 26, 1923. The American Unity League was advertising and trying to expand in the city at that time. *Indianapolis Star*, April 1, 1923.

10. A Klansman named Brock, formerly in charge of the Indianapolis headquarters, was reportedly involved in the theft. *Dawn*, May 19, 1923; and *The Fiery Cross*, April 2, 1923. See also *Chicago Daily News*, June 3, 1923.

11. Considerable controversy also surrounded Klansman Dory C. Blacker, who owned a string of chili houses and was accused by *Tolerance* of hiring Klan help exclusively.

12. The Indianapolis Klan was another instance where imperial officials delayed as long as possible before chartering a chapter in order to reap financial benefit at the expense of local members. Testimony of Robert W. Lyons, *Senatorial Campaign Expenditures*, p. 2113.

13. On July 28, 1923, 5000 Indianapolis Klansmen drove to Shelbyville Fairgrounds for a demonstration. *Indianapolis Star*, July 5 and 29, 1923; *The Fiery Cross*, December 29, 1922; *The Imperial Night-Hawk*, January 2, 1924; and *The Fiery Cross*, October 5, 1923. In September 1923, some 65,000 out-of-town Klansmen descended on Indianapolis for a meeting at the Fairgrounds. *Searchlight*, September 29, 1923.

14. The Brightwood neighborhood was a center of Klan strength.

15. Trusty made the mistake of inviting Catholic Bishop Joseph Chartrand as guest lecturer for the YMCA. Leibowitz, p. 213; and *Indianapolis News*, May 12, 1924.

16. Ed Jackson campaigned for the Negro vote by advertising in its newspapers, but most colored citizens voted for Shank. *Indianapolis World,* May 2, 1924; and *Indianapolis News,* May 8, 1924.

17. The *Indianapolis News,* on May 12, 1924, estimated a Marion County membership of between 50,000 and 60,000.

18. This estimate of neighborhood Klan strength is based upon the controversial list mentioned earlier, the location of Klan meeting places, cross-burnings, and sympathetic churches, and an analysis of election returns.

19. As early as January 1923 there were reports that the Indiana Klan counted between 50 and 60 members of the state legislature among its 225,000 Knights. *Tolerance,* February 4, 1923. Other estimates of Hoosier membership ranged between 170,000 and 500,000. Testimony of Emmons, *Senatorial Campaign Expenditures,* pp. 425-427.

20. Grand Dragon Walter F. Bossert to all Hydras, Titans, Furies, Exalted Cyclopes, Province Kleepers, Unit officers, and all Klansmen of the Realm of Indiana (Mimeographed), Indianapolis, August 11, 1924. Indiana Klan Papers, Indiana State Library.

21. "I was not a member of the Ku Klux Klan. I never was." Testimony of Senator James E. Watson, *Senatorial Campaign Expenditures,* p. 2140. He was unquestionably a good friend of the secret order, however. Testimony of Hugh Pat Emmons, *Senatorial Campaign Expenditures,* p. 2045; and testimony of George W. Meyers, *Senatorial Campaign Expenditures,* pp. 2254-64. See also Louis Francis Budenz, "There's Mud on Indiana's White Robes," *The Nation,* CXXV (July 27, 1927), 81-2; John Bartlow Martin, *Indiana: An Interpretation* (New York, 1947), pp. 193-5; and Leibowitz, p. 192. *Detroit News,* May 8, 1924.

22. *Chicago Broad Ax,* July 12, 1924; and *Indianapolis World,* June 13, 1923, and February 22, 1924.

23. Grand Dragon Walter Bossert to all Grand Officers, Titans, Exalted Cyclopes, Kligrapps and Unit Officials, Indianapolis, October 25, 1924. Mimeographed. Indiana Klan Papers, Indiana State Library.

24. The Klan demonstrated its control of the House of Representatives by passing (67-22) a bill, clearly aimed at Catholic nuns, to prevent the wearing of distinctive religious garb by public school teachers. Testimony of D. C. Stephenson, *Indiana* v. *Klan; The Fiery Cross,* November 14, 1924; and *Indianapolis Star,* November 5, 1924. Jackson received 53.4 per cent of the Indiana vote and 54.4 per cent of the Marion County vote. Testimony of Stephenson, *Indiana* v. *Klan,* Reel 201.

25. One year later, when an investigating committee asked Duvall if he were a member of the Klan, he replied: "I don't think I am paid up, but I am." Testimony of John Duvall, *Senatorial Campaign Expenditures,* p. 2293. A past grand master of the Indiana Masonic

Grand Lodge, Orbison was one of the most prominent Klansmen in the state and a member of the Imperial Kloncilium. *Minutes of the Imperial Kloncilium*, meeting of May 1 and 2, 1923, p. 6-8.

26. Duvall had expected to carry the city by at least 20,000 votes. Republican boss William H. Armitage reported that he bribed Negro precinct committeemen for $25 each. *Indianapolis News*, November 2 and 5, 1925. The Klan was also successful in Evansville, electing Mayor Herbert Males and Congressman Harry Rowbottom.

27. Testimony of John L. Duvall, *Senatorial Campaign Expenditures*, pp. 2290-93; and testimony of Walter Bossert, *Senatorial Campaign Expenditures*, pp. 2282-3.

28. Two of Stephenson's sidekicks, Earl Klinck and Earl Gentry, were acquitted of the same charge. Stephenson always maintained his innocence, but he was not released from prison until 1950. According to one observer, "the only crime that Stephenson has not committed is the one for which he was convicted." The official records of the struggle may be examined in the Indiana State Library. See also Merritt, pp. 465-7; and John Bartlow Martin, "Beauty and the Beast: The Downfall of D. C. Stephenson, Grand Dragon of Indiana," *Harper's Magazine*, CLXXXIX (September 1924), 319-29.

29. The resultant disgust of the Indianapolis citizenry was reflected in a special election of the same year, when the city-manager system was successful by a five-to-one margin.

30. Some 3000 Marion County Klansmen reportedly resigned in 1925 because they did not want to work with county Republican chairman George Coffin. Testimony of Robert F. McNay, *Senatorial Campaign Expenditures*, p. 2124.

31. Testimony of Rollie C. J. Granger, *Senatorial Campaign Expenditures*, p. 2227; and testimony of Emmons, *Senatorial Campaign Expenditures*, p. 2051.

32. Morton Harrison, "Gentleman from Indiana," *The Atlantic Monthly*, CXLI (May 1928), 676-7; Leibowitz, p. 214; and *Indiana* v. *Klan*, Reel 200, pp. 54 and 425-7.

CHAPTER 11

1. The New York *World*, September 7, 1921; *The Fiery Cross*, May 11, 1923; and *The Imperial Night-Hawk*, July 9, 1924.

2. *Wisconsin Kourier*, November 21, 1924, and December 5, 1924; *The Badger-American*, April 1923, p. 2; *Dawn*, September 8, 1923; *Tolerance*, December 24, 1922; and *Searchlight*, January 16, 1922.

3. See particularly the incisive chapter "A Kansan in Babylon" in Walter Johnson, *William Allen White's America* (New York, 1947), pp. 375-400. See also *The Fiery Cross*, March 23 and September 28, 1923; *Kourier*, December 1926, p. 19; and *Searchlight*, December 9, 1922.

4. David M. Chalmers, *Hooded Americanism: The First Century of the Ku Klux Klan* (Garden City, N. Y., 1965), pp. 138-40. See also Benjamin H. Avin, "The Ku Klux Klan, 1912-1925: A Study in Religious Intolerance" (unpub. Ph.D. diss., Georgetown University, 1952), pp. 85 and 139.

5. The Ohio organization was much less influential than its Hoosier counterpart, however, due to the smaller total population of Indiana, where perhaps 20 per cent of the adult population owed allegiance to the Invisible Empire.

6. Customary practice was to charter only one klavern per county, but the number of Hamilton County klaverns may have been as high as fourteen. Embrey B. Howson, "The Ku Klux Klan in Ohio After World War I" (unpub. Master's thesis, Ohio State University, 1951), *passim*. See also *Columbus Dispatch*, August 30, 1925; *Searchlight*, June 3, 1922; *Dayton Journal*, August 7, 1924; the New York *World*, September 9, 1921; and testimony of Ramsey, *Indiana* v. *Klan*.

7. See particularly testimony of Frank Ramsey, *Indiana* v. *Klan*, pp. 13-58; *Dayton Journal*, November 5, 1924; *Dayton Daily News*, December 30, 1923; *The Fiery Cross*, January 11, 1924; and New York *Evening Post*, March 26, 1928.

8. Two huge meetings were held at Buckeye Lake: the first on July 12, 1923, and the second on August 29, 1925. More than 75,000 persons were present on both occasions. *Columbus Citizen*, July 13, 1923; *Columbus Dispatch*, August 30, 1925; *Searchlight*, September 23, 1922; *Cleveland Plain-Dealer*, May 8, 1923; and *Indiana* v. *Klan, passim*.

9. Testimony of James R. Ramsey, Commander of the Grand Dragon's Guard, *Indiana* v. *Klan*, pp. 3-10; *The Pitchfork*, January 27, 1926; *Akron Beacon Journal*, February 20, 1966; *Searchlight*, August 5, 1922; and *The Fiery Cross*, February 23, 1923, to February 1, 1924.

10. *American Civil Liberties Union Annual Report for 1923* (New York, 1924), pp. 19-20; *The Fiery Cross*, December 14 and 28, 1923; and *Akron Beacon Journal*, February 20, 1966.

11. It is worthy of note that the valley was not rural, and the bulk of the population was not Protestant. Yet in 1923, five cities in the area, including Akron and Youngstown, elected Klan mayors.

12. In a closely related vote the Klan successfully supported Bible-reading legislation in 1924.

13. The November vote in the 1924 Ohio election was:

(D) Vic Donahey	1,051,159	(D) Davis	470,492
(R) Harry Davis	884,573	(R) Coolidge	1,148,423
		(P) La Follette	346,468

Dayton Journal, August 10, November 7 and 8, 1924; *Cleveland Plain-Dealer*, November 11, 1923; and testimony of James Ramsey, *Indiana* v. *Klan*, p. 58.

CHAPTER 12

1. New York *World,* September 7, 1921.
2. The NAACP asked Harvard to expel its Klan students. *Dawn,* October 27, 1923; *The Fiery Cross* (Kentucky), November 2, 1923; and *The New York Times,* November 1 and 2, 1923.
3. The study by Emerson Hunsberger Loucks, *The Ku Klux Klan in Pennsylvania* (Harrisburg, 1936), is excellent. See also testimony of Harry E. A. McNeel, a Pennsylvania kleagle from November 25, 1921, to September 23, 1924, in *Indiana* v. *Klan,* Reel 201, pp. 30 and 44-6.
4. Testimony of Arthur L. Cotton and Roy F. Barclay, *Indiana* v. *Klan,* Reel 201, pp. 95-108 and 180-82; *Searchlight,* February 25, 1922; *Chicago Tribune,* April 9, 1923; and *The New York Times,* April 2, 1923.
5. The Klan side of the incident is recorded in the pamphlet *The Martyred Klansman, in Which Events Leading Up to the Shooting to Death of Klansman Thomas Rankin Abbott, on August 25, 1923, Are Related, Together with a Record of the Court Proceedings That Followed* (Pittsburgh, 1923).
6. Loucks, pp. 25 and 169; *Searchlight,* December 9, 1922; *The New York Times,* December 5, 1921; New York *World,* September 9, 1921; and testimony of Joseph R. Shoemaker, *Indiana* v. *Klan,* Reel 201, pp. 109-10.
7. Dixon Merritt, "The Klan on Parade," *The Outlook,* CXVIII (August 19, 1925) 554, reported that the Washington Parade was, except for Virginia and Kentucky, "in the main a Northern parade."
8. Buffalo *Express,* July 1 to November 15, 1924; and Buffalo *Evening News,* September 1, 1924, to January 31, 1925.
9. Testimony of C. Anderson Wright, *Klan Hearings,* p. 19; New York *World,* September 8 to 26, 1921; *Chicago Defender,* December 30, 1922; *The New York Times,* July 12, 1923; and *Searchlight,* January 13, 1923. New York City's total membership probably never exceeded 15,000.
10. Part of Wheeler's enthusiasm stemmed from his desire to receive the contract for a proposed $400,000 Klan propaganda film. New York *World,* September 25, 1921. See also *The Kourier,* July 1929, p. 15; and *The New World,* May 4, 1923.
11. "New York's Anti-Klan Outburst," *The Literary Digest,* LXXV (December 23, 1922), 32; *Searchlight,* December 9, 1922; and *Chicago Defender,* December 16, 1922.
12. Announcement was made in advance that the Klansman would speak, and the church was crowded. *Searchlight,* February 24, 1923; and *Tolerance,* December 24, 1922.
13. *The New York Times,* December 5 and 12, 1922, and May 5,

1923; *Dawn,* July 21, 1923; and David Fellman, *The Constitutional Right of Association* (Chicago, 1963), Chapter V.

14. Frank Parker Stockbridge, "The Ku Klux Klan Revived," *Current History Magazine,* XIV (April 1921), 19-25; and *Tolerance,* December 24, 1922.

15. The pro-Klan account of the incident is included in Paul M. Winter, *What Price Tolerance?* (Hewlett, N. Y., 1928), pp. 32-47.

16. *The Watcher on the Tower,* October 27, 1923, p. 12; R. L. Duffus, "Ancestry and End of the Ku Klux Klan," *The World's Work,* XLVI (September 1923), 535; *The New York Times,* October 19, 1924; and Chalmers, *Hooded Americanism,* pp. 256-68.

17. In 1923, the minutes of a Klan meeting in Atlantic City were stolen from the pockets of Klansman Herman Z. Ross of Hoboken. New York *World,* September 6, 15, and 17, 1921; "The Klan Celebrates Mother's Day," *The Christian Century,* XLII (May 21, 1925), 677; and *The New York Times,* May 3, 1923; June 18, 1923; and August 6, 1924.

18. Everett R. Meves to Attorney General Harlan Stone, October 30, 1924, in Justice Department File 43-48-1, National Archives, Washington.

19. *Washington Post* estimates of Klan strength usually erred on the side of exaggeration, however. *Washington Post,* November 25, 1922, and November 2, 1930.

20. Merritt, "The Klan on Parade," p. 554.

21. The circus was planned for the Fourth Regiment Armory in Baltimore, but officials refused its use at the last moment. *The Fiery Cross,* December 21, 1923; *Searchlight,* December 9, 1922, May 26, 1923, and December 1, 1923.

22. Late in 1922 Grand Goblin A. J. Padon claimed 45,000 in Connecticut, 25,000 in Massachusetts, 10,000 each in Vermont and New Hampshire, 8000 in Maine, and 2000 in Rhode Island. Although the estimates were probably too high, it is worthy of note that the Know-Nothing movement was perhaps strongest in Massachusetts, where Irish immigration threatened Protestant control of large cities.

23. True to its tradition, the American Civil Liberties Union fought Mayor Curley's ban against meetings of the Klan and of birth control advocates. *ACLU 1924 Annual Report,* pp. 24-5; *The New York Times,* October 22, 1923; and Ralph G. Martin, *The Bosses* (New York, 1964), p. 237.

24. "The Ballots Behind the Ku Klux Klan," *The World's Work,* LV (January 1928), 249. See also Kenneth T. Jackson, "The Decline of the Ku Klux Klan, 1924-1932" (unpub. Master's thesis, University of Chicago, 1963), p. 73.

25. Hiram Wesley Evans, "Alienism in the Democracy," *The Kourier,* April 1927, pp. 2-4.

CHAPTER 13

1. The pro-Klan account of the affair is contained in *The Inglewood Raiders: The Story of the Celebrated Ku Klux Case at Los Angeles and Speeches to the Jury* (Los Angeles, 1923). See also report of William S. Coburn to Acting Imperial Wizard Clarke, reprinted in *Senator from Texas*, p. 689; and *Los Angeles Times*, April 25, 1922.

2. Coburn, who later became the Klan's Imperial Representative to the United States, was murdered in Atlanta in 1923 by Phillip Fox as an outgrowth of the Simmons-Evans dispute.

3. *Searchlight*, March 18 to June 17, 1922; *Watcher on the Tower*, August 25, 1923; David M. Chalmers, *Hooded Americanism: The First Century of the Ku Klux Klan* (Garden City, N. Y., 1965), pp. 122-4; and *Los Angeles Times*, March to August 1922, *passim.*

4. Between 1910 and 1920 Los Angeles Negroes increased from 7599 to 15,579 and Orientals from 6292 to 14,230, but these increases were not significantly greater than that for the city as a whole. *Census, 1920, Population*, II, 53. In 1894 the American Protective Association newspaper *Tocsin* was published in Los Angeles. Donald Kinzer, *An Episode in Anti-Catholicism: The American Protective Association* (Seattle, 1964), p. 95.

5. All three men maintained that they had resigned after short memberships. See Joseph Burke, U.S. Attorney, to the United States Attorney General, May 16, 1922, Justice Department File 221718, National Archives.

6. W. L. Limerian to R. P. Shuler, Los Angeles, August 15, 1924, Anaheim Klan Papers, Library of Congress. See also *Searchlight*, November 4, 1922; *Watcher on the Tower*, September 22, 1923; and *Wisconsin Kourier*, December 1924.

7. The Klan estimate on Wobbly Hill was 25,000. The largest class was listed as 1500. *The Imperial Night-Hawk*, January 16 and April 2, 1924; and *Watcher on the Tower*, July 21, 1923.

8. A list of the Anaheim Klan members is available in the Manuscript Division of the Library of Congress. See also W. L. Limerian to R. P. Shuler, Los Angeles, August 15, 1924, Anaheim Klan Papers, Manuscript Division, Library of Congress.

9. *Orange County Plain Dealer*, February 2, 1925; *Anaheim Bulletin*, January 27, 1925, and February 4, 1925; *Anaheim Gazette*, January 29, 1925, to February 4, 1925.

10. The Reverend Leon Myers resigned from the Christian Church in Anaheim and moved to the First Christian Church of Dodge City, Kansas, effective December 1, 1924. *Anaheim Gazette*, February 4 and 5, 1925.

11. Ku Klux Klan Broadsides, dated October 2, 1939, in possession of the Anti-Defamation League, Chicago office. See also *A.D.L. Memorandum*, September 29, 1939.

12. *Anti-Defamation League Memorandums* dated January 29, 1940, November 9, 1941, and October 27, 1942. Chicago Regional Office, Anti-Defamation League.

13. Clark, Abraham Lincoln, *Why the Ku Klux Klan?* (Spokane, Wash., 1924), *passim; The Watcher on the Tower*, August 4 and 18, 1923; and *The Morning Oregonian*, October 30, 1924.

14. As will be related later, Powell was also an important figure in the Oregon Klan. *Searchlight*, March 11, 1922, and March 31, 1923; *The Imperial Night-Hawk*, September 10, 1924; and *The Watcher on the Tower*, July 28 to August 18, 1923.

15. The population of Seattle in 1920 was 315,312. Between 1910 and 1920 the percentage of Orientals in the city increased slightly to 9.1 per cent while that for Negroes fell from 1 per cent to 0.9 per cent in the same period.

16. *Seattle Post-Intelligencer*, November 1 to November 26, 1924, *passim;* and *Oregon Daily Journal*, November 15, 1922.

CHAPTER 14

1. *Harpoon*, I (April 1924), 2; and Vincent Throop, "The Suburban Zone of Metropolitan Portland, Oregon" (unpub. Ph.D. diss., University of Chicago, 1948), pp. 4-5. In 1910 the city's population was 207,000 and in 1930 was 301,000. Donald J. Bogue, *Population Growth in Standard Metropolitan Areas, 1900-1950* (Washington, 1953), p. 68.

2. Justice Department File 221187, National Archives. See also "The Ku-Kluxing of Oregon," *The Outlook*, CXIII (March 14, 1923), 490-91; *The Kourier*, July, 1931; and Lawrence J. Saalfeld, "Forces of Prejudice in Oregon, 1920-25" (unpub. Master's thesis, Catholic University of America, 1950), pp. 9-10.

3. Just fourteen months later the governor remarked that, "the KKK has been and is an active menace in Oregon," *Oregon Daily Journal*, November 23, 1922.

4. *Oregon Voter*, March 25, 1922; *Harpoon*, p. 7; and Lem A. Dever, *Masks Off: Confessions of an Imperial Klansman . . .* (Portland, Ore., 1925), p. 38.

5. R. H. Sawyer, *The Truth About The Invisible Empire, Knights of the Ku Klux Klan* (Portland, Ore., 1925), pp. 1-16.

6. *Oregon Daily Journal*, May 10, and 11, 1922. Whether or not Mayor Baker was actually a member of the Klan was a subject of constant conjecture and cannot be ascertained with certainty. He definitely had a strong Klan association and was under the influence of Fred Gifford.

7. In 1924 when the local Klan was less powerful, John Hammrick removed the "100%" from his movie advertisements.

8. In the spring of 1922, Gifford claimed that there were already some 14,000 members of the Klan in Oregon of which 9000 were

members in Portland. *Oregon Voter,* March 25, 1922; *Searchlight,* May 20, 1922; *The Morning Oregonian,* October 27, 1924; April 11, 1927; and *Oregon Daily Journal,* November 14, 1922; and November 11, 1923.

9. *The Watcher on the Tower,* July 21, 1923; and *Searchlight,* September 30, 1922.

10. *Dawn,* May 26, 1923. Actually the extent of anti-Oriental prejudice on the part of the Klan in the Far West has been much over-emphasized. The percentage of Chinese and Japanese in Portland fell from 10 per cent in 1900 to 1.5 per cent in 1920 and declined absolutely from 7217 in 1910 to 3771 in 1920. *1920 Census, II, Population,* 57.

11. The leading A.P.A. newspaper in Oregon was the *Portlander.* Donald Kinzer, *An Episode in Anti-Catholicism: The American Protective Association* (Seattle, 1964), p. 95.

12. Nativistic prejudice in Oregon was not confined to the uneducated. In 1922 University of Oregon librarian M. H. Douglass reported that Lothrop Stoddard's *Rising Tide of Color* was one of the most popular books on campus. *Oregon Daily Journal,* November 22, 1922, and November 10, 1923; *Western American,* May 23 and 30, 1923; and Saalfeld, pp. 23-41.

13. Executive Department Proclamation, State of Oregon, May 13, 1922, Salem, Oregon; as printed in A. B. Cain, *The Oregon School Fight* (Portland, Ore., 1924).

14. McArthur also incurred the wrath of the American Legion because he was one of the few men who voted against the soldier bonus. *The Morning Oregonian,* May 18 and 23, 1922; *Searchlight,* June 3, 1922.

15. The vote for governor was 43,009 to 42,499.

16. Upon deciding that Pierce was acceptable, The Klan discouraged a move to run Hall as an independent. *Catholic Sentinel,* September 14, 1922; *Searchlight,* August 5, 1922, and September 30, 1922; *Oregon Daily Journal,* May 1 to November 2, 1922.

17. It may be recalled that the initiative, as well as the direct primary, referendum, and recall, was part of the so-called Oregon system, which in the early years of the twentieth century especially placed the state on the frontiers of progressive democracy.

18. Although George C. Brown, Grand Master of the Masons in Oregon, denied that they fostered and promoted the school bill, and although some Masons went to the extent of advertising against the bill, their Supreme Council quietly passed out petitions to various lodges in Oregon, and it was no secret that most pro-compulsory education newspaper advertisements were paid for by the Ancient and Accepted Order of Scottish Rite Masons.

19. With the exception of the *Telegram,* Portland newspapers were noncommittal on compulsory education as was the Taxpayer's League.

20. At least twenty nuns did in fact teach in Oregon public schools in such Catholic communities as Sublimity, St. Paul, St. Louis, and Mt. Angel. Saalfeld, pp. 125-6; *The Morning Oregonian*, April 18, 1937.

21. The city's only Democratic newspaper, the *Oregon Daily Journal*, supported Pierce and labeled his campaign, "one of the finest instances of single-handed political fighting in the history of Oregon." The emphasis of the Democrat was on tax reduction.

22. The compulsory school bill received 55.5 per cent of the vote in Portland and 51.5 per cent of the vote in the rest of the state. *Oregon Daily Journal*, November 9, 1922; Dudley G. Wooten, *Remember Oregon* (Denver, 1924), p. 3; *Tolerance*, December 24, 1922.

23. Although Pierce received only 55.3 per cent of the Portland vote, while gathering 58.4 per cent in the rest of the state, his strength in the city was surprising because low agricultural prices induced the incumbent Republican administration to concentrate on the urban vote.

24. Watkins, who was probably a Klansman, defeated McArthur 36,703 to 35,677.

25. In defense of Pierce and Baker it was said that neither executive knew that the Klan was sponsoring the banquet.

26. Estimates of the city's peak membership range from 9000 to 25,000. *Oregon Daily Journal*, November 15, 1922; "The Ku Kluxing of Oregon," p. 491; Dever, p. 43; *Savannah Tribune*, December 21, 1922; Saalfeld, p. 31.

27. According to Dever, the Ladd and Tilton Bank staff was especially well represented in the Klan, as was the American Legion, which threatened to split over the Klan issue. Dever, p. 31; *Portland Telegram*, March 12, 1923; *The Morning Oregonian*, April 18, 1937; *Oregon Daily Journal*, May 14, 1922; and *Tolerance*, December 24, 1922.

28. Articles of Incorporation for the Ladies of the Invisible Empire were filed in Salem on July 6, 1922, by Sawyer, Powell, Davis, and Gifford. Dever, pp. 37 and 46; *Portland Telegram*, November 19, 1922; *Tolerance*, December 31, 1922; and *Searchlight*, September 30, 1922. The Riders later became known as the American Krusaders.

29. The only other overt instance of Klan-related violence in Portland came in January 1923 when a woman was branded on her chest by two robed and masked men so "she won't wear any more low-neck dresses." *Tolerance*, February 4, 1923; Dever, p. 38; and *The Morning Oregonian*, April 11, 1927.

30. Previous to the establishment of the Klan journal, there was another Portland magazine of the same name which was a part of the Americanization movement. It opposed the Klan and most of its doctrines and changed its name to the *United American* because of "the odium that had become attached to the title since the Klan

adopted the same title for a publication." *United American*, August 1923; Dever, p. 32; *Tolerance*, December 24, 1922; *Western American*, January 4 and February 8, 1924.

31. In 1922 Governor Olcott had complained that the Klan was so strong "that the metropolitan papers of the state said not one word against them." Percy Maddux, *City on the Willamette: The Story of Portland, Oregon* (Portland, Ore., 1952), p. 154; *The Morning Oregonian*, April 18, 1927. See also, *Governor's Conference Proceedings*, p. 138; and *Oregon Daily Journal*, May 1 and 17, 1922, and November 30, 1923.

32. Only $6000 was finally contributed by the Klan to the W.C.T.U. project. Saalfeld, pp. 85-7; Dever, p. 31.

33. The letter was signed by Jacques De Nyse and reprinted in the *Harpoon*, pp. 22-3.

34. *Western American*, February 1, 1924; *Catholic Sentinel*, May 22, 1924.

35. It is interesting to note, however, that the Oregon delegation to the 1924 Democratic National Convention voted solidly against the anti-Klan plank and against Al Smith.

36. Gifford tried to maintain that the Klan had no interest in the election, however. *The Morning Oregonian*, November 2, 1924.

37. The re-election of George Baker established a precedent as he was the first man to serve as mayor for three consecutive terms. He went on to a fourth term in 1928 and completed his service to the city in 1933 after sixteen years as mayor. *The Morning Oregonian*, November 4 to 6, 1924; and Maddux, pp. 214-15.

38. Dever, pp. 25-54; *Harpoon*, p. 1; and Charles M. Smith to U.S.A. Club, Anaheim, California, January 16, 1925. Anaheim Klan Papers, Library of Congress.

39. Tom Akers, former publisher of the *Phoenix Gazette* and chief of the Imperial Klan Intelligence Division, was the editor of the *Western American* in its waning months.

40. *Pierce* v. *Society of Sisters*, 268 U.S. 510 (1925).

CHAPTER 15

1. The total population of the city was 213,000 in 1910 and 287,000 in 1930. See *1920 Census, III, Population*, p. 138; *Religious Bodies: 1926*, pp. 406-7; and William F. Christians, "Land Utilization in Denver" (unpub. Ph.D. diss., University of Chicago, 1938), pp. 2 and 17.

2. Edward Keating, *The Gentleman from Colorado; A Memoir* (Denver, 1964), pp. 59-62. See also Samuel Wallace Johnson, *Autobiography* (Denver, 1960), pp. 90-92; Frank Thomas Johnson, *Autobiography of a Centenarian* (Denver, 1961), p. 106; and Donald Kinzer, *An Episode in Anti-Catholicism: The American Protective Association* (Seattle, 1964), pp. 95 and 255.

3. Don Zylstra, "When the Ku Klux Klan Ran Denver," *Denver Post Roundup*, January 5, 1958, pp. 5-7.
4. Padon was transferred to Boston on July 1, 1921. New York *World*, September 9, 1921; *Denver Times*, June 17, 1921.
5. Zylstra, p. 7; and James H. Davis, "The Ku Klux Klan in Colorado" (unpub. Master's thesis, University of Denver, 1962), p. 50.
6. *Searchlight*, January 16 and July 22, 1922; *Denver Express*, January 3, 1925; and *Denver Catholic Register*, January 26, 1922.
7. *Searchlight*, February 17, 1923.
8. Zylstra, pp. 6-7. See also Davis, pp. 25-6, 47; and *Denver Catholic Register*, June 19, 1923.
9. The Colorado Klan applied for incorporation in March 1922.
10. One of the ironies of Locke's Klan career was his loyalty to his private secretary, a Catholic, whom he refused to fire despite pressure from the national office. Zylstra, p. 7; *Denver Post*, August 14, 1924; Lee Casey, "When the Ku Klux Klan Controlled Colorado," *Rocky Mountain News*, June 18, 1946, p. 12; *Denver Post*, April 6, 1935.
11. *Denver Express*, June 27, 1923; *Denver Times*, May 25, 1923; and *Denver Post*, August 2, 1923.
12. The Klan made preparations to circulate a recall petition of its own when Stapleton refused to follow orders. *Denver Post*, August 11, 1924.
13. Former Mayor George D. Begole implied that at one time the Klan had control of the civil service commission as well as the fire and police departments. *Denver Post*, August 27, 1947. See also *Denver Express*, March 27, 1924; and *ADL Records*.
14. These calculations are based upon election returns and a list of more than 4000 Denver Klansmen now in the author's possession. It is interesting to note that the Colorado Klan was antagonistic to organized labor despite its lower-middle-class base. After careful investigation the *Denver Express* reported on April 24, 1924, that neither union leaders nor business agents were Klansmen. See also Zylstra, pp. 5-6.
15. Under the Klan administration, the Denver Gas and Electric Company did not pay what anti-Klan forces regarded as a fair price for the privilege of doing business in Denver.
16. *Denver Post*, August 3 to 9, 1924.
17. According to the Klan, Bailey was a Papist opponent. *The Fiery Cross*, August 29, 1924; *Denver Post* August 10 to 13, 1924; and *Denver Express*, August 8, 1924.
18. Locke also remarked that Americans had been losing ground through indifference and the dying out of families. Now they were going to regain that ground with the Klan leading the way. *Denver Post*, August 13 and 14, 1924.
19. In addition to the Klan vote, however, there was an important element of voters that did not side with the Klan but who felt that

recall was wrong as a matter of principle. *Denver Express,* August 13, 1924; and *Denver Post,* August 13, 1924.

20. *Denver Post,* August 5, 1924; *Denver Express,* August 5, 1924; and *Detroit News,* October 6, 1924.

21. The vote in the major races was as follows:

	Denver	Colorado
Means	44,844	152,658
Shafroth	41,897	138,006
Morley	50,961	165,477
Sweet	40,317	142,222
Milliken	56,335	169,883
Humphrey	30,387	100,957

22. The favorable estimate is that of John Gunther, *Inside U.S.A.,* rev. ed. (New York, 1951), p. 217.

23. Lindsey, Benjamin Barr, "My Fight with the Ku Klux Klan," *The Survey Graphic,* June 1, 1925, pp. 271-4; and J. B. Ozier to A. W. Murray, Nashville, February 18, 1927; Klan No. 14 Papers.

24. Except for one four-year period Ben Stapleton remained mayor for almost a quarter of a century until the late 1940's.

25. In 1942 Kleagle A. W. Lease of Colorado Springs made an unsuccessful attempt to reorganize the Colorado Klan. *Anti-Defamation League Memorandum,* October 27, 1942.

PART V

1. For example, see John Higham, *Strangers in the Land: Patterns of American Nativism, 1860-1925* (New Brunswick, N.J., 1955), pp. 264-99; John M. Blum, *et al., The National Experience: A History of the United States* (New York, 1963), pp. 610-15; Andrew Sinclair, *Prohibition, the Era of Excess* (Boston, 1962), *passim;* Richard Hofstadter, *The Age of Reform* (New York, 1955), pp. 289-299; and William E. Leuchtenberg, *Perils of Prosperity, 1914-1932* (Chicago, 1958), pp. 204-40.

CHAPTER 16

1. Complete records may never have existed because Imperial Wizard Simmons testified in 1921 that the Klan did not maintain a printed roster of the membership. On the local level, the National Council of Grand Dragons and Titans decided at Buckeye Lake, Ohio, in 1925 to continue to conceal membership records. Testimony of Simmons, *Klan Hearings,* p. 182; and *The New York Times,* August 28, 1925.

2. The lower estimate is that of Noel P. Gist, "Secret Societies: A

Cultural Study of Fraternalism in the United States," *University of Missouri Studies*, XV (October 1940), 36. The figure of 9 million, which includes such oddities as an estimate of 890,000 for Michigan, was offered by the *Washington Post*, November 2, 1930.

3. It is interesting to note that the Klan itself rarely boasted of more than 2 million members. See *The Kourier*, January 1925, p. 10; *Dawn*, September 1, 1923; *Searchlight*, February 24, 1923; *Tolerance*, February 4, 1923; Robert L. Duffus, "The Ku Klux Klan in the Middle West," *The World's Work*, XLVI (August 1923), 363; New York *World*, January 3, 1923; *The New York Times*, February 21, 1926; and *Detroit News*, September 17, 1937.

4. Henry P. Fry, *The Modern Ku Klux Klan* (Boston, 1922), p. 60; Guy B. Johnson, "The New Ku Klux Klan Movement," (unpub. Master's thesis, University of Chicago, 1922), pp. 36-7; and Arthur Corning White, "An American Fascismo," *The Forum*, LXXII (November 1924), 636-42.

5. Irving Leibowitz, *My Indiana* (Englewood Cliffs, N.J., 1964), p. 211; Charles C. Alexander, *The Ku Klux Klan in the Southwest* (Lexington, Ky., 1965), p. 18; Hofstadter, *The Age of Reform*, pp. 292-3; and Frederick Lewis Allen, *Only Yesterday* (New York, 1931), p. 47.

6. This conclusion is based primarily upon: (1) the official chapter records of Knox County Klan No. 14 in Tennessee and Winchester Klan No. 72 in Illinois; (2) membership lists of the klaverns of Denver, Indianapolis, Chicago, and Anaheim, California; and (3) precinct returns, particularly of local elections in Atlanta, Denver, Detroit, Memphis, Chicago, Dallas, Portland, and Indianapolis. Voting results are only semi-reliable, however, because the secret order often received support from upper-middle-class elements that were not sufficiently threatened by minority groups to take an extreme position and actually join the Klan.

7. The author used the Spearman rank correlation coefficient to measure the association between the percentage growth of a city between 1910 and 1930, and the percentage of white natives who joined the Klan. Eighteen cities were ranked according to the two criteria, and the resulting correlation between city growth and Klan size was .627. This correlation is significant at the .01 confidence level.

8. Perhaps the best sources of information relative to Klan violence are the weekly bulletins and annual reports of the American Civil Liberties Union. In 1922, the ACLU reported that most Klan victims were white. The New York *World* maintained that the secret order was morally responsible for crimes committed by white-sheeted men even if technically innocent. *ACLU 1924 Annual Report*, pp. 5-7; "The Rise and Fall of the K.K.K.," *The New Republic*, LIII (November 30, 1927), 33; "The Klan as a Victim of Mob Violence," *The Literary Digest*, LXXVIII (September 18, 1923),

12-13; New York *World,* September 20, 1921; and *Chicago Tribune,* March 24, 1922. Significant also is the fact that relatively few re- ports of Klan-related violence between 1915 and 1944 are con- tained in the files of the United States Department of Justice.

9. For example, in 1920 approximately 74 per cent of all Negroes and 84 per cent of all Negro heads of households who were then living in Chicago were born in the southern and southwestern states, predominantly in rural areas of Tennessee, Alabama, Geor- gia, and Kentucky. Irene Graham, "Negroes in Chicago, 1920: An Analysis of United States Census Data" (unpub. Master's thesis, University of Chicago, 1929), p. 13.

10. The tendency of the Negro community to segregate within itself on the basis of occupations, intelligence, and ambition has long been recognized. For instance, in Chicago in the 1920's, Negro physicians, lawyers, and musicians sought to escape the deluge of poor and disorganized colored families by moving into the select Woodlawn community west of Cottage Grove Avenue. But these families were soon overwhelmed by the same poor people from whom they had escaped, with the unhappy result that resistance to the movement of the Negro increased solely because of his color. E. Franklin Frazier, *The Negro Family in Chicago* (Chicago, 1932), pp. 97-110.

11. The term and the concept are borrowed from Robert A. Woods and Albert J. Kennedy, *The Zone of Emergence,* Sam B. Warner, ed. (Cambridge, 1962).

12. It is interesting to note that "the only significant association between socio-economic status and level of support for Barry Goldwater in 1964 that appeared to be independent of region was a slight bulge at the lower-middle income level." Irving Crespi, "The Structural Basis for Right-wing Conservatism: The Goldwater Case," *Public Opinion Quarterly,* XXIX (Winter 1966), 537-9.

13. For instance, the Klan supported the Sterling-Towner Federal Aid to Education Bill largely in the hope that it would aid public schools and weaken parochial education. Even the Klan's campaign against the Communists and union organizers in the 1930's could not be considered to be based primarily upon economic self-interest.

EPILOGUE

1. Arthur Schlesinger, Sr., ascribed the general decline of all secret fraternal orders after the mid-1920's to the cheap motorcar, talking movies, radios, and the growth of International Rotary and similar businessmen's luncheon clubs. Such factors no doubt contributed to the ultimate decline of the Klan, but initially they spurred its growth. Schlesinger, "Biography of a Nation of Joiners," *American Historical Review,* L (October 1944), 1-25.

Acknowledgments

The Woodrow Wilson National Fellowship Foundation has twice expressed confidence in my ability: in 1961-1962, with a grant for the initial stages of my graduate study, and in 1964-1965, with a dissertation year fellowship. This inquiry is the result of the latter award, which enabled me to devote a full year to uninterrupted research in various cities of the United States. I shall always be grateful to Sir Hugh Taylor and the various selection committees for this support.

Among the many persons who assisted me in the quest for Klan source materials the following were particularly helpful: Frank Burke of the Library of Congress, Esther Wolfson of the Chicago office of the Anti-Defamation League, Mrs. Mary R. Davis and Miss Ann Sasnett of the Emory University Library, Margaret Pierson of the Indiana State Archives, Mrs. Katie Drew of the Memphis *Commercial-Appeal*, Ruth P. Braun of the *Detroit News*, and Mrs. Dale Curry of the *Atlanta Constitution*. I am also appreciative of the co-operation and courtesies extended by the National Archives, the Atlanta Historical Society, the Chicago Historical Society, the Wisconsin Historical Society, the New York Public Library, the Newberry Library, the Boston Public Library, and the libraries of

Columbia, Denver, Harvard, Illinois, Michigan, Northwestern, Oregon, Syracuse, Vanderbilt, Virginia, and Wisconsin universities. Special mention must be made of the kindness, generosity, and continual helpfulness of Miss Helen M. Smith and Miss Judy Lola of the University of Chicago Library.

Intellectually, my heaviest debt is to Professor Richard C. Wade of the University of Chicago. This study developed from his suggestion in 1962, and he has since been a wise and steadfast counselor. I am also under a deep obligation to Professor Walter Johnson for his careful reading of the entire manuscript and for his support and encouragement over the past five years.

Other persons who offered specific suggestions helpful to the research or who read portions of the manucript include James Harvey Young of Emory University, Arthur Thurner of DePaul University, the late Enoch L. Mitchell of Memphis State University, Bessie Louise Pierce, Daniel J. Boorstin, and John Hope Franklin of the University of Chicago, Ralph McGill and Harold Martin of the *Atlanta Constitution*, Stanley K. Schultz of the University of Wisconsin, and the Honorable Clifford Davis of Washington, D.C. I owe a special debt of gratitude to those former Klansmen who shared with me their recollections of the Invisible Empire.

The typing of the manuscript was accomplished with diligence and resourcefulness by Mrs. Norma Peachy of Dayton and Mr. Fred Duffel of Chicago.

My greatest debt is to my wife, Barbara. While performing admirably the duties of wife and mother, she accompanied me to Klan rallies, searched through endless reels of microfilm, edited and typed much of the manuscript, and shared every task from first draft to final correction. She is largely responsible for whatever merit this study may possess.

A Note on Sources

The following essay is a brief description of the pattern of the research and of the author's larger indebtedness to certain of the more helpful materials. The discussion is highly selective and does not even attempt to indicate all the sources with which the text is documented. A full bibliography, if required, can be found in my dissertation.

Primary Sources

Among the problems associated with research on the Klan, the most frustrating is the difficulty in finding former members who are willing to discuss their association with the Invisible Empire. Although more than two score former Klansmen were contacted by the author, only eight could be persuaded to reminisce at length, and all insisted upon remaining anonymous. A more willing interviewee was Calvin Craig, the present grand dragon of Georgia, but he knew relatively little about the movement in the 1920's.

Manuscript sources in the form of Klan membership rolls, correspondence, and financial records are few. Most local officers undoubtedly regarded such materials as dangerously implicating and chose not to preserve them. Fortunately, the void is not absolute. A particularly important collection of Knox County (Tennessee) Klan No. 14 Papers is available in the Department of Special Collections at Emory University. Included in these files are dozens of pieces of chapter correspondence, several hundred membership applications, and various dues records and financial reports to the national office, all dated between 1923 and 1929. Another excellent source of information is the Chicago office of the Anti-Defamation League, which kindly permitted this author to make use of the dues records of Winchester (Illinois) Klan No. 72 as well as membership lists for Indianapolis and Denver in the 1920's. The New York City office of the Anti-Defamation League has photostatic copies of several Klan charters, and an especially rich collection of information on Klan activities since 1939.

The Indiana State Library and Archives in Indianapolis has an exceptional number of Klan manuscript pieces and Klan testimony filed under the general heading of Indiana Klan Papers. At the Library of Congress there is important material relating to Klan activity in Anaheim, California, including membership lists, local newspaper accounts, and some pieces of correspondence. The files of the United States Department of Justice in the National Archives contain records of complaints regarding Klan-inspired violence as well as a helpful "Memorandum on the Activities of the Ku Klux Klan in the State of Oregon" (File 198589). The Paul M. Angle Collection at the Chicago Historical Society includes much of the material Angle gathered while doing research on Klan violence in southern Illinois. The Stetson Kennedy Papers in the Schomberg Collection of Negro History at the New York Public Library have some relevant papers, but are strongest for the post-1940 period. The membership list of the Pond Creek (Kentucky) Klan (1926-1927) is available at the University of Kentucky, and various records of the Waco, Texas, chapter after World War II are on file at Baylor University. The author did not use the alleged Klan membership list which was published in the Buffalo Evening News in September, 1924.

Relevant materials in the papers of individuals who were not themselves members of the Klan are few. Among the collections examined with little positive result were the Shailer Matthews and Julius Rosenwald Papers at the University of Chicago, the Josephus Daniels, John Sharp Williams, William Jennings Bryan, and Clarence Darrow Papers at the Library of Congress, the Ben Wilson Olcott Papers at the University of Oregon, and the Socialist Party of America Papers at Duke University. The papers at the Library of Congress of Stone Mountain sculptor and sometime Klansman Gutzon Borglum contain some information regarding his relationship with the Klan's inner circle.

The relative lack of local and national Klan records is partially made up by the abundance of official Klan publications, most of which are available at either the Library of Congress or the New York Public Library. The most helpful items are the *Klansman's Manual. Compiled and Issued Under Direction and Authority of the Ku Klux Klan* (Atlanta, 1924), which explains the types of membership, the duties of officers, and the functions of meetings; and the *Kloran, Knights of the Ku Klux Klan: First Degree Character* (Atlanta, 1916), which contains the ritual. Among the other important publications are: *Constitution and Laws of the Knights of the Ku Klux Klan* (Atlanta, 1921); *The A.B.C. of the Knights of the Ku Klux Klan* (Atlanta, 1917); *Ideals of the Ku Klux Klan* (Atlanta, 1923); *The K.K.K. Katechism: Pertinent Questions, Pointed Answers* (Columbus, Ohio, 1924); *Delivery of Charter. Issued by the Imperial Palace, Knights of the Ku Klux Klan* (Atlanta, 1923); *Catalogue of Official Robes and Banners* (Atlanta, 1925); *America for Americans* (Atlanta, 1922); and *Klan Building: An Outline of Proven Klan Methods for Successfully Applying the Art of Klankraft in Building and Operating Local Klans* (Atlanta, 1923). The proceedings of important Klan gatherings may be partially consulted in *Papers Read at the Meeting of Grand Dragons, Knights of the Ku Klux Klan, at Their First Annual Meeting, held at Asheville, North Carolina, July 1923. Together with Other Articles of Interest to Klansmen* (Asheville, N. C., 1923); *Minutes of the Imperial Kloncilium, Knights of the Ku Klux Klan, Meeting of May 1 and 2, 1923. Which Ratified W. J. Simmons' Agreement with the Knights of the Ku Klux Klan, Together with Certified Copies of all Litigation Instituted by W. J. Simmons Against the Imperial Wizard and the Knights of the Ku Klux Klan* (Atlanta, 1923); and *Inspirational Addresses Delivered at the Second Imperial Klonvokation Held in Kansas City, Missouri, September 23, 24, 25, and 26, 1924* (Kansas City, 1924).

In addition to the official pamphlets and books that flowed from the Klan press, the semi-official literature was also vast. C. Lewis Fowler, *The Ku Klux Klan: Its Origin, Meaning and Scope of Operations* (Atlanta, 1922) was a pamphlet which complimented Fowler's lectures on Americanism; J. O. Wood, *Are You a Citizen? The Klansman's Guide* (Atlanta, 1923) expressed the pro-Klan sentiments of an Atlanta city official; Luther Ivan Powell, *The Old Cedar School* (Seattle, 1923) emphasized the Klan's hostility to parochial education; and E. H. Lougher, *The Kall of the Klan in Kentucky* (Greenfield, Ind., 1924) was a recruiting pamphlet. Walter Carl Wright, *Religious and Patriotic Ideals of the Ku Klux Klan* (Waco, Texas, 1926) and John Stephen Fleming, *What is Kluxism? Let Americans Answer—Aliens Only Muddy the Waters* (Birmingham, 1923) are virulent defenses of the Klan movement. Billy Parker, *The Bloody Trail of Romanism* (n.p., n.d.); Samuel H. Campbell, *The Jewish Problem in the United States* (Atlanta, 1923); and George Estes, *The Roman Katholic Kingdom and the Ku Klux Klan* (Portland, 1923) are droll recitals of anti-Catholic and anti-Semitic thought.

Neither the founder of the Klan, William Joseph Simmons, nor his successor as imperial wizard, Hiram Wesley Evans, had any difficulty getting published. Simmons's early work *The Practice of Klannishness* (Atlanta, 1918) emphasizes the fraternal side of the secret order, while his study *America's Menace: or, The Enemy Within* (Atlanta, 1926) is a typical nativist polemic. The founder's thoughts on the purposes, method, and organization of the Invisible Empire are presented in *The Klan Unmasked* (Atlanta, 1924), and his account of the internal struggle for control of the imperial palace is given in William G. Shepherd, "The Fiery Double Cross," *Collier's*, LXXXII (July 28, 1928), 8-9, 47-49.

Evans, who was even more prolific with the pen than his predecessor, ordered published *The Whole Truth Behind the Effort to Destroy the Ku Klux Klan* (Atlanta, 1923) in order to show that the Simmons camp was led by avaricious men who hoped to rule the Klan for personal gain. Evans also authored a number of short pamphlets defending the Klan's narrow definition of Americanism, the most important of which were: *The Attitude of the Ku Klux Klan Toward the Roman Catholic Hierarchy* (Atlanta, 1923); *The Attitude of the Ku Klux Klan Toward the Jew* (Atlanta, 1923); *Negro Suffrage: Its False Theory* (Atlanta, 1923); and *The Attitude of the Ku Klux Klan Toward Immigration* (Atlanta, 1923). In addition to such diatribes, the Dallas dentist wrote often for public consumption. Among the more revealing items are: "The Ballots Behind the Ku Klux Klan," *World's Work*, LV (January 1928), 243-52; "The Klan: Defender of Americanism," *Forum*, LXXIV (December 1925), 801-14; "The Catholic Question as Viewed by the Ku Klux Klan," *Current History Magazine* XXVI (July 1927), 563-8; and "The Klan's Fight for Americanism," *North American Review*, CCXXIII (March 1926), 33-63. Reuben H. Sawyer, *The Truth About the Invisible Empire, Knights of the Ku Klux Klan* (Portland, 1923), the transcript of a lecture delivered at the Municipal Auditorium in Portland, Oregon, on December 22, 1921, indicates the tendency of Klan speakers to emphasize "respectability" and "law and order."

A complete listing of Klan and pro-Klan newspapers and magazines would run to more than sixty titles. Almost all of these publications had a local circulation and an ephemeral life; only the most important ever reached a library. The following were the most useful of those examined: *Searchlight*, published weekly in Atlanta from 1919 to 1924 and now partially available on microfilm at the Universities of Chicago and Texas; *The Imperial Night-Hawk*, published weekly in Atlanta from April 1923 until September 1924 and available now at Chicago, the Library of Congress, and the New York Public Library; *The Kourier*, published monthly in Atlanta (various state editions were also issued) from 1924 to 1936 and available now at Chicago and the Library of Congress; *Dawn*, published weekly in Chicago from October 1922 until February 1924 and available now at the Library of Congress; *The Fiery Cross*, published weekly in Indianapolis (and in half a dozen state editions) from 1923 until 1925 and available now on microfilm at the New York Public Library; *The Watcher on the Tower*, published weekly in Seattle from 1923 to 1924 and available now at the Library of Congress; *The American Standard*, published twice monthly in New York City from 1924 to 1926 and available now at the Newberry Library in Chicago; and *The Badger-American*, published monthly in Milwaukee from 1923 to 1924 and partially available now at the State Historical Society of Wisconsin. The pro-Klan newspaper *Fellowship Forum*, published in Washington, D.C., is available at the Library of Congress. Less useful, but also available for research on the Klan are scattered issues of *Col. Mayfield's Weekly* (Houston), *The Texas 100 Per Cent American* (Dallas), *The Western American* (Portland), *The Fort Worth American Citizen*, *The Caldwell* (La.) *Watchman*, the Mississippi Realm Office *Official Monthly Bulletin*, and *The Wisconsin Kourier*.

General metropolitan newspapers yielded information on many aspects of Klan activity, and particularly on the extent of political involvement. The author's heavy reliance upon the eighty newspapers he consulted with varying degrees of completeness is evident from the citations in the text. In addition to *The New York Times*, the index of which was invaluable, the following were searched most systematically: *Atlanta Constitution, Atlanta Journal, Chicago Daily News, Chicago Tribune, The Commercial-Appeal* (Memphis), *Dallas Morning News, Denver Post, Denver Times, Detroit News, Indianapolis News, Indianapolis Star, Memphis News Scimitar, Knoxville Journal, The Morning Oregonian* (Portland), the *Oregon Daily Journal* (Portland), the *Portland Telegram*, and the *World* (New York). In a special category are Catholic and Negro newspapers such as the *Chicago Defender, Indianapolis Freeman, Savannah Tribune, New World* (Chicago), and *Denver Catholic Register*, which covered Klan activities with uncommon diligence. The most valuable of all newspaper sources were scattered issues of *Tolerance*, a publication of the American Unity League which the author fortuitously discovered while examining the court records of a Klan-related libel suit.

Legal documents in general provide unique data on the inner workings of the Klan. The evidence and depositions of at least a dozen relevant cases in Chicago's Cook County Superior Court have been preserved. Two of the more important cases are *William R. Johnston v. Tolerance Publishing Company* (Case #223-23-S-386399 in Cook

County Superior Court, 1923) and *Grady K. Rutledge, et al.* v. *Robert E. Shepherd, et al.* (Case #B-93874 in Cook County Circuit Court, 1923). An especially rich source of information is a collection of testimony, never tried, which was gathered by the Indiana Attorney General between 1925 and 1929, and which is now available, due to the efforts of Norman Weaver, in the Indiana State Archives under the heading of *State of Indiana* v. *The Knights of the Ku Klux Klan, et al.* (Case #41769 in Marion County Circuit Court). A fairly complete record of the murder trial of David C. Stephenson is also available there. Other helpful court cases are *Clayton C. Gilliland* v. *Symwa Club, Ku Klux Klan, A Michigan Corporation* (Case #117851 in Wayne County Circuit Court, 1925); *Henry C. Warner* v. *Arthur S. Nichols, et al.* (Case #132314 in Wayne County Circuit Court, 1928); *People of Colorado* v. *W. R. Given* (Case #26632 in Denver County District Court, 2nd Judicial District, Division 5); and *Knights of the Ku Klux Klan* v. *Rev. John F. Strayer, et al.* (Case #1897 in Equity in the Federal District Court, Pittsburgh, Pa.). The legal battle over the Oregon compulsory public education law may be consulted in *Pierce* v. *Society of Sisters*, 268 U.S. 510 (1924). Unfortunately, the court litigation for control of the national Klan office in Atlanta, *William Joseph Simmons* v. *Hiram Wesley Evans, et al.* (Case #556,553 in Fulton County Superior Court), has been destroyed in accord with Georgia law.

On three occasions the federal government investigated the activities of the Klan. In 1921, largely as a result of the New York *World* exposé, the House Committee on Rules conducted *Hearings on the Ku Klux Klan* (67th Cong., 1st Sess., 1921). The inquiry featured the lengthy personal testimony of Klan founder William Joseph Simmons, and it resulted in no punitive action. Soon after the 1922 election to the Senate of Klansman Earle B. Mayfield from Texas, the Senate Committee on Privileges and Elections launched an extensive review of alleged campaign irregularities and Klan participation in the contest, the proceedings of which were published as *Senator from Texas: Hearings* (68th Cong., 1st and 2nd Sess., 1924). In 1926, a Special Committee Investigating Expenditures in Senatorial Primary and General Elections (69th Cong., 1st Sess., 1926), headed by Senator Reed of Missouri, revealed the extent of Klan dominance over the government of Indiana. All three investigations are rich in the testimony of Klan officials and are easily accessible in most libraries. The author also made extensive use of the various publications of the U.S. Bureau of the Census, particularly the *Census of Religious Bodies: 1926* and *Negroes in the United States, 1920-1932.*

Secondary Sources

The most useful general history of the 1920's is William E. Leuchtenberg's breezy *The Perils of Prosperity, 1914-1932* (Chicago, 1958).
Frederick Lewis Allen, *Only Yesterday* (New York, 1931) is an ab-
sorbing social history of the decade that is only slightly less useful than
the final two volumes of Mark Sullivan, *Our Times: The United States,
1900-1925* (New York, 1935). Preston W. Slosson, *The Great Crusade
and After, 1914-1928* (New York, 1930) and Arthur M. Schlesinger,
Jr., *The Crisis of the Old Order, 1919-1933* (Boston, 1957) are also
valuable accounts of the period. Henry F. May, "Shifting Perspectives
on the 1920's," *Mississippi Valley Historical Review*, XLIII (December 1956), 405-27, emphasizes how changing intellectual currents have
altered interpretations of the decade. The best account of the fate of
progressivism in the 1920's is Richard Hofstadter's controversial, *The
Age of Reform: From Bryan to F.D.R.* (New York, 1955).

The history of nativism in America is treated in a number of works,
of varying merit. The only general account is Gustavus Myers's ram-
bling, superficial, and uneven *History of Bigotry in the United States*
(New York, 1943). Ray Allen Billington, *The Protestant Crusade,
1880-1860: A Study of the Origins of American Nativism* (New York,
1938) is standard on anti-Catholicism before the Civil War. William
Darrell Overdyke, *The Know-Nothing Party in the South* (Baton
Rouge, 1960) is good on nativist politics. The ebb and flow of the
movement for immigration restriction is analyzed in John Higham's
careful *Strangers in the Land: Patterns of American Nativism, 1860-
1925* (New Brunswick, N.J., 1955). Donald Kinzer, *An Episode in
Anti-Catholicism: The American Protective Association* (Seattle, 1964)
adds significantly to our understanding of nativism in the 1890's. Oscar
Handlin, *Race and Nationality in American Life* (New York, 1957)
considers the effect of immigration on the growth of religious intolerance, while Arthur Mann's essay "Gompers and the Irony of Racism,"
Antioch Review, XIII (1953), 203-14, examines the relationship between organized labor and nativism. Maldwyn Allen Jones, *American
Immigration* (Chicago, 1958) is a helpful general account.

The broad subject of racism has recently been treated by Thomas
F. Gossett, *Race: The History of an Idea in America* (Dallas, 1963).
John Hope Franklin, *From Slavery to Freedom: A History of American
Negroes*, 2nd ed. (New York, 1956) is the best complete history.
Gunnar Myrdal, *An American Dilemma: The Negro Problem and
Modern Democracy*, 2 vols. (New York, 1941) is an encyclopedic
study that covers all aspects of Negro life. Two important recent books

are I. A. Newby, *Jim Crow's Defense: Anti-Negro Thought in the United States, 1900-1930* (Baton Rouge, 1965) and August Meier, *Negro Thought in America, 1880-1915: Racial Ideologies in the Age of Booker T. Washington* (Ann Arbor, 1963). On the urban migration of Negroes, T. J. Woofter, Jr., *Negro Problems in Cities* (Garden City, 1929) was extremely useful, as were E. Franklin Frazier, *The Negro Family in the United States* (Chicago, 1939) and Robert H. Mugge, "Negro Migrants to Atlanta" (unpub. Ph.D. diss., University of Chicago (1957). Frederick G. Detweiler, *The Negro Press in the United States* (Chicago, 1922) is an indispensable reference that is regrettably out of print. On urban race riots, the best accounts are: Robert Shogan and Tom Craig, *The Detroit Race Riot: A Study in Violence* (Philadelphia, 1964); Chicago Commission on Race Relations, *The Negro in Chicago: A Study of Race Relations and a Race Riot* (Chicago, 1922); and Arthur I. Waskow, *From Race Riot to Sit-in, 1919 and the 1960's: A Study in the Connections Between Conflict and Violence* (Garden City, 1966).

The best analysis of the growth of civil liberties is John P. Roche, *The Quest for the Dream: The Development of Civil Rights and Human Relations in Modern America* (New York, 1963). On the controversy surrounding the anti-mask laws, see David Fellman, *The Constitutional Right of Association* (Chicago, 1963) and Jack Swertfeger, Jr., "Anti-Mask and Anti-Klan Laws," *Journal of Public Law,* I (Spring 1952), 182-97. *Unmasking the Klan: The Story of the Anti-Mask Laws* (Chicago, 1949) is a short pamphlet with emphasis on the period immediately after World War II. On the general problem of adult fraternalism, see Arthur M. Schlesinger, Sr., "Biography of a Nation of Joiners," *American Historical Review,* L (October 1944), 1-25; Noel P. Gist, "Secret Societies: A Cultural Study of Fraternalism in the United States," *University of Missouri Studies,* XV (October 1940), 1-115; and Charles W. Ferguson, *Fifty Million Brothers: A Panorama of American Lodges and Clubs* (New York, 1937). Gordon W. Allport, *The Nature of Prejudice* (Garden City, 1958) is a readable and comprehensive interpretation of group intolerance.

The best general history of the Invisible Empire is David Mark Chalmers, *Hooded Americanism: The First Century of the Ku Klux Klan* (Garden City, 1965). Although lacking cohesiveness, it is an impressive compendium of information that is exceptionally strong on local Klan activities in the 1920's. William Peirce Randel, *The Ku Klux Klan: A Century of Infamy* (Philadelphia, 1965) is essentially a "revisionist" history of the Reconstruction Klan that is shallow on the 1920's. Stanley Frost, *The Challenge of the Klan* (Indianapolis, 1924) is particularly informative on the Evans regime, though entirely too favorable to him. The book was reportedly written in conjunction with Milton Elrod, the editor of the Klan's *Fiery Cross*, and is basically a synthesis and expansion of a series of magazine articles done earlier. Two recently published, mass-market paperbacks, *KKK* (Evanston, Ill., 1963), by Ben Haas, and *Inside Ku Klux Klan* (New York, 1965), by Paul Gillette and Eugene Tillinger, are unreliable and tasteless. More helpful are Charles C. Alexander, "Kleagles and Cash: The Ku Klux Klan as a Business Organization, 1915-1930," *Business History Review*, XXXIX (Autumn, 1965), 348-67; Charles O. Jackson, "The Ku Klux Klan: A Study in Leadership (unpub. Master's thesis, Emory University, 1962); and Benjamin Herzl Avin, "The Ku Klux Klan, 1915-1925: A Study in Religious Intolerance" (unpub. Ph.D. diss., Georgetown University, 1952).

The interpretive literature on the Klan is of uneven quality. John Moffatt Mecklin, *The Ku Klux Klan: A Study of the American Mind* (New York, 1924) is a sociological treatment reportedly based upon interviews and questionnaires with representative numbers of Klansmen. It takes little note of internal developments in the Klan after 1921. Frank Tannenbaum considers the origin of the Klan spirit in a perceptive chapter in *Darker Phases of the South* (New York, 1924) and in "The Ku Klux Klan: Its Social Origin in the South," *Century Magazine*, CV (April 1923), 873-82. William Starr Myers, "The Ku Klux Klan of Today," *North American Review*, CCXXIII (June 1926), 304-9, and Guy B. Johnson, "Sociological Interpretations of the New Ku Klux Movement," *Journal of Social Forces*, I (May 1923), 44-5, both avoid the error of premature judgment. Frank Bohn, "The Ku Klux Klan Interpreted," *American Journal of Sociology*, XXX (January 1925), 385-407, is based largely on Marion County, Ohio. Carl N. Degler, "A Century of the Klans: A Review Article," *Journal of Southern History*, XXXI (November 1965), 435-43, is a summation of very recent scholarship. Paul L. Murphy, "Sources and Nature of Intolerance in the 1920's," *Journal of American History*, LI (June 1964), 60-76, is an interpretive article that traces post-war intolerance to the late Progressive period and describes the Klan as "content to draw its money and support largely from private citizens in small towns and rural communities."

As might be expected, much of the published literature on the Invisible Empire is either uncritically laudatory or savagely hostile. Among the books that view the hooded order as the greatest organization in America, Ben Bogard, *Ku Klux Klan Exposed: Inside Facts Laid Bare and Explained* (Little Rock, 1924) and Leroy Amos Curry, *The Ku Klux Klan Under the Searchlight* (Kansas City, Mo., 1924) are particularly valuable. Crusading evangelist Alma White wrote several book-length apologies for the Klan, the most useful of which is a commentary on the secret order's political actions entitled, *The Ku Klux Klan in Prophecy* (Zarephath, N.J., 1925). E. F. Stanton, *Christ and Other Klansmen, or, Lives of Love: The Cream of the Bible Spread Upon Klanism* (Kansas City, 1924) is a strange mixture of Biblical tales and stories of Klansmen. A disjointed piece of propaganda based largely upon interviews with Imperial Wizard Simmons is Winfield Jones, *The Story of the Ku Klux Klan* (Washington, 1921). Adding some new information on Evans and Colescott, Jones republished the study twenty years later under the title of *The Knights of the Ku Klux Klan* (New York, 1941).

Among the more revealing of the anti-Klan sources is the revelation of ex-Kleagle Edgar I. Fuller, *The Maelstrom: The Visible of the Invisible Empire* (Denver, 1925). Under the pseudonym of Marion Monteval, Fuller also authored *The Klan Inside Out* (Claremore, Okla., 1928), a book which demonstrates an intimate knowledge of the inner councils of the secret order. Henry Peck Fry, an ex-Kleagle from Tennessee, wrote *The Modern Ku Klux Klan* (Boston, 1922) largely as an elaboration of the New York *World* exposé. Perceptive and carefully phrased, it focuses heavily on the nature of Klan leadership. Another former Klansman who turned against the Invisible Empire was Lem A. Dever, whose *Masks Off: The Confessions of an Imperial Klansman* (Portland, Ore., 1925) did much to wreck the Klan in the Pacific Northwest. Peter Paul Kruszka, *You Wouldn't Believe It: An Astonishing Documentary Exposé of the "Hooded Empire"* (Chicago, 1939) is an egotistical volume emphasizing the virtue of its author. William M. Likins, *The Trail of the Serpent* (n.p., 1928) is a reckless and superficial account of Klan atrocities in Pennsylvania. In a similar vein are Likins, *Patriotism Capitalized; or, Religion Turned into Gold* (Uniontown, Pa., 1925) and A. V. Dalrymple, *Liberty Dethroned: An Indictment of the Ku Klux Klan* (Philadelphia, 1923).

Thomas Dixon's novel, *The Clansman: An Historical Romance of the Ku Klux Klan* (New York, 1905), which reinforced the traditional southern view of Negro rule during Reconstruction, provides insight into the appeal of the modern Klan. A careful study of D. W. Griffith's epic motion picture is Tom Murray White, "*The Birth of a Nation: An Examination of Its Sources, Content, and Historical Assertions About Reconstruction*" (unpub. Master's thesis, University of Chicago, 1952). A much shorter account is Everett Carter, "Cultural History Written with Lightning: The Significance of *The Birth of a Nation,*" *American Quarterly,* XII (Fall 1960), 347-57. The best items on the early growth of the Klan are Littel McClung, "The Klan Again in the South," *The New York Times,* September 1, 1918; Ward Greene, "Notes for a History of the Klan," *American Mercury*, V (June 1925), 240-43; William G. Shepherd, "How I Put Over the Klan," *Collier's*, LXXXII (July 14, 1928), 5-7, 32-5; Robert L. Duffus, "Salesmen of Hate: The Ku Klux Klan," *World's Work*, XLVI (May 1923), 31-8; "For and Against the Ku Klux Klan," *Literary Digest*, LXX (September 24, 1921), 38; Frank Parker Stockbridge, "The Ku Klux Klan Revival," *Current History*, XIV (April 1921), 19-25; and Walter F. White, "Reviving the Klan," *Forum*, LXV (April 1921), 426-34. Ralph McGill, *The South and the Southerner* (Boston, 1959) contains an interesting character sketch of William Joseph Simmons as well as an autobiographical commentary on the long career of the Klan in Atlanta.

The best regional study of the secret order is Charles C. Alexander, *The Ku Klux Klan in the Southwest* (Lexington, 1965), which pulls together several earlier articles as well as a shorter book, *Crusade for Conformity: The Ku Klux Klan in Texas, 1920-1930* (Houston, 1962). Alexander advances the basic hypothesis that, at least in the Southwest, the Klan was primarily a movement for "moral and social conformity." I would agree that a desire to return America to older values was almost everywhere characteristic of Klansmen, but it is no less true that in most parts of the country the Klan was either unable or unwilling to enforce its moral code upon the community, as it was in the habit of doing in the Southwest. In addition to Alexander's exhaustive studies, the most helpful sources on the Klan in the Southwest are Howard A. Tucker, *History of Governor Walton's War on the Klan* (Oklahoma City, 1923); Walter C. Witcher, *The Reign of Terror in Oklahoma* (Fort Worth, 1923); Sam Acheson, *35,000 Days in Texas: A History of the Dallas News and Its Forbears* (New York, 1938); Stanley Frost, "Night Riding Reformers: The Regeneration of Oklahoma," *Outlook*, CXXXV (November 14, 1923), 439; and Max Bentley, "The Ku Klux Klan in Texas," *McClure's*, LVII (May 1924), 11-21. Aldrich Blake, a Muskogee publicity agent who served as Governor Walton's chief advisor, wrote *The Ku Klux Kraze: A Lecture* (Oklahoma City, 1924) and "Oklahoma's Klan Fighting Governor," *Nation*, CXVII (October 3, 1923), 353. Angie Debo, *Prairie City: The Story of an American City* (New York, 1944) contains a good chapter on the impact of the Klan in Marshall, Oklahoma. Lois E. Torrence, "The Ku Klux Klan in Dallas, 1915-1928: An American Paradox" (unpub. Master's thesis, Southern Methodist University, 1948) is much more general than the title might indicate. John William Rogers, *The Lusty Texans of Dallas* (New York, 1951) is unsatisfactory.

Every serious student of the Klan in the Southeast should begin with W. J. Cash's penetrating, if not at every point convincing, analysis of *The Mind of the South* (New York, 1941). After almost twenty years,

V. O. Key, *Southern Politics in State and Nation* (New York, 1949) remains the most thorough study of twentieth-century southern politics. Arnold Rice, *The Ku Klux Klan in American Politics* (Washington, 1962) is a brief study which focuses heavily on the elections of 1924 and 1928 and on local Klan activities below the Mason and Dixon Line. The very readable autobiography of William Alexander Percy, *Lanterns on the Levee: Recollections of a Planter's Son* (New York, 1941) contains a revealing chapter "The Klan Comes to Town." On the career of Tom Watson, a noted Georgia progressive whose later career was marred by crude invective against Catholics, Negroes, and Jews, C. Vann Woodward, *Tom Watson, Agrarian Rebel* (New York, 1938) is standard. The somewhat ironic relationship between liberal economic reform and demagogic racism is also examined by Albert D. Kirwan, *Revolt of the Rednecks: Mississippi Politics, 1876-1926* (Lexington, Ky., 1951). Wilma Dykeman and James Stokley, *Seeds of Southern Change: The Life of Will Alexander* (Chicago, 1962) is the biography of a white southerner who devoted his life to the improvement of race relations. David Chalmers, "The Ku Klux Klan in the Sunshine State: The 1920's," *Florida Historical Quarterly*, XLIII (January 1964), 209-15; Virginia Phillips, "Rowlett Paine, Mayor of Memphis, 1920-1924," *West Tennessee Historical Society Papers*, XIII (1959), 95-116; and William D. Miller, *Mr. Crump of Memphis* (Baton Rouge, 1964) are helpful on local activities of the Klan in the South.

The best source on the Klan in the Midwest is Robert L. Duffus, the author of a number of trenchant contemporary articles in *World's Work*. Among his best contributions are: "Ancestry and End of the Ku Klux Klan," *World's Work*, XLVI (September 1923), 527-36; and "The Ku Klux Klan in the Middle West," *World's Work*, XLVI (August 1923), 363-72. The Klan of Muncie, Indiana, is considered by Robert and Helen Lynd in their classic analysis *Middletown: A Study in Contemporary American Culture* (New York, 1929). Walter Johnson examines the crusade against Kluxism by the editor from Emporia, Kansas, in *William Allen White's America* (New York, 1947). Norman F. Weaver, "The Ku Klux Klan in Indiana, Wisconsin, Ohio, and Michigan" (unpub. Ph.D. diss., University of Wisconsin, 1954) is a solid study that is particularly good on Wisconsin and Indiana. Embrey B. Howson, "The Ku Klux Klan in Ohio After World War I" (unpub. Master's thesis, Ohio State University, 1951) has very limited value.

Unfortunately, Bessie Louise Pierce's multi-volumed *History of Chicago* (New York, 1933-   ) has not yet been brought past 1900. Background information for this study was provided by Harold F. Gosnell, *Negro Politicians: The Rise of Negro Politics in Chicago* (Chicago,

1935); Roi Ottley, *The Lonely Warrior: The Life and Times of Robert S. Abbott* (Chicago, 1955); E. Franklin Frazier, *The Negro Family in Chicago* (Chicago, 1932); and Carroll Hill Woody, *The Chicago Primary of 1926: A Study of Election Methods* (Chicago, 1926). Louis Wirth, *The Ghetto* (Chicago, 1928) and St. Clair Drake and Horace M. Clayton, *Black Metropolis: A Study of Negro Life in a Northern City* (New York, 1945) remain indispensable classics. More specifically oriented toward the Windy City Klan are Grady K. Rutledge, *The Flag Draped Skeleton* (Chicago, 1923) and George C. Sikes, "Thompson Rule in Chicago Ended," *Outlook*, CXIII (March 4, 1923), 480-82. Relevant background information regarding the Klan in Detroit may be consulted in June Baber Woodson, "A Century with the Negroes of Detroit" (unpub. Master's thesis, Wayne University, 1949); Robert C. Adams, "Social Reasons Bring Negroes to Detroit," *Detroiter*, XIV (August 30, 1923), 7-9; Irving Stone, *Clarence Darrow for the Defense* (Garden City, 1941); and William P. Lovett, *Detroit Rules Itself* (Boston, 1930). David Greenstone, *A Report on the Politics of Detroit* (Cambridge, Mass., 1961) is a helpful general analysis.

The extraordinary career of Indiana Grand Dragon David C. Stephenson has not yet been the subject of a good biography. His trial for murder and rape and its ramifications are considered in John Bartlow Martin, *Indiana, An Interpretation* (New York, 1947); Dixon Merritt, "Klan and Anti-Klan in Indiana," *Outlook*, CXX (December 8, 1926), 465-7; Louis Francis Budenz, "There's Mud on Indiana's White Robes," *Nation*, CXXV (July 27, 1927), 81-2; Alva W. Taylor, "What the Klan Did in Indiana," *New Republic*, XLVII (November 18, 1927), 330-32; and Harry E. Hodsden, *Stephenson Was Framed in a Political Conspiracy: Recent Editorials and News Articles with Text of Petition in the LaPorte Circuit Court and Argument of Counsel* (n.p., 1936). A former Klan official, Edgar Allen Booth, gives the ins and outs of the case as well as his own disjointed revelations about chicanery within the Indiana organization from 1922 to 1926 in *The Mad Mullah of America* (Columbus, O., 1927). Robert A. Butler, *So They Framed Stephenson* (Huntington, Ind., 1940) is favorable to the Grand Dragon. A good study of the political impact of the secret order, or lack of it, is Emma Lou Thornbrough, "Segregation in Indiana During the Klan Era of the 1920's," *Mississippi Valley Historical Review*, XLVII (March, 1961), 594-619. There is also good material on the Indiana Klan in Robert Coughlan, "Klonklave in Kokomo," in *The Aspirin Age*, Isabel Leighton, ed. (New York, 1949); Irving Leibowitz, *My Indiana* (Englewood Cliffs, N.J., 1964); and Powell A. Moore, *The Calumet Region: Indiana's Last Frontier* (Indianapolis, 1959).

On the Klan in the Northeast, the best single source is Emerson

Hunsberger Loucks, *The Ku Klux Klan in Pennsylvania* (Harrisburg, Pa., 1936), a Columbia University doctoral dissertation that has lost none of its luster in the light of more recent scholarship. Loucks's work should be supplemented with Donald Crownover, "The Ku Klux Klan in Lancaster County, 1923-1924," *Journal of the Lancaster County Historical Society*, X (March 1964), 83-98; "The Klan Celebrates Mother's Day," *Christian Century*, XLII (May 21, 1923), 677; "New York's Anti-Klan Outburst," *Literary Digest*, LXXV (December 23, 1922), 31-2; F. L. Collins, "Way Down East with the Ku Klux Klan," *Collier's*, LXXVII (December 5, 1923), 12; and William R. Pattangall, "Is the Ku Klux Klan Un-American," *Forum*, LXXIV (1925), 321-32.

There is no general account of the Klan in the West; Chalmers's *Hooded Americanism* is the most valuable source. The movement in Colorado is considered by Ben B. Lindsey, "My Fight with the Ku Klux Klan," *Survey Graphic*, June 1, 1925, pp. 271-4; Lee Casey, "When the Ku Klux Klan Controlled Colorado," *Rocky Mountain News*, June 17-19, 1946; Don Zylstra, "When the Ku Klux Klan Ran Denver," *Denver Post Roundup*, January 5, 1958; and James H. Davis, "The Ku Klux Klan in Colorado" (unpub. Master's thesis, University of Denver, 1963). The Klan experience in Oregon may be consulted in A. B. Cain, *The Oregon School Fight* (Portland, 1924); "The Ku Kluxing of Oregon," *Outlook*, CXIII (March 14, 1923), 490-91; Edwin V. O'Hara, *Pioneer Catholic History of Oregon* (Paterson, N.J., 1939); Lawrence Saalfield, "Forces of Prejudice in Oregon, 1920-1925" (unpub. Master's thesis, Catholic University of America, 1950); and Charles Easton Rothwell, "The Ku Klux Klan in the State of Oregon" (unpub. Bachelor's thesis, Reed College, 1924). Percy Maddux, *City on the Willamette: The Story of Portland, Oregon* (Portland, 1952) is a vapid urban history.

On the relationship between the Klan and violence, the annual reports and weekly bulletins of the American Civil Liberties Union are particularly good. Support for my contention that violence has been over-emphasized as a facet of Klan activity is provided in "The Klan as a Victim of Mob Violence," *Literary Digest*, LXXVIII (September 18, 1923), 12-13; and "The Rise and Fall of the K.K.K.," *New Republic*, LIII (November 30, 1927), 33. Among the many indictments of the Klan on the vigilante issue, see R. A. Patton, "A Ku Klux Klan Reign of Terror," *Current History Magazine*, XXVIII (April 1928), 51-5; Grady Kent, *Fogged by the Ku Klux Klan* (Cleveland, Tenn., 1942); John Rogers, *The Murders of Mer Rouge* (St. Louis, 1923); and Leonard L. Cline, "In Darkest Louisiana," *Nation*, CXVI (March 14, 1923), 292-3. Paul M. Angle has carefully re-created the Klan crusade in Herrin, Illinois, in *Bloody Williamson: A Chapter in American*

Lawlessness (New York, 1952). The Invisible Empire offered its account of the many altercations in which it was involved in a number of special pamphlets, among them *The Truth About the Niles Riot, November 1, 1924* (Elyria, O., 1925); *The Truth About the Notre Dame Riot on Saturday, May 17th, 1924* (Indianapolis, 1924); *The Martyred Klansman: In Which Events Leading Up to the Shooting to Death of Klansman Thomas Rankin Abbott, on August 25, 1923, Are Related, Together with a Record of the Court Proceedings That Followed* (Pittsburgh, 1923); and *The Inglewood Raiders: The Story of the Celebrated Ku Klux Case and Los Angeles and Speeches to the Jury* (Los Angeles, 1923).

The religious orientation of the Klan has been the subject of considerable exploration. Robert Moats Miller, "A Note on the Relationship Between the Protestant Churches and the Revival of the Ku Klux Klan," *Journal of Southern History,* XXII (August 1956), 355-68, is the best single inquiry. The subject is also probed by Laura L. Bradley, "Protestant Churches and the Ku Klux Klan in Mississippi During the 1920's" (unpub. Master's thesis, University of Mississippi, 1962); Martin J. Scott, "Catholics and the Ku Klux Klan," *North American Review,* CCXXIII (June 1926), 268-81; Thomas M. Conroy, "The Ku Klux Klan and the American Clergy," *Ecclesiastical Review,* LXX (January 1924), 47-58; and Everett Ross Clinchy, *All in the Name of God* (New York, 1934). Norman Furniss, *The Fundamentalist Controversy, 1918-1931* (New Haven, Conn., 1954) rightly advises caution in assuming a one-to-one relationship between the Klan and Fundamentalism as organized movements. Also helpful in providing background information are Paul A. Carter, *The Decline and Revival of the Social Gospel: Social and Political Liberalism in American Protestant Churches, 1920-1940* (Ithaca, N.Y., 1954); Kenneth K. Bailey, *Southern White Protestantism in the Twentieth Century* (New York, 1964); Robert M. Miller, *American Protestantism and Social Issues, 1919-1939* (Chapel Hill, 1958); William G. McLoughlin, Jr., *Billy Sunday Was His Real Name* (Chicago, 1955); and David M. Reimers, *White Protestantism and the Negro* (New York, 1965).

On the Klan crusade against Al Smith, Edmund A. Moore, *A Catholic Runs for President: The Campaign of 1928* (New York, 1956) is good on the religious angle. Michael Williams, a Catholic journalist, discusses the influence of the Klan in both the 1924 and 1928 elections in *The Shadow of the Pope* (New York, 1932). Also helpful are Roy V. Peel and Thomas C. Donnelly, *The 1928 Campaign: An Analysis* (New York, 1931); and William G. Carleton, "The Popish Plot of 1928," *Forum,* CXII (September, 1949), 141-7. Paul Meres Winter, *What Price Tolerance?* (New York, 1928) is a violently anti-Catholic and pro-Klan diatribe that was used in the campaign against Governor Smith.

There is fairly extensive periodical coverage of the fortunes of the Invisible Empire during the Depression decade; the most useful materials are "Hugo Black: The Early Years," *Catholic University Law Review*, X (1959), 103-16; Heywood Broun, "Up Pops the Wizard," *New Republic*, XCIX (June 21, 1939), 186-7; Theodore Irwin, "The Klan Kicks Up Again," *American Mercury*, L (August 1940), 470-76; and Richard H. Rovere, "The Klan Rides Again," *Nation*, CLI 445-6. A valuable account of the Klan-related Black Legion in the 1930's is Morris Janowitz, "Black Legions on the March," in Daniel Aaron, ed., *America in Crisis: Fourteen Crucial Episodes in American History* (New York, 1952). Although emphasizing the post–World War II period, two books by Stetson Kennedy, *Southern Exposure* (Garden City, N.Y., 1946) and *I Rode with the Ku Klux Klan* (London, 1954), offer a considerable amount of firsthand testimony. John Roy Carlson (pseudonym), *Under Cover: Four Years in the Nazi Underground, 1939-1943* (New York, 1943) is an inflammatory account of Axis undercover work that ties the Klan to the German-American Bund and other extreme right-wing groups.

Index

Abbott, Robert S., 102
Abbott, Thomas, 171
Adams, Thomas, 159
Advertisers in Klan publications, 238; in *Dawn*, 101, 121; in *Searchlight*, 33; in *The Fiery Cross*, 147–8
Agnes Scott College, 37
Akers, Tom, 186, 286
Akron, Ohio, 166–8, 236, 239, 279
Alabama, 7, 26, 236; Klan membership, 237
Aldridge, Clara, 149
Aldridge, Shawnie R., 69
Alexander, Charles, 237, 240, 265
Alexander, Will, 145
Alger, Horatio, 245
Allen, Frederick Lewis, 240
Alley, J. P., 46
Allison, V. K., 201
All-Nations Rally, 105
Allport, Gordon, 246
American Civic Association, 175
American Civil Liberties Union, 241, 289

American Debating Society, 254
American Fascisti, 163; *see also* Fascists
American Hellenic Educational Progressive Association, 35
American Journal of Sociology, 90
American Legion, 69, 190, 284–5
American Protective Association, 128, 201, 215, 226, 267, 272, 284
American Standard, The, 175–6, 238
American Unity League, 102–3, 112–13, 115, 276; activities in Indianapolis, 148–9; decline, 115–17; establishment of *Tolerance*, 103–4; informants, 106–7
Americanism. *See* Patriotism
Anaheim Bulletin, 192–3
Anaheim, Calif., 190, 192–3
Anaheim Gazette, 192–3
Anderson, Albert O., 109
Anderson, John Wood, 199
Anderson, Sherwood, 90
Anglo-Saxon Clubs of America, 82
Anti-Catholicism, 20–21, 23, 175–

Kenneth T. Jackson is Jacques Barzun Professor of History and the Social Sciences at Columbia University, where he has taught since 1968. In addition to *The Ku Klux Klan in the City*, he is the author of *Crabgrass Frontier: The Suburbanization of the United States,* which received the Bancroft Prize and the Francis Parkman Award, and *Silent Cities: The Evolution of the American Cemetery.* Mr. Jackson is also editor-in-chief of the *Encyclopedia of New York City.*

ELEPHANT PAPERBACKS

American History and American Studies
Stephen Vincent Benét, *John Brown's Body*, EL10
Henry W. Berger, ed., *A William Appleman Williams Reader*, EL126
Andrew Bergman, *We're in the Money*, EL124
Paul Boyer, ed., *Reagan as President*, EL117
Robert V. Bruce, *1877: Year of Violence*, EL102
George Dangerfield, *The Era of Good Feelings*, EL110
Clarence Darrow, *Verdicts Out of Court*, EL2
Floyd Dell, *Intellectual Vagabondage*, EL13
Elisha P. Douglass, *Rebels and Democrats*, EL108
Theodore Draper, *The Roots of American Communism*, EL105
Joseph Epstein, *Ambition*, EL7
Lloyd C. Gardner, *Spheres of Influence*, EL131
Paul W. Glad, *McKinley, Bryan, and the People*, EL119
Daniel Horowitz, *The Morality of Spending*, EL122
Kenneth T. Jackson, *The Ku Klux Klan in the City, 1915–1930*, EL123
Edward Chase Kirkland, *Dream and Thought in the Business Community, 1860–1900*, EL114
Herbert S Klein, *Slavery in the Americas*, EL103
Aileen S. Kraditor, *Means and Ends in American Abolitionism*, EL111
Leonard W. Levy, *Jefferson and Civil Liberties: The Darker Side*, EL107
Seymour J. Mandelbaum, *Boss Tweed's New York*, EL112
Thomas J. McCormick, *China Market*, EL115
Walter Millis, *The Martial Spirit*, EL104
Nicolaus Mills, ed., *Culture in an Age of Money*, EL302
Nicolaus Mills, *Like a Holy Crusade*, EL129
Roderick Nash, *The Nervous Generation*, EL113
William L. O'Neill, ed., *Echoes of Revolt: The Masses, 1911–1917*, EL5
Glenn Porter and Harold C. Livesay, *Merchants and Manufacturers*, EL106
Edward Reynolds, *Stand the Storm*, EL128
Geoffrey S. Smith, *To Save a Nation*, EL125
Bernard Sternsher, ed., *Hitting Home: The Great Depression in Town and Country*, EL109
Athan Theoharis, *From the Secret Files of J. Edgar Hoover*, EL127
Nicholas von Hoffman, *We Are the People Our Parents Warned Us Against*, EL301
Norman Ware, *The Industrial Worker, 1840–1860*, EL116
Tom Wicker, *JFK and LBJ: The Influence of Personality upon Politics*, EL120
Robert H. Wiebe, *Businessmen and Reform*, EL101
T. Harry Williams, *McClellan, Sherman and Grant*, EL121
Miles Wolff, *Lunch at the 5 & 10*, EL118
Randall B. Woods and Howard Jones, *Dawning of the Cold War*, EL130

European and World History
Mark Frankland, *The Patriots' Revolution*, EL201
Lloyd C. Gardner, *Spheres of Influence*, EL131
Thomas A. Idinopulos, *Jerusalem*, EL204
Ronnie S. Landau, *The Nazi Holocaust*, EL203
Clive Ponting, *1940: Myth and Reality*, EL202